Pocket Rough Guide

BERLIN

written and researched by

PAUL SULLIVAN

Contents

INTRODUCTION TO
BERLIN

Of all today's European capitals, Berlin carries the biggest buzz. In the two decades or so since it was reunified, the city has developed into a heady meld of grit and glamour that's vastly different from anywhere else in Germany – or the rest of the world for that matter. Its edgy cultural and fashion scenes, burgeoning nightlife and radical anti-gentrification agenda regularly make global headlines, as does its reputation as "poor but sexy" – a term coined by mayor Klaus Wowereit and quickly adopted as the city's unofficial motto.

PRATER BEER GARDEN

Best place for a Currywurst

Berliners argue endlessly over where to find the best *Currywurst* – sliced pork sausage covered with a unique blend of ketchup and curry powder. While everyone has their favourite *Currywurst* outlet, ours is *Konnopke's Imbiss*, underneath the Eberswalder Str. U-Bahn. SEE > p.95

The crackle of youthful energy that characterizes much of the inner city – especially areas such as trendy Mitte (Spandauer Vorstadt and around) and student-heavy Friedrichshain – mingles incongruously with the scars of Berlin's less glamorous past. Holocaust memorials, concentration camps and a wealth of thought-provoking museums, such as Daniel Libeskind's celebrated Jewish Museum, join bullet holes and empty spaces to provide visitors with constant reminders of the horrors of National Socialism and World War II. The fragments of the Berlin Wall scattered around the city like broken concrete teeth testify to its painful division – sometimes still reflected in the mindsets of the city's formerly divided neighbourhoods, many of which have retained their pre-reunification identities.

So overwhelming is Berlin's twentieth-century history and its twenty-first century grab for the future that it's easy to forget that the city has a longer and more illustrious history. Originally two cities – Cölln, an island in the middle of the city, now the site of the Museum Island, and Alt Berlin, formerly a fishing village – Berlin was formed in 1237. Located at the intersection of significant trade routes, it quickly prospered, rising to power as the seat of the Hohenzollern dynasty following the Thirty Years' War. During the eighteenth century, Frederick the Great (1712–86) established Berlin – and neighbouring Potsdam with its magnificent summer palace Sanssouci – as a grand capital for the Prussian monarchy; it was during this time that many of the buildings on Unter den Linden were constructed. When Germany was united in 1871, Berlin became its capital and the Reichstag its parliament.

Following the defeat of World War I, during the Weimar Republic (1919–33) Berlin rivalled Paris as a centre for the cultural avant-garde, the legacy and spirit of which live on in contemporary Berlin. World War II reduced seventy percent of the city to ruins, and it was partitioned into American, British and French zones in the West and a Soviet zone in the East. The three Western-occupied zones eventually merged into West

OYE RECORD STORE IN PRENZLAUER BERG

Berlin is a great city to visit at any time of year with plenty to do and see – but like most places, it really comes alive in the warmer months. If you're not a fan of cold weather, be warned that the winter months can be brutally chilly thanks to winds blowing in from the east. In general though, the city enjoys a cool and humid climate with an average summer temperature of around 25°C as well as the occasional heat wave. Spring and autumn are often lovely seasons.

Berlin, while the Soviet zone in the East remained defiantly separate – the city's division was fully realized with the building of the Berlin Wall in August 1961 by the East German government.

The fall of the Wall in 1989 provided a rare opportunity for a late twentieth-century rebirth. Berlin still carries an unfinished air and change remains an exciting constant in the city, though it's not without its growing pains, with gentrification a red-hot topic: Prenzlauer Berg and Mitte have been yuppified beyond recognition and in Friedrichshain and Kreuzberg cars are torched and windows smashed in an effort to resist.

Political forces and ideals continue to battle it out in Berlin, rendering the city a vibrant and vertiginous place to be, an irresistible combination of entrepreneurial possibility and creative energy rubbing shoulders with a fully developed tourist city overflowing with museums, sights and events. What's not to like?

CYCLISTS AT TEMPELHOFER PARK

BERLIN AT A GLANCE

>> SHOPPING

Despite Karl Lagerfeld's public dismissal of it in 2010, Berlin's fashion scene has been going from strength to strength in the past decade or so, with a string of local designers constantly upping the ante. The city is awash with small boutiques, with clusters around Neue Schönhauser Strasse and Munzstrasse in Spandauer Vorstadt (Mitte) and between Kantstrasse and Ku'damm in Charlottenburg, while Kreuzberg and Friedrichshain have a surfeit of street fashion stores. More commercial shopping can be found around Hackescher Markt and along Ku'damm.

>> DRINKING

The majority of bars are independent and relaxed licensing laws means they can usually close when they like. Though there are a decent spread of bars everywhere, the biggest concentration are around Mitte, Prenzlauer Berg and Kreuzberg, with many operating as cafés during the day serving snacks and light meals, then bars later on, all the way through to the early hours.

>> EATING

The dining scene in Berlin has come on leaps and bounds since the Wall fell. Cheap eats are abundant all over the city, with snack stalls, *Imbisses,* hawking everything from burgers and *Currywurst* to Asian food. At the other end, you can dine in style at a decent selection of high-end, Michelin-starred spots – particularly in upscale areas such as Unter den Linden, Potsdamer Platz and Charlottenburg. The area in between – mid-priced restaurants – make up the majority of eating options, again all over the city, and vary from authentic German cuisine to stylish dens of cool. A particular Berlin favourite is the weekend brunch buffet, served in cafés across the city – Prenzlauer Berg is a good bet for these.

>> NIGHTLIFE

Berlin's nightlife scene is the envy of, well, most of the world, and its large creative scene means that people have fairly flexible schedules. The city's nightclubs not only stay open later than most (some don't close for days) but also purvey some of the most cutting-edge house and techno around, attracting clubbers from around the globe who come to the city just to party the weekend away at heavyweight places like *Berghain*, *Watergate*, *Tresor* and *Cookies*. There's a strong concentration of clubs in Friedrichshain and East Kreuzberg, particularly along the river Spree, which divides these two neighbourhoods.

OUR RECOMMENDATIONS FOR WHERE TO EAT, DRINK AND SHOP ARE LISTED AT THE END OF EACH CHAPTER.

Day One in Berlin

Breakfast > p.52. The café of the Deutsches Historisches Museum is a refined and classic place to start the day before throwing yourself into the museum.

1 Deutsches Historisches Museum > p.52. Check out two thousand years of German history neatly and thoughtfully arranged throughout this beautiful museum.

2 Neue Wache > p.53. Visit Schinkel's famous Neoclassical monument and its emotive Käthe Kollwitz sculpture Mother with her Dead Son.

Lunch > For a budget option in the area try sushi at *Ishin* (p.61); for classic Austrian dishes opt for *Café Einstein* (p.62).

3 Berlin Story > p.60. Pop into this sprawling shop to pick up books, souvenirs, DVDs or just about anything else on Berlin.

4 Brandenburg Gate > p.57. Berlin's foremost landmark and one of its biggest tourist attractions. A must see for first-time visitors.

5 Reichstag > p.58. Climb the dome of this historic building to find great views across the city. Make sure you book a tour ahead.

6 Memorial to the Murdered Jews of Europe > p.58. Visit the controversial memorial with its rows of stelae above ground and sobering visitor centre below.

Dinner > p.60. End the day with high-quality Italian cuisine at *Bocca di Bacco*.

Day Two in Berlin

Breakfast > p.135. West Berlin's *Schwarzes Café* (right) is a vaguely bohemian 24-hour café with a wonderful interior (upstairs) and decent breakfasts.

1 Berlin Zoo and Aquarium > p.124. One of the biggest zoos in Europe, with an equally comprehensive aquarium right around the corner.

2 Kaiser-Wilhelm-Gedächtnis-Kirche > p.128. Don't let the shattered spire put you off, this memorial church has a wonderful interior to investigate.

3 Käthe Kollwitz Museum > p.128. The biggest collection of work from Berlin's pre-eminent sculptor collected in a lovely villa.

Lunch > p.134. Linger over coffee or lunch right next door at elegant café/restaurant *Café im Literaturhaus* (right).

4 Story of Berlin > p.128. This museum does precisely what it says on the tin, in an insightful and impressive manner.

5 Shopping on Ku'damm > p.130. Since you're on the mighty Kurfürstendamm it'd be a shame not to indulge in some retail therapy. Don't forget to check the side streets too for a host of excellent, independent boutiques.

Dinner > p.133. Try some thoroughly old-fashioned Silesian and Pomeranian food at *Marjellchen*, a wonderful timewarp.

GDR Berlin

Take an "Ostalgie" tour through former East Berlin, its monumental sights, kitsch icons and memorials to the city's divided past.

1 DDR Museum > p.66. Get hands on with GDR culture at this fun and interactive museum. Nearby is the Marx-Engels-Forum, an imposing square with its Marx and Engel monuments, offering a fascinating glimpse into East German communist ideology.

2 The Fernsehturm > p.65. Gape at the bleak GDR architecture of Alexanderplatz before taking a trip up the Fernsehturm for tremendous views over the city.

3 Karl-Marx-Allee > p.101. Admire the Soviet architecture along this impressive historical boulevard, formerly known as Stalinallee, including the original Kino International, as featured in the film *Goodbye Lenin!*

Coffee > p.105. Grab coffee and cake (or ice cream) at *Café Sybille* (above), which also hosts a small but informative museum about Karl-Marx-Allee.

4 East Side Gallery > p.100. Finish up at the largest remaining section of the Berlin wall, also one of the world's largest open-air galleries.

Sleep > p.151. For a complete Ostalgie experience, book a night at the GDR-themed *Ostel* in Friedrichshain, which is also well placed for the neighbourhood's nightlife.

Budget Berlin

Berlin's not necessarily an expensive city, and there are plenty of fun ways to explore the city on the cheap.

1 Take the bus > p.156. Public buses #100 and #200 will give you a guided tour of some of the city's main sights at a fraction of the cost.

2 Contemporary art > p.74 & p.54. For free contemporary art, check out Daimler Contemporary (always free) and Deutsche Guggenheim (free Mon).

Lunch > p.81. *Joseph Roth Diele* (right), a charming restaurant near Potsdamer Platz, is dedicated to the Jewish author and has excellent lunch deals.

3 Topography of Terror > p.110. Built on the grounds of the former SS Headquarters, this memorial of Gestapo horrors will leave you reeling.

4 Gedenkstätte Berliner Mauer > p.84. The Wall memorial on Bernaur Strasse has fascinating indoor and outdoor exhibitions for free.

5 Cheap and quirky museums > p.67 & p.117. The Buchstabenmuseum (Museum of Letters) offers a collection of letters for €2.50 while you can access the Museum der Dinge (Museum of Things) for just €4.

Drinks > p.43. Drink and make merry at one of the *Weinerei* bars (above left), low-key hipsters hangouts where you pay what you feel is fair for the wine.

BEST OF BERLIN

Big sights

DEM DEUTSCHEN VOLKE

1 **The Reichstag** Having survived fascism, revolution, bombardment and neglect, the Reichstag is today a symbol of the city's reunification. > **p.58**

2 East Side Gallery The largest section of the Berlin Wall still standing is also the world's largest open-air art gallery. > **p.100**

3 Memorial to the Murdered Jews of Europe Nineteen thousand square metres of dramatic, disorienting concrete stelae plus a highly emotive underground museum. > **p.58**

4 The Museum Island A treasure trove of ancient and modern art spread over five world-class museums. > **p.46**

5 Brandenburg Gate This imposing former city gate is one of Berlin's most recognizable symbols. > **p.57**

Architecture

1 Jewish Museum Daniel Libeskind's Jewish Museum is notable not only for its content but for its complex structural prowess. **> p.111**

2 **Schloss Charlottenburg** The largest palace in Berlin is also a fine example of Prussian-era architecture, built in stunning Rococo and Baroque style. > **p.128**

3 **Tempelhof airport** One of the last remaining examples of Nazi architecture is now an expansive leisure area. > **p.112**

4 **Berliner Dom** Berlin's towering neo-Renaissance cathedral has much to admire both inside and out. > **p.46**

5 **Neue Nationalgalerie** This beautiful "temple of light and glass" was designed by Bauhaus maestro Ludwig Mies van der Rohe. > **p.77**

Museums and galleries

1 Hamburger Bahnhof This former train station now houses Berlin's largest collection of cutting-edge, international art. > **p.36**

2 Topography of Terror Located where the SS headquarters used to be, this museum unflinchingly explores the rise of the Nazi party and its atrocities. > **p.110**

3 Gemäldegalerie The undisputed heavyweight of the Kulturforum boasts hundreds of exquisite Old Masters. > **p.74**

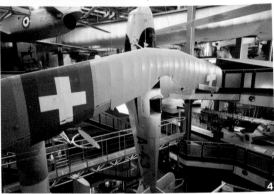

4 Deutsches Technikmuseum A jaw-dropping ensemble of German technical innovations, past and present. > **p.110**

5 Pergamonmuseum If you only get to see one of the Museum Island's big guns, make sure it's this one. > **p.49**

Berlin nightlife

1 Salon zur Wilden Renate A two-floor villa run by artists and dedicated to unbridled hedonism. > **p.107**

3 Clärchen's Ballhaus Harking back to an earlier era of Berlin nightlife, *Clärchen's* brilliantly mixes live bands, cheesy disco and ballroom dancing. > **p.44**

2 White Trash Fast Food One of the main places to catch up-and-coming local and international live acts. Great burgers too. > **p.45**

4 Tresor The third version of one of Berlin's most pioneering clubs offers three floors of muscular techno action. > **p.123**

5 Club der Visionaere This popular, floating summer hangout often has unannounced sets from big-name DJs like Ricardo Villalobos. > **p.121**

Family and kids

1 Onkel Albert Try one of Berlin's "kindercafés", a place to enjoy a proper coffee while the little ones roam free. > **p.42**

2 Strandbad Wannsee The most popular lakeside retreat in the city. Wannsee also has one of the largest lidos in Europe. > **p.145**

4 Legoland Play with as much lego as you can get your hands on down in Potsdamer Platz. > **p.72**

3 Tiergarten Formerly the hunting grounds of Friedrich I, this vast urban park is a great place to kick back or run around with the family. > **p.79**

5 Berlin Zoo and Aquarium One of the largest zoos in Europe with pandas, elephants, giraffes and more – plus a comprehensive aquarium around the corner. > **p.124**

Kaffee und Kuchen

1 Anna Blume Poetry, flowers and cake mingle harmoniously in this Art Deco Prenzlauer Berg favourite, with attractive outdoor seating as well.
> p.95

3 Café Buchwald This place has been serving up *Baumkuchen* and more for 130 years. Needless to say, they're quite good. > **p.82**

2 Operncafé in Opernpalais A sumptuous Baroque place, the opera house café offers nostalgic elegance and wonderful cakes. > **p.62**

4 Barcomi's Cynthia Barcomi's cheesecake is very difficult to beat. Her Berlin-roasted coffees are pretty special too. > **p.41**

5 Café Einstein A taste of old Vienna in a gorgeous villa once owned and managed by Goebbels. > **p.138**

Viewpoints

1 Siegessäule The viewing platform at the top of the Victory Column offers vistas across Tiergarten and beyond. **> p.80**

2 Panoramapunkt The lift at the Kollhoff Tower will whisk you up to the 24th floor in no time. It's worth the ride. **> p.73**

3 The Reichstag There's a restaurant in the Reichstag but the views from the glass dome are – quite literally – the highlight. **> p.58**

4 Fernsehturm Buy a timed ticket online to beat the queues to the top of this Berlin landmark for superb views across the whole city. **> p.65**

5 Viktoriapark At 66m, the cross at the top of Schinkel's monument in this Kreuzberg park is officially the highest point in Berlin. **> p.108**

PLACES

Spandauer Vorstadt

Arcing elegantly above the Spree between Friedrichstrasse and Alexanderplatz, the Spandauer Vorstadt was an eighteenth-century suburb that today serves as Berlin's primary "downtown" area, and is the heart of the Mitte district. Before World War II it was a significant hub for Jewish and French Huguenot exiles; after the Wall fell it became an artists' enclave, playing a vital role in the transferral of the city's art scene from West to East. Two decades of commercialization have resulted in a vibrant but touristic part of the city that's dense with boutiques, bars and restaurants, mainly around Hackescher Markt and the adjacent Oranienburger Strasse, as well as galleries, along Augustsstrasse and Torstrasse. Key insights into local Jewish life remain at the Neue Synagoge, the Jewish cemetery on Grosse Hamburger Strasse, and a trio of museums in the Haus Schwarzenberg.

HACKESCHE HÖFE

Rosenthaler Str. 40/41 & Sophienstr. 6
Ⓢ Hackescher Markt ☎ 030/28 09 80 10,
Ⓦ www.hackesche-hoefe.com. Open various hours (residential parts close 10pm).
MAP P.32–33, POCKET MAP E12

The extensive series of interconnected courtyards known as the Hackesche Höfe, located just across from S-Bahn station Hackescher Markt, are one of the best-known sights in this area. Having formerly hosted a Jewish girls' club, ballroom, factories, apartments – even a poets' society – the courtyards were remixed post-Wall into a more commercial enterprise albeit with a vaguely arty twist. Today you'll find a cinema, several theatres, including the Chameleon Theatre, Hackesche Höfe Theatre and Theatre of Yiddish Culture, a jumble of smart restaurants and shops – and a throng of tourists, attracted by the impressive Art Nouveau restoration.

HACKESCHE HÖFE

THE HAUS SCHWARZENBERG MUSEUMS

Rosenthaler Str. 39 Ⓢ Hackescher Markt
Ⓦ www.haus-schwarzenberg.org.
MAP P.32–33, POCKET MAP E12

Haus Schwarzenberg is the unapologetically grungy alternative to the gentrified Hackesche Höfe, located just a couple of doors away. It has only been minimally

refurbished and at least part of its allure are its wonderful crumbling facades. Inside is an aptly unpretentious selection of cafés, bars and shops plus a cinema and galleries (street art lovers will want to visit Neurotitan Gallery). Of particular interest are a trio of small museums that explore Jewish life in the area during the Third Reich. The **Gedenkstätte Stille Helden** (☎030/23 45 79 19, Ⓦwww.gedenkstaette-stille-helden.de; daily 10am–8pm; free) commemorates local residents who risked their lives to rescue persecuted Jews, documenting both heroic successes and tragic failures via photographs, documents and oral testimonies. Among the heroes is Otto Weidt, a German entrepreneur who helped save a number of his Jewish employees – all of whom were blind – at his workshop. Now called the **Museum Blinden-werkstatt Otto Weidt** (☎030/28 59 94 07, Ⓦwww.museum-blindenwerkstatt.de; daily 10am–8pm; free), it preserves photographs and personal mementoes of Weidt and his workers and the claustrophobic, hidden room, located behind a backless wardrobe, where he hid Jewish

families when the Gestapo came knocking. Finally, the **Anne-Frank-Zentrum** (☎030/28 88 65 600, Ⓦwww.annefrank.de; Tues–Sun 10am–6pm; €5) is a modern, surprisingly engaging exhibition on her life.

SAMMLUNG HOFFMANN

Sophie-Gips-Höfe, Sophienstr. 21
Ⓢ Hackescher Markt ☎030/28 49 91 20.
Ⓦ www.sammlung-hoffmann.de. Sat
11am–4pm, closed Aug. €8.
MAP P.32–33. POCKET MAP D11

Started by avid art collectors Erika and Rolf Hoffmann, this sizeable private museum displays their personal collection of contemporary art, which spans painting, sculpture, photography and video over three floors filled with natural light. Organized subjectively – there are no names, descriptions or over-arching curatorial themes – the exhibition features internationally renowned names such as Jean-Michel Basquiat, Andy Warhol and Bruce Nauman. The collection is changed around every year. Entry is by guided tour (English tours available) – a pleasantly interactive and informative way of experiencing such major works.

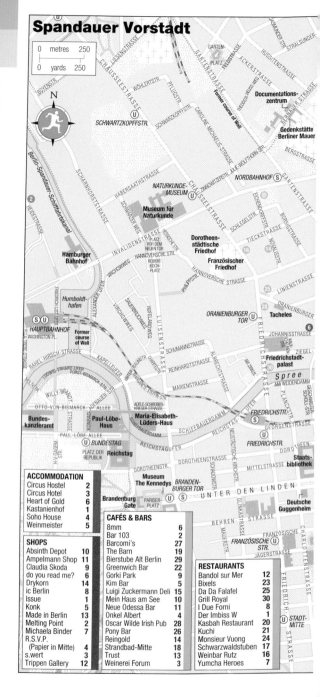

Spandauer Vorstadt

| 0 | metres | 250 |
| 0 | yards | 250 |

ACCOMMODATION

Circus Hostel	3
Circus Hotel	3
Heart of Gold	6
Kastanienhof	1
Soho House	4
Weinmeister	5

SHOPS

Absinth Depot	10
Ampelmann Shop	11
Claudia Skoda	9
do you read me?	6
Drykorn	14
ic Berlin	8
Issue	5
Konk	5
Made in Berlin	13
Melting Point	2
Michaela Binder	7
R.S.V.P. (Papier in Mitte)	4
s.wert	3
Trippen Gallery	12

CAFÉS & BARS

8mm	6
Bar 103	2
Barcomi's	27
The Barn	19
Bierstube Alt Berlin	29
Greenwich Bar	22
Gorki Park	9
Kim Bar	7
Luigi Zuckermann Deli	15
Mein Haus am See	10
Neue Odessa Bar	11
Onkel Albert	4
Oscar Wilde Irish Pub	28
Pony Bar	26
Reingold	14
Strandbad-Mitte	18
Trust	13
Weinerei Forum	3

RESTAURANTS

Bandol sur Mer	12
Bixels	23
Da Da Falafel	25
Grill Royal	30
I Due Forni	8
Der Imbiss W	1
Kasbah Restaurant	20
Kuchi	21
Monsieur Vuong	24
Schwarzwaldstuben	17
Weinbar Rutz	16
Yumcha Heroes	7

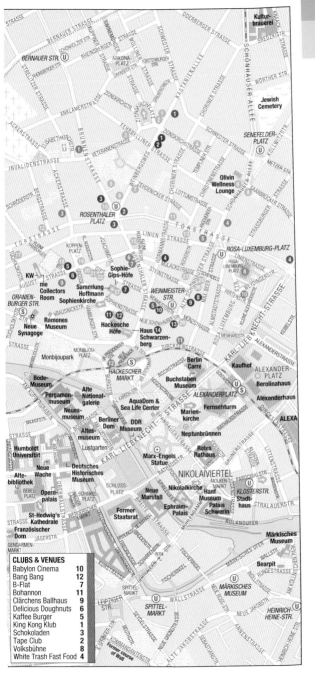

CLUBS & VENUES

Babylon Cinema	10
Bang Bang	12
B-Flat	7
Bohannon	11
Clärchens Ballhaus	9
Delicious Doughnuts	6
Kaffee Burger	5
King Kong Klub	1
Schokoladen	3
Tape Club	2
Volksbühne	8
White Trash Fast Food	4

RAMONES MUSEUM

Krausnickstr. 23 ⓢ Oranienburger Str.
☎ 030/75 52 88 90, ⓦ www.ramonesmuseum
.com. Mon–Thurs 9am–6pm, Fri 9am–8pm, Sat
10am–8pm, Sun noon–8pm. €3.50 (concerts
vary but mostly free). MAP P.32–33, POCKET MAP D11

Berlin's own shrine to the
American proto-punks, the
Ramones Museum was started
by music editor Flo Hayler two
decades ago. Back then the
collection amounted to a few
signed posters and some
T-shirts, but today it has
expanded to over three hundred
items of memorabilia. It's
certainly an eclectic assortment,
ranging from childhood photos
of the group to gig set lists and
flyers. The museum also hosts
film screenings, the odd
acoustic show from artists as
well known as Fran Healy from
Travis and special events.
There's a decent café (Mania)
next door selling coffee, beer
and snacks.

NEUE SYNAGOGE

Oranienburger Str. 28–30 ⓢ Oranienburger
Str. ☎ 030/88 02 83 00, ⓦ www.cjudaicum.de.
April–Sept Sun & Mon 10am–8pm, Tues–Thurs
10am–6pm, Fri 10am–5pm; March & Oct Sun
& Mon 10am–8pm, Tues–Thurs 10am–6pm,
Fri 10am–2pm; Nov–Feb Sun–Thurs
10am–6pm, Fri 10am–2pm. €3.
MAP P.32–33, POCKET MAP D12

Topped with a golden,
glittering dome that almost
rivals the Reichstag's for
prowess and recognition, the
Moorish Neue Synagoge (New
Synagogue) is a building with a
long and largely brutal history.
Consecrated on Rosh
Hashanah in 1866, it quickly
became the most important
synagogue in Berlin; in its
prime it could house over three
thousand worshippers. Its
fortunes changed under the
Nazis and the synagogue was
heavily vandalized during
Kristallnacht (1938), bombed

NEUE SYNAGOGE

by Allied planes (1945) and
demolished by the GDR in the
1950s. Rebuilt and restored in
the 1990s, it stands proudly
today both as a memorial to
Jewish suffering in Germany
and a depository of local Jewish
culture. Sadly it wasn't possible
to restore all of the synagogue
and its interior, so the front
section (or **Centrum
Judaicum**) displays the oldest
surviving elements – original
carvings, entrance vestibules
and anterooms – and hosts
exhibitions, which mostly focus
on the history of the building
and Jewish Berlin. You can get
an idea of the building's former
dimensions by visiting a
gravel-covered area outside,
which marks the original layout
of the synagogue.

ME COLLECTORS ROOM

Auguststr. 68 ⓢ Oranienburger Str. ☎ 030/86
00 85 10, ⓦ www.me-berlin.com. Tues–Sun
noon–6pm. €6. MAP P.32–33, POCKET MAP D11

The latest gallery to join
Auguststrasse's art scene, Me
Collectors Room was conceived
and built by chemist and
endocrinologist Thomas
Olbricht to showcase his
private art collection – which
happens to be among the most
comprehensive in Europe,

including works by John Currin, Franz Gertsch, Marlene Dumas and Gerhard Richter – via a series of alternating exhibitions. The "me" here is not misplaced egotism but an acronym for "moving energies": the collection spans painting, sculpture, photography, installation and new media works from the early sixteenth century to the present day. A permanent part of the museum is the **Wunderkammer**, which rekindles an older tradition, popular during the Renaissance period, of bringing together eccentric curiosities and "wonders" from around the world. The spacious café downstairs serves coffee and snacks (Tues–Sun 11.30am–6.30pm).

KW INSTITUTE FOR CONTEMPORARY ART

Auguststr. 69 ⑤ Oranienburger Str.
☎ 030/243 45 90, ⓦ www.kw-berlin.de.
Tues–Sun noon–7pm, Thurs noon–9pm. €6.
MAP P.32–33, POCKET MAP D11

The Kunst Werke Institute was one of the prime movers in the post-*Wende* (reunification) transformation of Auguststrasse into what has been dubbed Berlin's "art mile". Once a nineteenth-century margarine factory, KW was turned into a dedicated art space by Klaus Biesenbach in the early 1990s. The elegant facade leads into a lovely, tree-filled courtyard surrounded by six artist studios, a glass-walled café (designed by American artist Dan Graham) and a series of modern, white spaces that includes an exhibition hall by Berlin architect Hans Düttmann. The institute mainly exhibits cutting-edge international works from both up-and-coming and major names such as Doug Aitken, Dinos and Jake Chapman and Paul Pfeiffer. KW also runs Berlin's immensely popular Art Biennale.

TACHELES

Oranienburger Str. 54–56A ⑤ Oranienburger Str. ☎ 030/28 26 185, ⓦ www.tacheles.de.
Opening hours and admission varies.
MAP P.32–33, POCKET MAP C11

In the two decades since squatters took over this dilapidated former department store, Tacheles has become an unofficial symbol of the city's alternative art and politics movements as well as a major tourist landmark. Named after the Jewish word for "disclose, reveal or speak clearly" as well as slang for "bring to an end", the ramshackle, non-profit venue comprises a series of artist studios (around fifty, most open to visitors), bars, cinema, live music venue and a huge back yard that hosts exhibitions and more throughout the summer. While its fate currently hangs in the balance mainly thanks to commercial prospectors hungry to develop the site, the owners are confident that the immense public support the venue enjoys is enough to keep the Tacheles spirit alive for some time yet.

TACHELES

FRIEDRICHSTADTPALAST

Friedrichstr. 107 ⑤ Friedrichstr.
☎ 030/23 26 23 26, ⓦ www.show-palace.eu.
MAP P.32–33, POCKET MAP C12

Founded in the 1860s, this
theatre has a long and
distinguished history, having
been a market hall, circus,
theatre and, during the Nazi
era, the Theater des Volkes
when it staged bourgeois
operettas. Its current
incarnation – an imposing
GDR-style block – was opened
in 1984. The main hall is a
whopping 2800 square metres
and holds up to two thousand
people for its programme of
broadway shows, musicals and
high-profile pop shows.

MUSEUM FÜR NATURKUNDE

Invalidenstr. 43 ⓤ Naturekundemuseum
☎ 030/20 93 85 91, ⓦ www
.naturkundemuseum-berlin.de. Tues–Fri
9.30am–6pm, Sat & Sun 10am–6pm.€5.
MAP P.32–33, POCKET MAP A10

Inaugurated in 1889 by
Emperor Wilhelm II, Berlin's
natural history museum is the
largest of its kind in Germany,
counting some thirty million
objects within its collections.
Highlights include the dinosaur
hall, which includes the largest
mounted dinosaur in the world
– a Brachiosaurus Brancai
composed of fossilized bones
recovered by German
paleontologist Werner Janensch
from Tanzania in the early
1900s – and a wonderfully

preserved Archaeopteryx, the
earliest known bird.

HAMBURGER BAHNHOF

Invalidenstr. 50 ⑤ &ⓤ Hauptbahnhof
☎ 030/26 64 24 242, ⓦ www
.hamburgerbahnhof.de. Tues–Fri 10am–6pm,
Sat 11am–8pm, Sun 11am–6pm. €12. Free
guided tours (in English) Sat & Sun noon.
MAP P.32–33, POCKET MAP A11

Berlin's museum for
contemporary art (Museum für
Gegenwart) is one of the city's
major modern art venues.
Occupying a capacious and
architecturally interesting space
(formerly one of the city's first
terminal stations) its
permanent collection focuses
on the major movements of the
late twentieth century up to the
present day. There's an
emphasis on video and film,
built from a vast array of 1970s
video art gifted by Mike
Steiner, and the expansive
Joseph Beuys archive, to which
the entire west wing is
dedicated. The museum's Marx
Collection has works by
Anselm Kiefer and Andy
Warhol, while Friedrich
Christian Flic's collection –
donated in 2008 – added 166
works by artists like John Cage,
Bruce Nauman and Wolfgang
Tillmans. Alongside rotating
showcases from these
permanent collections, the
museum hosts temporary
exhibitions by international
artists usually at the forefront
of their respective fields.

Shops

ABSINTH DEPOT

Weinmeisterstr. 4 ⓊWeinmeisterstr.
☎030/28 16 789. Mon–Fri 2pm–midnight, Sat
1pm–midnight. MAP P.32–33, POCKET MAP E11
The place not only to find all
kinds of "Green Fairy" liquor
but also a wide variety of props
for the true absinth experience.
You can even have a little taste
should you feel the urge.

AMPELMANN SHOP

Rosenthaler Str. 40–41 ⓊWeinmeisterstr.
☎030/44 72 64 38, Ⓦwww.ampelmann.de.
Mon–Fri 9.30am–10pm, Sat 10am–7pm.
MAP P.32–33, POCKET MAP D11
Everything here is based on the
Ampelmännchen – the
distinctive (and stylish) traffic
light men once present on all
East German traffic lights, who
were saved from extinction
after the Wall fell by various
high-profile campaigns.

CLAUDIA SKODA

Alte Schönhauser Str. 35 ⓊWeinmeisterstr.
☎030/28 07 211. Mon–Fri noon–8pm, Sat
11am–7pm. MAP P.32–33, POCKET MAP E11
This beautiful shop is filled
with Skoda's renowned and
instantly recognizable knitwear.
Unapologetically chic (and
correspondingly expensive), the
clothes are geared mostly for
women but there's a small
men's section too.

DO YOU READ ME?

Auguststr. 28 ⓊRosenthaler Platz
☎030/69 54 96 95, Mon–Sat 10am–7.30pm.
MAP P.32–33, POCKET MAP D11
A magazine lover's paradise,
this multi-lingual store offers a
vast assortment of magazines
and reading material from
around the world, covering
fashion and photography, art
and architecture. Check the
website for regular readings
and events.

DRYKORN

Neue Schönhauser Str. 14 ⓊWeinmeisterstr.
☎030/28 35 010. Mon–Fri noon–8pm, Sat
noon–7pm. MAP P.32–33, POCKET MAP E12
Drykorn sells a good range of
smart urban clothing created
by the likes of Grisby, Karl
Lagerfeld, Bonser, Cinque and
more.

IC BERLIN

Max-Beer-Str. 17 ⓊWeinmeisterstr.
☎030/41 71 770. Mon–Sat 11am–8pm.
MAP P.32–33, POCKET MAP E11
Internationally famous thanks
to owner Ralph Anderl's
handmade screwless frames
and fantastic designs, the
glasses here have been bought
by everyone from Tom Cruise
to Shakira. They're not cheap,
but they are beautiful.

ISSUE

Kastanienallee 58 ⓊEberswalder Str.
☎030/44 32 70 89. Mon–Sat noon–8pm.
MAP P.32–33, POCKET MAP E10
Magazine and bookstore with a
broad range of creative, arty
magazines, from familiar
monthlies to obscure one-offs
and signed collectors items, all
neatly laid out on makeshift
black crates and tables.

AMPELMANN SHOP

MADE IN BERLIN

Neue Schönhauser Str. 19 ⓤ Weinmeisterstr.
☎ 030/21 23 06 01. Mon–Sat noon–8pm.
MAP P.32–33, POCKET MAP E12

One of four shops in the city
that sell cutting-edge, mostly
vintage clothes for girls and
boys. You'll find everything
from hats and shoes to blouses
and faintly bizarre appendages.
Tuesday noon till 3pm is happy
hour (20 percent off all vintage).

MELTING POINT

Kastanienallee 55 ⓤ Rosenthaler Platz
☎ 030/44 04 71 31. Mon–Sat noon–8pm.
MAP P.32–33, POCKET MAP E10

Opened in the mid-1990s
Melting Point records has stayed
true to Berlin's techno and house
culture, though it also sells funk,
Afro, Latin and more. Masses of
vinyl and a small CD section.

MICHAELA BINDER

Gipsstr. 13 ⓤ Weinmeisterstr. ☎ 030/28 38
48 69. Tues–Fri noon–7pm, Sat noon–4pm.
MAP P.32–33, POCKET MAP E11

Michaela Binder's smart shop
stocks her stylish rings,
bracelets, ear studs and
necklaces in clean, basic
shapes, from silver and gold.
There's also a line of (cheaper)
steel and stone vases.

KONK

Kleine Hamburger Str. 15 ⓢ Oranienburger
Str. ☎ 030/28 09 78 39. Mon–Fri noon–8pm,
Sat noon–6pm. MAP P.32–33, POCKET MAP D11

Featuring collections from
many of Berlin's esteemed
labels (C. Neeon, Anntian and
Boessert/Schorn), this women's
boutique features cutting-edge
fashions, jewellery and other
glamorous accessories that flit
between fashion and art.

R.S.V.P. (PAPIER IN MITTE)

Mulackstr. 14 ⓤ Weinmeisterstr.
☎ 030/28 09 46 44. Mon–Sat noon–7pm.
MAP P.32–33, POCKET MAP E11

From rare international
notebooks to the store's own
unique printed cards and
journals, R.S.V.P. sells elegant
stationery, including classic
brands like Moleskine and
Caran D'ache plus smaller
products from international
artists.

S.WERT

Brunnenstr. 191 ⓤ Rosenthaler Platz
☎ 030/40 05 66 55. Mon–Fri 11am–7pm, Sat
11am–6pm. MAP P.32–33, POCKET MAP D10

Interested in special Berliner
Skyline curtains, or unique
designs of 1960s wrapping
paper? s.wert sells all this and
more, including stylish
drinking glasses, dresses and
pillows, all in a vibrant and
friendly setting.

TRIPPEN GALLERY

Hackesche Höfe, Hofs 4 & 6, Rosenthaler Str.
40/41 ⓢ Hackescher Markt (also Knaackstr.
26, Prenzlauer Berg) ☎ 030/24 63 22 84.
Mon–Sat noon–7pm. MAP P.32–33, POCKET MAP D11

Trippen sells men's and
women's shoes for every
occasion in a range of
materials. There are several
branches in the city, but this
flagship store has the biggest
range. Footwear can also be
made to order.

Restaurants

BANDOL SUR MER

Torstr. 167 ⓤ Rosenthaler Platz ☎ 030/67 30 20 51. Daily 6pm–late. MAP P.32–33, POCKET MAP D11

A former kebab kiosk refurbished into a tiny but casually upmarket French restaurant, *Bandol sur Mer* is hugely popular. The menu, chalked up on the all-black walls, consists of fine French cuisine like snails, entrecôte and foie gras. There's not too much innovation for the price (mains around €18) but the food is consistently good.

BIXELS

Mulackstr. 38 ⓤ Rosa-Luxemburg-Platz ☎ 0178 13 19 320, ⓦ www.danielbixel.com. Mon–Sat noon–9pm. MAP P.32–33, POCKET MAP E11

This small, hip, all-black restaurant is dedicated to one thing: the humble baked potato. Not the first thing you'd expect on a trendy Mitte street but then these aren't ordinary potatoes. Baked in a vintage oven, they come with suitably sumptuous fillings (from €5.50); wine and beer available.

DA DA FALAFEL

Linienstr. 132 ⓤ Oranienburger Tor ☎ 0171 35 97 392, ⓦ www.dadafalafel.de. Mon–Sat 9am–6pm. MAP P.32–33, POCKET MAP C11

Berlin isn't exactly short of falafels but *Da Da* stands out from the crowd, thanks to fresh salads and an excellent array of sauces. The Dada Teller (€6.50) will set you up for a day's sightseeing, though you may find a long queue at lunchtimes.

GRILL ROYAL

Friedrichstr. 105b ⓤ Oranienburger Tor ☎ 030/28 87 92 88, ⓦ www.grillroyal.com. Daily from 6pm. MAP P.32–33, POCKET MAP C12

The steaks are definitely high end at this celeb-friendly restaurant. Some of the best

Argentine, German and French cuts in town are served, as well as excellent seafood and wines. In summer try and reserve a seat out on the Spree-facing terrace. Mains from €16.

I DUE FORNI

Schönhauser Allee 12 ⓤ Senefelderplatz ☎ 030/44 01 73 33. Daily noon–midnight. MAP P.32–33, POCKET MAP H2

This famous Italian joint serves up cheap and tasty brick-oven pizzas (€5.50–€8.50) and pasta dishes, in an idiosyncratic atmosphere, aided by the punk staff (all Italian) and – in summer – a large beer garden. Service is appropriately blasé.

DER IMBISS W

Kastanienallee 49 ⓤ Senefelderplatz ☎ 030/43 35 22 06, ⓦ www.w-derimbiss.de. Daily: summer noon–midnight; winter 12.30–11.30pm. MAP P.32–33, POCKET MAP H2

Easily identified by its cheekily inverted *McDonald's* sign (and orange tables), *Imbiss W* serves up fusion food that includes such unusual items as naan pizza and other bright ideas. The results can be a bit hit and miss, but they're generally good and the reasonable prices (items begin at €2) and outdoor seating make this a good budget option.

BANDOL SUR MER

KASBAH RESTAURANT

Gipsstr. 2 ⊕ Rosenthaler Platz ☎ 030/27 59 43 61. ⓦ www.kasbah-berlin.de. Tues–Sun 6pm–midnight. MAP P.32–33, POCKET MAP D11

One of the few spots in Berlin to find authentic Moroccan cuisine, *Kasbah* has the experience down to a tee, from the rose-water hand-rinsing ritual and flickering lanterns to the tasty tagines and couscous dishes (from €11). Good Moroccan wines available.

KUCHI

Gipsstr. 3 ⊕ Rosenthaler Platz ☎ 030/28 38 66 22, ⓦ www.kuchi.de. Mon–Sat noon–midnight, Sun 6pm–midnight. MAP P.32–33, POCKET MAP D11

Kuchi might not serve the best sushi in Berlin, but it's definitely the buzziest place to eat the stuff in, with a classy interior, hipster clientele and upbeat atmosphere. The menu ranges beyond sushi (nigiri from €4) to noodles and tempura. At peak times expect to share a table. The tiny shop next door serves the best ramen in town.

MONSIEUR VUONG

Alte Schönhauser Str. 46 ⊕ Rosa-Luxemburg-Platz ☎ 030/99 29 69 24, ⓦ www.monsieurvuong.de. Daily noon–midnight. MAP P.32–33, POCKET MAP E11

The light, simple and cheap Vietnamese food served at

Monsieur Vuong has made it one of the most popular dining spots in Mitte. The menu changes every few days but there's always good fresh soups, noodle salads and fruit cocktails. You may have to wait for a table, especially at peak times. Specials from €7.

SCHWARZWALDSTUBEN

Tucholskystr. 48 ⓢ Oranienburger Str. ☎ 030/28 09 80 84. Mon–Wed & Sun 9am–11pm, Thurs–Sat 9am–midnight. MAP P.32–33, POCKET MAP C11

This Mitte mainstay doubles as a casual restaurant serving hearty Swabian food – think Sauerkraut, *Maultaschen* (filled pasta) and *Flammkuchen* (a type of thin-crust pizza, from €8.90) – and a friendly bar in the evenings with decent German beers on draught.

WEINBAR RUTZ

Chausseestr. 8 ⊕ Naturkundemuseum ☎ 030/24 62 87 60, ⓦ www.rutz-weinbar.de. Tues–Sat: wine bar 4–11pm; restaurant 6.30–10.30pm. MAP P.32–33, POCKET MAP B11

Michelin-starred cuisine on the second floor and over a thousand international wines on offer at the ground-floor bar make this a de rigeur stop for foodies. It's expensive – multi-course menus range from €90 to €122 – but the bar sells slightly cheaper (but still great) home-style dishes.

YUMCHA HEROES

Weinbergsweg 8 ⊕ Rosenthaler Platz ☎ 030/76 21 30 35, ⓦ www.yumchaheroes.de. Daily noon–midnight. MAP P.32–33, POCKET MAP E16

With the same owners as nearby Portuguese café *Galao*, *Yumcha Heroes* is *the* place in Mitte for dumplings – steamed, baked or in a tasty broth. The food is handmade and MSG-free, cooked in an open kitchen and served in a small, but stylish interior.

YUMCHA HEROES

Cafés and bars

8MM

Schönhauser Allee 177 Ⓤ Senefelderplatz
☎ 030/40 50 06 24, Ⓦ www.8mmbar.com.
Daily 9pm–close. MAP P.32–33, POCKET MAP F10

It's just a small, blacked-out room with a small bar, a DJ spinning anything from rock to northern soul and 8mm films projected onto one wall – but it's a superb place for low-key, late-night hedonism.

BAR 103

Kastanienallee 49 Ⓤ Senefelderplatz/
Rosenthaler Platz ☎ 030/44 34 11 03,
Ⓦ www.agentur103.de. Daily 9am–3am.
MAP P.32–33, POCKET MAP H2

A relative veteran of the Kastanienallee scene, *103* doubles as chic café and bar hangout. Its location, right on the intersection of Zionskirchplatz and "Casting Alley", makes it a prime people-watching spot. Staff can be cool bordering on nonchalant but the food, while slightly pricey, is decent enough.

BARCOMI'S

Sophienstr. 21, Sophie-Gips-Höfe
Ⓤ Weinmeisterstr. ☎ 030/28 59 83 63,
Ⓦ www.barcomis.de. Mon–Sat 9am–9pm,
Sun 10am–9pm. MAP P.32–33, POCKET MAP O11

This second outlet from American baker Cynthia Barcomi is tucked away in a lovely courtyard and offers excellent bagels, brunches, coffee and cakes – the cheesecake is justly famous – as well as a particularly lively vibe. Reservations essential at weekends.

THE BARN

Auguststr. 58 Ⓤ Rosenthaler Platz ☎ 0151
24 10 51 36, Ⓦ www.thebarn.de. Mon–Fri
8am–6pm, Sat 10am–6pm, Sun noon–6pm.
MAP P.32–33, POCKET MAP O11

Staff in lumberjack shirts, wooden shelves stacked with

BARCOMI'S

delicious products for sale, and some of the best coffee in town make *The Barn* well worth a visit. The sandwiches, quiches and cakes are all freshly made and organic too.

BIERSTUBE ALT BERLIN

Münzstr. 23 Ⓤ Weinmeisterstr. ☎ 030/28 19
687. Daily from 8pm. MAP P.32–33, POCKET MAP E12

A traditional corner pub, *Alt Berlin* has successfully resisted time (and gentrification) in an area that's all but lost to modern cosmopolitanism. Traditional jazz or Tom Waits features on the stereo, and since it's a small place that values atmosphere, don't show up in a large group as you'll likely be turfed out.

GORKI PARK

Weinbergsweg 25 Ⓤ Rosenthaler Platz
☎ 030/44 87 28 6, Ⓦ www.gorki-park.de.
Mon–Sat 9.30am–2am, Sun 10am–2pm.
MAP P.32–33, POCKET MAP E10

Gorki Park comprises a network of lounge-style rooms decked out with interesting furniture and retro wallpaper. Despite the Russian theme, mostly evident in the name and the blini and borscht available, there's a distinctly Berlin-esque "Wohnzimmer" (living room) feel to the place.

GREENWICH BAR

Gipsstr. 5 ⓤ Rosenthaler Platz ☎ 030/28 09
55 66, ⓦ www.greenwichbar.com. Mon–Sat
9am–6pm. MAP P.32–33, POCKET MAP D11

Though past its heyday, this
New York-style cocktail bar is
still a decent place for a
cocktail or two. Quiet in the
week, it's popular with a dressy
crowd at weekends, who hang
out at the long bar and admire
the fish-tank or lounge on the
(slightly tatty) leather sofas at
the back.

KIM BAR

Brunnenstr. 10 ⓤ Rosenthaler Platz ⓦ www
.kim-in-berlin.com. Mon & Wed–Sat 9pm–
late. MAP P.32–33, POCKET MAP D10

Art space, bar and locals'
hangout, *Kim* is a firm favourite
among Mitte's trend-conscious
residents. There's no sign on the
door, just a glass facade (the
entrance is through the adjacent
courtyard) onto a perpetually
dark, white-walled space. Check
the website for information on
art, film and DJ nights.

LUIGI ZUCKERMANN DELI

Rosenthaler Str. 67 ⓤ Rosenthaler Platz
ⓦ www.luigizuckermann.com. Daily 7am–late.
MAP P.32–33, POCKET MAP E11

This gourmet Italian–Israeli
deli does a brisk trade thanks
to its large and considered
range of speciality sandwiches
and decent coffee (soy options
included): the ingredients are
fresh, staff are cheerful, and it's
open more or less round the
clock at weekends.

MEIN HAUS AM SEE

Brunnenstr. 197–198 ⓤ Rosenthaler Platz
☎ 030/23 88 35 61, ⓦ www.mein
-haus-am-see.blogspot.com. Open 24hr.
MAP P.32–33, POCKET MAP D16

A spacious café/bar, stumbling
distance from Rosenthaler Platz,
Mein Haus am See is filled with
comfy flea-market furnishings
and serves as a great spot for
some book reading or a chat
during the day, and a more
upbeat drink late at night when
DJs play anything from disco to
Latin.

NEUE ODESSA BAR

Torstr. 89 ⓤ Rosenthaler Platz/
Rosa-Luxemburg-Platz ☎ 0171 83 98 991.
ⓦ www.neueodessabar.de. Daily from 7pm.
MAP P.32–33, POCKET MAP E10

This newish bar has become a
bit of a place-to-be thanks to a
well thought out combination
of attractive, swanky interior,
reasonably made cocktails and
table service. Perpetually busy
but never too overbearing.

ONKEL ALBERT

Zionskirchstr. 63 ⓤ Senefelderplatz
☎ 030/44 04 56 10, ⓦ www.onkelalbert.de.
Mon–Fri 10am–7pm, Sat & Sun 2–7pm.
MAP P.32–33, POCKET MAP E10

This breezy, colourful
"kindercafé" is a great place for
visiting parents to let the kids
run around while they enjoy a
coffee or spot of lunch. There's
a seating area upstairs with
sofas and tables, an adjacent
play area with plentiful toys,
books and a kids' kitchen, plus
second-hand children's clothes
shop below.

ONKEL ALBERT

OSCAR WILDE IRISH PUB

Friedrichstr. 112A ⓤ Oranienburger Tor
☎ 030/28 28 166. Mon–Thurs noon–2am, Fri
& Sat noon–3am, Sun noon–midnight.
MAP P.32–33, POCKET MAP C11

Every city's got one, and this is
Berlin's quintessential Irish bar.
Guinness, Kilkenny and
Strongbow on draught (as well
as German beers), a good
selection of whiskies, Irish
breakfasts and televised
sporting events make this
perennially popular.

PONY BAR

Alte Schönhauser Str. 44 ⓤ Rosenthaler
Platz ☎ 016 37 75 66 03, Mon–Sat from noon,
Sun from 6pm. MAP P.32–33, POCKET MAP E11

Just along from *Monsieur
Vuong* lies the equally popular
Pony Bar – a small but perfectly
formed drinking spot that
serves bottled beers and
cocktails (and finger food).

REINGOLD

Novalisstr. 11 ⓤ Oranienburger Tor ☎ 030/28
38 76 76, ⓦ www.reingold.de. Daily 7pm–3am.
MAP P.32–33, POCKET MAP C11

Featuring one of the most
impressive bars in town –
certainly one of the longest –
this classy watering hole offers
impeccably attired waiters who
make meticulous cocktails
while you lounge on a leather
sofa and listen to 1920s jazz.

STRANDBAD-MITTE

Kleine Hamburger Str. 16 ⓢ Oranienburger Str.
☎ 030/24 62 89 63, ⓦ www.strandbad-mitte.de.
Daily 9am–2am. MAP P.32–33, POCKET MAP D11

This laid-back café, with breezy,
green-tiled seaside-themed
decor, is slightly hidden from
the tourist routes and has a
correspondingly local vibe. The
food and coffee are good, the
staff friendly and there are
magazines to read too. Check
out the weekend breakfasts as
well as the delicious cakes.

WEINEREI

TRUST

Torstr. 72 ⓤ Rosa-Luxemburg-Platz.
Tues–Sat 8pm–late. MAP P.32–33, POCKET MAP E11

Founded by the owners of
Cookies Cream (see p.61) and
Weekend (see p.71), this bar is
every bit as cool and clubby as
you'd expect. Ring a bell at the
unmarked door to be ushered
into a bunker-esque space that's
all unfinished walls and cosy
spaces. The bar only serves
bottles of champagne or vodka
(in small or large versions) and
the toilets are unisex and
interconnected. Trust indeed.

WEINEREI FORUM

Shop: Veteranenstr. 14; bar: Fehrbellnir Str.
57 ⓤ Rosenthaler Platz ☎ 030/44 06 983,
ⓦ www.weinerei.com. Shop: Mon–Fri 1–8pm,
Sat 11am–8pm; bars 8pm–midnight. MAP
P.32–33, POCKET MAP E10

This "underground" members
club-style wine shop and bar
operates on an honesty-box
system after 8pm: you pay
what you feel is fair for your
drinks when you leave. As such
it's popular with a mix of leftie
sympathizers, students and
freeloaders. The wine is
decidedly average but the
atmosphere is friendly. The
owners run similar ventures
nearby – *Perlin* (Griebenowstr.
5) and *Fra Rosa* (Zionskirchstr.
40). Seek and you shall find...

Clubs and venues

BABYLON CINEMA

Rosa-Luxemburg-Str. 30 ⑩ Rosa-Luxemburg-Platz ☏ 030/24 25 969, ⓦ www.babylonberlin.de. MAP P.32–33, POCKET MAP F11

This striking Berlin *Kino* opened in 1929 and remains one of the defining architectural landmarks of Rosa-Luxemburg-Platz. Today the cinema shows a mix of indie, trash and cult movies, as well as hosting concerts.

BANG BANG

Neue Promenade 10 ⓢ Hackescher Markt ☏ 030/60 40 53 10, ⓦ www.bangbangclub.net. Tues–Sat 9pm–late. MAP P.32–33, POCKET MAP D12

A small venue, a stone's throw from Hackescher Markt, that packs a decent punch when it comes to putting on live music: expect everything from avant-garde to British and US indie acts as well as soul, rock and electro DJs. The crowd tends to be young and musically aware.

B-FLAT

Rosenthaler Str. 13 ⑩ Rosenthaler Platz ☏ 030/28 33 123, ⓦ www.b-flat-berlin.de. Mon–Sat from 9/10pm. MAP P.32–33, POCKET MAP E11

This cosy jazz bar, with windows facing onto the street and small bar at the back, offers a mix of local musicians and the occasional international act. Popular at weekends, there's also a free jam session on Wednesdays (from 9pm) that gets busy.

BOHANNON

Dircksenstr. 40 ⓢ Hackescher Markt ☏ 030/69 50 52 87, ⓦ www.bohannon.de. Mon & Thurs–Sat 10pm–late. MAP P.32–33, POCKET MAP E12

Named after funk legend Hamilton Bohannon, this club is one of the few places in the city with regular hip-hop, funk and dancehall sets, though, despite the considered music policy, the sound system could be better.

CLÄRCHENS BALLHAUS

Auguststr. 24 ⑩ Rosenthaler Platz ☏ 030/28 29 29 5, ⓦ www.ballhaus.de. Daily 10am–late. MAP P.32–33, POCKET MAP D11

A night at *Clärchens* is a bit like attending someone else's wedding – in a good way. An authentic prewar ballroom, it still hosts dance classes, but at weekends the downstairs is taken over by one of the most diverse crowds (young, old, straight, gay) in Berlin, who are attracted by the unique atmosphere of a live covers band and an unpretentious good time. Tasty pizzas and traditional cuisine served too.

DELICIOUS DOUGHNUTS

Rosenthaler Str. 9 ⑩ Rosenthaler Platz ☏ 030/28 09 92 74, ⓦ www.delicious -doughnuts.de. Daily 9pm–open end. MAP P.32–33, POCKET MAP E11

If there's one place in Mitte that's open to anybody, at any time of night, it's this place. Part club, part dive bar, *Doughnuts* comes into its own in the small hours, when it fills with post-club casualties, the odd transvestite and those looking to drink themselves to bed.

BABYLON CINEMA

lounge – albeit one with cheap drinks, a friendly atmosphere and a consistently good line-up of indie-pop bands and upcoming singer/songwriters.

TAPE CLUB

Heidestr. 14 ⓤ & ⓢ Hauptbahnhof ☎ 030/28 48 48 73, ⓦ www.tapeberlin.de. Fri midnight–8am, Sat midnight–9am. MAP P.32–33, POCKET MAP E3

Modelled on a New York club, *Tape* offers a gold-themed upstairs bar, and a slick, dark main room (watch out for the art tree) with a lovely, crisp sound system that plays house, techno and more. Every month or so the club hosts an art event "Tape Modern".

VOLKSBÜHNE

Linienstr. 227 ⓤ Rosa-Luxemburg-Platz ☎ 030/24 06 57 77, ⓦ www.volksbuehne -berlin.de. MAP P.32–33, POCKET MAP F11

Built just before World War I, the Volksbühne ("People's Theatre") has its origin in the free people's theatre movement. Damaged during World War II, it was rebuilt in the 1950s and since 1992 has been directed by Frank Castorf, who has established it as one of Germany's most experimental theatres. The venue also hosts club nights and concerts within its various rooms.

WHITE TRASH FAST FOOD

Schönhauser Allee 6–7 ⓤ Rosa-Luxemburg-Platz ☎ 030/ 50 34 86 68, ⓦ www .whitetrashfastfood.com. Mon–Fri noon–late, Sat & Sun 6pm–late. MAP P.32–33, POCKET MAP F11

This perennially popular den of kitsch acts as restaurant, bar and club/live venue. Kitted out with Wild West salon meets Chinese restaurant theme, the food here – mostly burgers and nachos – is decent enough and matches the informal nature of the crowd, who come to check out the regular DJs and bands.

KAFFEE BURGER

Torstr. 60 ⓤ Rosa-Luxemburg-Platz ☎ 030/28 04 64 95, ⓦ www.kaffeeburger.de. Mon–Thurs from 8pm, Fri & Sat from 9 or 10pm, Sun from 7pm. MAP P.32–33, POCKET MAP E11

Kaffee Burger has been throwing parties and events beloved of students and culture vultures for years. The bi-monthly Russian Disco night is most popular; check the website for poetry readings, film screenings and live music.

KING KONG KLUB

Brunnenstr. 173 ⓤ Rosenthaler Platz ☎ 030/91 20 68 60, ⓦ www.king-kong-klub .de. Daily 9pm–late. MAP P.32–33, POCKET MAP D10

All tattered leather sofas, subdued lighting and B-movie paraphernalia, this kitsch club is a fun place to spend a night. The music is mainly rock and electro and it's popular with students and local eccentrics. Drinks are relatively cheap and entry is usually just a euro or two "donation" for the DJ.

SCHOKOLADEN

Ackerstr. 169 ⓤ Rosenthaler Platz ☎ 030/28 26 527, ⓦ www.schokoladen-mitte.de. Daily from 9pm. MAP P.32–33, POCKET MAP D10

A small live venue (in a former chocolate factory) that is a bit like visiting a private

The Museum Island

The world-renowned Museum Island (Museumsinsel) comprises five of Berlin's most famous museums and is an absolute must for any visitor to Berlin, if only to stroll around and take in the lovely buildings and waterside atmosphere. Friedrich Wilhelm III commissioned the Royal Museum (now the Altes Museum) in 1830, but the plan for an island of museums – intended as the embodiment of Enlightenment ideas about culture – came to fruition under Friedrich Wilhelm IV of Prussia. The site was further developed under successive Prussian kings. The range of artwork and architecture is startling, spanning two thousand years and featuring such treasures as the Roman gate of Miletus and the bust of Nefertiti as well as a dizzying range of paintings and sculptures. Though badly damaged during World War II, with the collections divided during the Cold War, sensitive renovations have seen the buildings brought back to life. As well as the main five museums, the island also comprises the Lustgarten park, Berlin Cathedral and the site of the former Stadtschloss.

BERLINER DOM (CATHEDRAL)

Am Lustgarten 1 ☎ 030/20 26 91 36,
ⓦ www.berlinerdom.de. Mon–Sat 9am–8pm,
Sun noon–8pm, Oct–March closes 7pm. €5,
€8 with audio guide. Guided tours of the
dome are available (☎ 030/20 26 91 19).
MAP OPPOSITE, POCKET MAP D13

Designed by Julius Raschdorff in Baroque style with Italian Renaissance influences, Berlin's Protestant cathedral was intended as a counterpart to St Peter's Basilica in Rome. The present structure dates from

1905, but stands on the site of several earlier buildings, including the St Erasmus Chapel and a Neoclassical design by Schinkel dating from 1822. Restoration of the current interior began in 1984 and in 1993 the church reopened. It's a handsome and interesting building to explore, with notable eye candy including Sauer's organ, stained-glass windows designed by Anton von Werner and a marvellous dome intricately decorated with mosaics. You can get an excellent close-up view of the dome – and the entire interior – by climbing the 270 steps to the gallery. The most historically significant feature of the cathedral is its crypt, which holds more than eighty sarcophagi of Prussian royals, including those of Friedrich I and his queen, Sophie Charlotte.

LUSTGARTEN

MAP BELOW, POCKET MAP D13

Berlin's "Pleasure Garden" is a fundamental part of the Museum Island landscape. It's difficult to believe that this charming rectangular park, a great spot for picnics or taking a pause between museum visits, has been used variously as a military parade ground (for Wilhelm I and Napoleon), mass protests (a huge anti-Nazi demo here in 1933 prompted the banning of demonstrations) and rallies (Hitler addressed up to a million people here). Bombed in the War and renamed Marx-Engels-Platz by the GDR, its current incarnation harks back to Peter Joseph Lenné's early nineteenth-century design with a central 13m-high fountain, as re-envisioned by German landscape architect Hans Loidl.

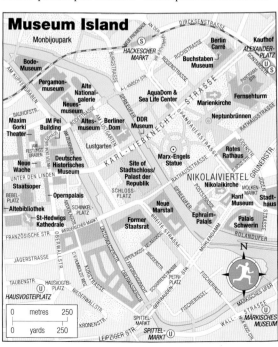

Museum Island practicalities

The **phone number** and **website** for all Museum Island enquiries are: ☎030/26 64 24 242 (Mon–Fri 9am–4pm), www.smb.museum. The nearest **station** for all museums is ⑤Hackescher Markt.

Three-day tickets for all state museums (including those in the Kulturforum, see pp.74–77) and a wealth of private museums can be bought for €19 (discounted €9.50), though these do not include special exhibitions. Note that entrance is always free for anyone under 18.

The **Berlin Welcome Card Museum Island** includes admission to many museums including the Museum Island, travel for up to 72 hours and up to 50 percent discount on many top attractions in Berlin for €34. See www.visitberlin.de.

The **City Tour Card** (www.citytourcard.com) offers a Museum Island addition to their visitor pass that includes entry to all Museum Island museums for €31.50 (valid for 72 hours in the tariff area Berlin AB).

A new museum called the James Simon-Galerie is scheduled to open in 2014 (between the Neues Museum and Kupfergraben), which will act as a welcome centre for the island and feature an auditorium, café, special exhibitions area and museum shop.

ALTES MUSEUM

Am Lustgarten. Mon–Wed & Fri–Sun 10am–6pm Thurs 10am–10pm. Guided tours by arrangement ☎030/266 36 66. €8. MAP P.47, POCKET MAP D13

The Altes Museum, built between 1823 and 1830 after a design by Karl Friedrich Schinkel, is Berlin's oldest museum. It's also one of the city's most important Classicist statements and a marvellous piece of architecture, all fluted Ionic columns, a beautiful rotunda filled with sculptures of Greek gods and a grand staircase that more than nods to Athens and Rome. As well as Greek statues downstairs, the upper floor contains a colossal range of Roman and Etruscan Art – urns, shields, sarcophagi, friezes – all chronologically and thematically arranged.

NEUES MUSEUM

www.neues-museum.de. Mon–Wed & Sun 10am–6pm, Thurs–Sat 10am–8pm. €10. MAP P.47, POCKET MAP D13

One of the Museum Island's undoubted highlights, the misleadingly named Neues Museum was opened in 1859 to cater for the overspill of the by-then over-crowded Altes Museum. Largely destroyed during World War II, it was only reopened in 2009, fully restored by British architect David Chipperfield. Over

NEUES MUSEUM

three floors you'll find no less than twenty exhibition halls, each impressively designed and connected via a stunning winding staircase. As well as the archeological collections of the Egyptian museum and papyrus collection, there's plenty of pre- and early history, as well as works from classical antiquity. The big draw is the bust of Egyptian Queen Nefertiti – famously described as "the world's most beautiful woman" – but you could happily spend an entire day absorbing the endless exhibits. Note that due to the popularity of the exhibitions you need to reserve a time slot, either by purchasing one from the nearby sales cabin or on the museum's website in advance.

PERGAMONMUSEUM

Am Kupfergraben 5, Mon–Wed & Fri–Sun 10am–6pm Thurs 10am–10pm €8. Guided tours ☎ 030/266 36 66. MAP P.47, POCKET MAP D12

The Pergamonmuseum was built by Alfred Mussel in 1930 to house the artefacts from the nineteenth-century excavations of German archeologists in Pergamon and Asia Minor, perhaps most famously the controversial "Priam's treasure" – a cache of gold and other artefacts discovered by classical archeologist Heinrich Schliemann, but whose authenticity and relationship to Homeric king Priam has long been in doubt. Essentially three museums in one, the museum offers a collection of Classical antiquities (part of which is also on display in the Altes Museum); the museum of the Ancient Near East; and the museum of Islamic Art. As with the Neues Museum, you can spend a day here easily, though the main highlights – a reconstructed (and mind-bogglingly large) Pergamon Altar from the second century BC, the Market Gate of Miletus (an important example of Roman architecture) and the bright blue glazed-brick Ishtar Gate of Babylon from the sixth century BC – can be viewed quickly if you're pushed for time. Also worth looking out for is the facade of the throne hall of King Nebuchadnezzar, a reconstructed Neo-Assyrian palace from the twelfth century BC and the seventeenth-century Aleppo Zimmer (Aleppo room).

ALTE NATIONALGALERIE

ALTE NATIONALGALERIE

Bodestr. 1–3. Tues–Wed & Fri–Sun
10am–6pm, Thurs 10am–10pm. €8.
MAP P.47, POCKET MAP D12

The Neoclassical Alte Nationalgalerie (Old National Gallery), designed to resemble a Greek temple, houses one of the country's most significant collections of nineteenth-century painting. Built between 1866 and 1876, the museum re-opened in 2001 to showcase its wealth of Classical, Romantic, Impressionist and early Modernist masterpieces. Highlights include the

Schlossplatz

The reconstruction of Berlin's **Stadtschloss** (City Palace) is just one of the many controversial components of Berlin's cityscape – not least because of its projected €552-million cost. The original palace, which featured architectural elements designed, built and inspired by Schlüter, Stüler, Schinkel and Goethe, among others, was the seat of the Prussian rulers (Hohenzollerns) from the fifteenth century onwards. The Stadtschloss was at the centre of the Revolution of 1848 and its last resident, Kaiser Wilhelm II, quit the palace and throne in 1918 following Germany's surrender in World War I.

The palace was damaged during World War II and pulled down in 1950 by the GDR, who replaced it with their own **Palast der Republik**, a bronze-tinted, blocky behemoth that became surprisingly popular with many East Germans. Nonetheless, after reunification this building was also pulled down, leaving a vast empty space and a lot of heated discussion about whether to rebuild the original palace or something more suited to the modern city. In 2007, the Bundestag (parliament) reached a compromise of sorts by deciding to rebuild the exterior facade with a modern interior – the new building is to be called the **Humboldt Forum** and will house parts of Humboldt University, the city library and various shops and restaurants. The empty space will remain for a while yet, however, since budget cuts have delayed the project until 2014, three years later than planned.

Goethe-era landscapes, works by Jakob Philipp Hackert and Anton Graff and Romantic paintings by the likes of Caspar David Friedrich and Karl Friedrich Schinkel (a gifted landscape painter as well as Berlin's foremost architect). The Impressionist section, with its international "big guns" Manet, Monet, Renoir and Rodin, is worth the visit alone.

BODE-MUSEUM

Am Kupfergraben 1. Mon–Wed & Fri–Sun 10am–6pm, Thurs 10am–10pm. €8.
MAP P.47, POCKET MAP D12

The stately Bode-Museum, with its recognizable dome, was originally called the Kaiser Friedrich Museum, and was renamed in 1956 after its inaugural curator Wilhelm van Bode. Opened after extensive refurbishments in 2006, the building is notable for its refined architectural details – the opulent staircases, monumental pilasters and demi-columns – as well as a wealth of art and artefacts from the Byzantine and Medieval periods. These are mainly from Germany but also come from major European art centres such as the Netherlands, Italy, France and Spain, and are culled from three major state museum collections: the sculpture collection, with highlights including the terracotta statues from Luca della Robbia, the Madonna from Donatello and the sculptures of Desiderio da Settignano; the Museum of Byzantine Art – the only one of its kind in Germany; and the Numismatic Collection, a vast and impressive collection of coins (and other forms of currency) that range from the seventh century BC to the twenty-first century.

THE BODE-MUSEUM

Unter den Linden and the government quarter

Berlin's grand boulevard, named for the Linden (lime) trees that line it, runs east–west from the site of the former royal palace to the Brandenburg Gate. The road originated as a bridle path for Duke Friedrich Wilhelm in the seventeenth century; by the nineteenth century it was a popular gathering place for many Berliners and Unter den Linden was furnished with new buildings, including the Neoclassical Neue Wache. Despite appearances, most of the buildings are reconstructions. Nonetheless it maintains its upscale aura, reflected in the fine-dining restaurants and expensive shops that predominate. Beyond the Brandenburg Gate lies the modern, yet no less authoritative Regierungsviertel ("government quarter"), a cluster of buildings starting with the Reichstag that stretch along the Spree. A stroll along the river past the striking Paul Löbe Haus and the Bundeskanzleramt, towards the Hauptbahnhof, is a pleasant and architecturally interesting way to pass a couple of hours.

DEUTSCHES HISTORISCHES MUSEUM

Unter den Linden 2 ⓤ/Ⓢ Friedrichstr.
☎ 030/20 30 44 44, ⓦ www.dhm.de. Daily 10am–6pm. Permanent exhibition
☎ 030/20 30 47 51, current exhibitions
☎ 030/20 30 47 50. €6. MAP P.54–55, POCKET MAP D13

The German Historical Museum (Deutsches Historisches Museum) is spread across two

DEUTSCHES HISTORISCHES MUSEUM

buildings: the unique Baroque Zeughaus (armoury) and a modern exhibition hall designed by Chinese-American architect I. M. Pei. The **Zeughaus** was first used as a museum for German history during the years of the GDR (1952–90), essentially to espouse the Marxist-Leninist concept of history. In 2006 a permanent exhibition "German history in images and artefacts" was inaugurated in the 300-year-old building (the oldest on Unter den Linden), which showcases two thousand years of German history via eight thousand objects from the museum's extensive collections. Supplementing this are special temporary exhibitions displayed on the four floors of the spacious **Pei building**, with its glass and steel lobby and winding staircase. There's also a very tasteful and little-known **cinema**, entered from the Spree side of the museum, with a historically protected interior.

NEUE WACHE

Unter den Linden 4 ⓤ/Ⓢ Friedrichstr. ☏ 030/25 00 25. Daily 10am–6pm.
MAP P.54–55, POCKET MAP D13

The Neue Wache (New Guard House) was Karl Friedrich Schinkel's first major commission in Berlin – he rose to the occasion by building a leading example of German Neoclassicism. Originally constructed as a guardhouse for the troops of the crown prince of Prussia, the building became a memorial to the Wars of Liberation (Napoleonic Wars) until 1918. From 1931 onwards it was a memorial for World War I, and the inner courtyard was covered over apart from a small opening in the roof letting through a slither of symbolic light. Post World War II, the GDR leadership turned it into the monument for the victims of fascism and militarism. An eternal flame was placed in a cube above the ashes of an unknown concentration camp prisoner and an unknown fallen soldier. After German reunification, the GDR memorial piece was removed and replaced by an enlarged version of Käthe Kollwitz's sculpture *Mother with her Dead Son* (*Pietá*). This sculpture is directly under the oculus, its exposure to the elements a metaphor for the suffering of civilians during World War II.

BEBELPLATZ

⊕ Französische Str. MAP BELOW, POCKET MAP C13

This historical square on the south side of the Unter den Linden was constructed between 1741 and 1743 and was originally known as Opernplatz. Though framed by the opulent **Staatsoper** (see p.63), a library and the swanky *Hotel de Rome* (see p.149), it remains best known for the 1933 Nazi book burning that took place here, as instigated by propaganda minister Joseph Goebbels. The Nazis burned some 20,000 books, including works by Thomas Mann, Erich Maria Remarque, Heinrich Heine and Karl Marx. At the centre of the square is a **memorial** of the burning by Micha Ullman, which consists of a glass-covered view into an underground chamber of empty bookshelves. Nearby, an engraving of a line from Heinrich Heine translates as: "Where they burn books, they ultimately burn people".

DEUTSCHE GUGGENHEIM

Unter den Linden 13 **⊕** Französische Str. **⊕** 030/20 20 930, **⊛** www.deutsche -guggenheim.de. Daily 10am–8pm. €4, free on Mon. MAP BELOW, POCKET MAP C13

Located on the ground floor of the Deutsche Bank, this museum is a collaboration between the Guggenheim Foundation and the bank. Though it opened relatively recently (1997), the museum has built a very good reputation in Berlin and beyond, attracting some 130,000 visitors each year. The small, minimalist space, designed by American architect Richard Gluckman, will doubtless surprise international art lovers used to the usual Guggenheim dimensions.

Unter den Linden

ACCOMMODATION	
Adlon Kempinski	3
Arcotel John F	5
Arte Luise Kunsthotel	1
Hotel de Rome	4
Westin Grand	2

SHOPS	
Berlin Story	2
Dussmann das KulturKaufhaus	1
Galeries Lafayette	3
Quartier 206	4

CLUBS & VENUES	
Komische Oper	4
Konzerthaus	3
Maxim Gorki Theater	2
Staatsoper	3
Tausend	1

Accordingly, the museum only holds three to four exhibitions per year, though they tend towards heavyweight contemporary figures such as Eduardo Chillida, Georg Baselitz and Gerhard Richter.

There are free daily tours of exhibitions at 6pm, shorter tours on Mondays (11am–8pm) and tour-plus-lunch deals on Wednesdays at 1pm. There's also a café, indoor courtyard and a small shop.

CAFÉS & BARS

Café Einstein	4
Café Nö!	14
Newton Bar	15
Operncafé in Opernpalais	5
Shochu Bar	9
Tadshikische Teestube	1
Windhorst	2

RESTAURANTS

Bocca di Bacco	8
Borchardt	10
Chipps	12
Cookies Cream	6
Fischers Fritz	7
Ishin	3
Lutter & Wegner	13
Vau	11

GENDARMENMARKT

⓾ Hausvogteiplatz/Französische Str./ Stadtmitte. MAP P.54–55, POCKET MAP C14

The Gendarmenmarkt, one of Berlin's most beautiful squares, was created at the end of the seventeenth century as a market place (then called the Linden Markt) but its current name comes from the Regiment Gens d'Armes that had their stables here from 1736 to 1773. Despite its inherent grandness, it's a surprisingly quiet place defined by three landmark buildings: the Französischer Dom, Deutscher Dom and the **Konzerthaus** (Concert Hall, see p.63), which frame a central statue of Friedrich Schiller. The **Französischer Dom** and **Deutscher Dom** are two seemingly identical churches facing each other across the square, poised in a stand off for visitor attention. The Französischer Dom (French Cathedral) is older, built between 1701 and 1705 by the Huguenot community, and contains a Huguenot museum, a restaurant on the top floor and a viewing platform. The pentagonal Deutscher Dom (German Cathedral), at the southern end of the square, was designed by Martin Grünberg,

built in 1708 by Giovanni Simonetti and modified in 1785 after a design by Carl von Gontard, who added the domed tower. A popular Christmas market is held on the square during the holidays.

AKADEMIE DER KÜNSTE

Pariser Platz 4 (and Hanseatenweg 10, Tiergarten) ⓾/Ⓢ Brandenburger Tor ☏ 030/20 05 72 000, Ⓦ www.adk.de. Daily 10am–10pm (general visits); Tues–Sun 10am–8pm (exhibitions). Admission varies. MAP P.54–55, POCKET MAP B14

Founded as the Prussian Academy of Arts in 1696 by Friedrich I, this public corporation continues its original mission to support and foster the arts. Its prestigious members have included Goethe, Mendelssohn-Bartholdy and

Brecht; Max Liebermann headed the institution in the 1920s after the academy introduced a literature section. Under Hitler it was used as a headquarters for architect Albert Speer to redesign Berlin into "Germania", before being bombed almost to the ground (only the exhibition halls remained intact). During the GDR era it was turned into studios for Academy members like the sculptor Fritz Cremer and several master scholars such as Wieland Förster and Werner Stötzer. They ran a print and photographic workshop known as the "Werkstätten für Druck und Fotografie". The glass-facade building, designed by Günter Behnisch, lies directly in front of what's left of the original academy, and its current members include German Nobel laureate Günter Grass, architects Daniel Libeskind and Sir Norman Foster and composer Sir Harrison Birtwistle. The venue holds a number of lectures, exhibits, and workshops.

BRANDENBURG GATE

Pariser Platz ⓤ/ⓈBrandenburger Tor
🕿 030/22 63 30 17. MAP P.54–55.
POCKET MAP A13

A former city gate (the only remaining of the period), the Brandenburg Gate (Branden-burger Tor) is one of the most recognizable icons of Berlin, if not Europe. Commissioned by Friedrich Wilhelm II of

Prussia as a sign of peace, and built by Carl Gotthard Langhans in 1788 from a design based upon the Propylaea (the gateway to the Acropolis in Athens), the gate has at various times been a symbol of victory, peace, division and unity. After the 1806 Prussian defeat at the Battle of Jena-Auerstedt, Napoleon took the Quadriga (added in 1793 by Johann Gottfried Schadow) to Paris. After Napoleon's defeat in 1814 and the Prussian occupation of Paris by General Ernst von Pfuel, the Quadriga was restored to Berlin. The Gate survived World War II and was one of the damaged structures still standing in the ruins of Pariser Platz in 1945. On December 21, 2000, the Brandenburg Gate was privately refurbished at a cost of €4-million by the Stiftung Denkmalschutz Berlin (Berlin Monument Conservation Foundation). Today, it still draws punters by the busload. The best way to enjoy it is to stroll towards it via Unter den Linden, taking in the trees and run of shops, glamorous theatres and excellent museums along the way. It's a very touristy spot, so for a bit of peace and quiet pop in the Room of Silence on the north side, built specifically for visitors to rest and reflect.

MEMORIAL TO THE MURDERED JEWS OF EUROPE

Cora-Berliner-Str. 1 Ⓤ/Ⓢ Brandenburger Tor ☎ 030/20 07 66 0, Ⓦ www .holocaust-mahnmal.de. Guided tours: ☎ 030/26 39 43 36, Memorial open 24hr; information centre Tues–Sun: April–Sept 10am–8pm (last entrance 7.15pm), Oct–March 10am–7pm (last entrance 6.15pm). MAP P.54-55, POCKET MAP A14

Peter Eisenman's hugely controversial 2711 sombre concrete slabs (stelae) are arranged in a neat grid spread across 19,000 square metres of prime Berlin real estate near the Brandenburg Gate, the memorial's grand scale intended as a reminder of the magnitude of the Holocaust. The slabs are purposefully varying in height to give visitors walking among them a sense of disorientation and confusion, though from above the slabs appear to make a wave-like form. Soon after construction began in 2003, a Swiss newspaper reported that a subsidiary of the company hired to produce the anti-graffiti substance to cover the stelae, Degussa, had created the poison gas used to exterminate so many in the Nazi death camps of the Holocaust. Rather

MEMORIAL TO THE MURDERED JEWS OF EUROPE WITH THE FERNSEHTURM

than spend an additional €2 million to undo the work and hire another company, work continued.

As impressive as the memorial is, it's really the 800-square-metre underground **information centre** (located in the southeastern corner) that leaves you reeling. The centre holds factual exhibits to balance the abstract memorial above, including personal information about many of the victims and a video archive ("Voices of Survival") where you can listen to Holocaust survivor testimonies in many languages, or even search for specific places, people or events in the database.

THE REICHSTAG

Platz der Republik 1 Ⓤ Bundestag ☎ 030/227 32 152, Ⓦ www.bundestag.de. Roof terrace and dome daily on pre-arranged guided tours only (free). MAP P.54-55, POCKET MAP A13

The Reichstag, the seat of the German Parliament, has played a crucial role in several of the city's most significant historic events. After the founding of the German Empire in 1872, German architect Paul Wallot was commissioned to create this imposing neo-Renaissance parliament building. It was constructed between 1884 and 1894 and mainly funded with wartime reparation money from France – following Prussia's defeat of France in 1871. The famous inscription "Dem Deutschen Volke" (To the German People) was added in 1916 by Wilhelm II. In 1933 a fire destroyed much of the Reichstag. Though it remains uncertain how the fire started, the Communists were blamed, giving a boost to Hitler and the Nazis, who would soon come to power. The building was further damaged at the end of

the War, when the Soviets entered Berlin. The picture of a Red Army soldier raising the Soviet flag on the Reichstag is one of the most famous twentieth-century images and symbolized Germany's defeat. The Reichstag was rebuilt between 1958 and 1972, but the central dome and most of the ornamentation were removed. During Berlin's division the West German parliament assembled here once a year as a way to indicate that Bonn was only a temporary capital – and indeed, after reunification, the Bundestag relocated here. The building was renovated again from 1995 to 1999, when the glass dome designed by Sir Norman Foster was added. At first the subject of much controversy, the dome has become one of the city's most recognized landmarks. Since April 1999, the Reichstag is once again the seat of the Bundestag – and also one of the city's largest attractions. Not all of the building is open to the public: the most popular (and accessible) part is the glass dome, which features a roof terrace, restaurant (9am–4.30pm & 6.30pm– midnight; ☎030/226 29 933) and fantastic views over the

city. It's currently only open to visitors with a restaurant reservation, who have registered to attend a sitting or lecture, or who sign up in advance for a guided tour. The audio guides (free) last twenty minutes and give all the important facts about the building and the surroundings as you ascend and descend the 230-metre spiral staircase to the top.

MUSEUM THE KENNEDYS

Pariser Platz 4a ⓤ/Ⓢ Brandenburger Tor ☎ 030/20 65 35 70, ⓦ www.thekennedys.de. Daily 10am–6pm. €7, changing special exhibitions included in the admission price. MAP P.54–55, POCKET MAP B13

Yes, an entire museum dedicated to JFK and his family, mainly centred on his world-renowned "Ich bin ein Berliner" speech and Kennedy's 1963 Berlin trip, but expanding into many other surprisingly fascinating areas. Books, films, historical documents and roughly 200 photographs pertain to the man's life, family and political career. The exhibit also houses some of JFK's personal property including his black Hermès briefcase, a Louis Vuitton suitcase, a pair of reading glasses and one of Jackie's pillbox hats.

Shops

BERLIN STORY

Unter den Linden 26 Ⓤ/Ⓢ Brandenburger Tor ☏ 030/20 45 38 42. Daily 10am–8pm. MAP P.54–55, POCKET MAP C13

The only bookshop in Berlin that is exclusively devoted to Berlin. Over 10,000 titles in twelve languages, including English, that cover everything from Prussian kings and the Third Reich to architecture and children's books. There's a café, theatre and bar and an associated history festival.

DUSSMANN DAS KULTURKAUFHAUS

Friedrichstr. 90 Ⓤ/Ⓢ Friedrichstr. ☏ 030/20 25 11 11. Mon–Sat 10am–midnight. MAP P.54–55, POCKET MAP C13

This giant store has five levels of books, CDs and…more books. A small shop at the back also features books about music and musical notation.

GALERIES LAFAYETTE

Friedrichstr. 76–78 Ⓤ Stadtmitte ☏ 030/20 948. Mon–Sat 10am–8pm. MAP P.54–55, POCKET MAP C14

This elegant branch of the Parisian store opened in 1996. Housed in a glass temple designed by Jean Nouvel, it

SHOPPER AT GALERIES LAFAYETTE

stocks every super-exclusive brand you can think of, from Agent Provocateur to Yves Saint Laurent. There's also a vast variety of gourmet foods.

QUARTIER 206

Friedrichstr. 71 Ⓤ Stadtmitte ☏ 030/20 94 68 00. Mon–Fri 10.30am–7.30pm, Sat 10am–6pm. MAP P.54–55, POCKET MAP C14

Unapologetically posh department store with everything from stationery to furniture and cosmetics, all with a luxe-designer twist.

Restaurants

BOCCA DI BACCO

Friedrichstr. 167 Ⓤ Französische Str. ☏ 030/20 67 28 28, ⓦ www.boccadibacco.de. Mon–Sat noon–midnight, Sun 6pm–midnight. MAP P.54–55, POCKET MAP C14

Bocca di Bacco blends a down-to-earth atmosphere with high-quality cuisine that takes its inspiration from Tuscany and other parts of Italy. The menu includes pasta, game and fish and plenty of wonderful desserts. The three-course lunch is a pretty good deal at €19.50.

BORCHARDT

Französische Str. 47 Ⓤ Französische Str. ☏ 030/81 88 62 62. Daily. noon–1am, kitchen till midnight. MAP P.54–55, POCKET MAP C14

The original *Borchardt* was at no. 48, but that was in the late nineteenth century when it was a meeting place for high society. *Borchardt* mark two is a tasteful facsimile with marble columns, plush seating and an Art Nouveau mosaic that was discovered during renovations. The place draws politicians, celebrities and tourists, cuisine is high-quality French-German though if you're not a regular, service will be offhand at best.

CHIPPS

Jägerstr. 35 ⓤ Hausvogteiplatz ☎ 030/28 08 806. ⓦ www.chipps.eu. Mon–Fri 8am–late, Sat & Sun 9am–late. MAP P.54–55, POCKET MAP D14

This venture from the owner of *Cookies Cream* features panoramic windows, a light-filled, sleek interior and terrace. The open kitchen serves seasonal and regional ingredients. You can mix and match your dishes (meat and fish are served as side orders – evening dishes from €12), while hearty breakfasts include the "hangover". A second *Chipps* is at Friedrichstr. 120.

COOKIES CREAM

Behrenstr. 55 ⓤ Französische Str. ☎ 030/27 49 29 40. ⓦ www.cookiescream.de. Tues–Sat 7pm–midnight. MAP P.54–55, POCKET MAP C13

Deliberately difficult to find (see website for creative directions, it's behind the *Westin Grand* on Friedrichstr.) this stylish restaurant is worth seeking out. Chef Stephan Hentschel has made this one of the best vegetarian restaurants in the city. At €32 for a three-course menu and €18 for a main, it's pricey but far from prohibitive, and the seasonal, inventive food is worth it.

FISCHERS FRITZ

The Regent, Charlottenstr. 49 ⓤ Französische Str. ☎ 030/20 33 63 63. ⓦ www .fischersfritzberlin.com. Daily noon–2pm & 6.30–10.30pm. MAP P.54–55, POCKET MAP C14

Fischers Fritz is the domain of Christian Lohse, whose way with fish and seafood has earned him numerous accolades (including two Michelin stars). This is imaginative stuff, bursting with originality in terms of presentation, flavours and ideas. There's a price of course, namely €110 for four courses; for a cheaper option, check the lunch deals.

ISHIN

ISHIN

Mittelstr. 24 ⓤ/Ⓢ Brandenburger Tor/ Friedrichstr. ☎ 030/20 67 48 29. ⓦ www .ishin.de. Mon–Sat 11am–10pm (kitchen till 9.30pm). MAP P.54–55, POCKET MAP C13

There are four *Ishin* restaurants in Berlin. The interior of this central one is slightly functional but the decent, fresh sushi, good prices and quick service make it very popular, especially for lunch. There's a happy hour every day until 4pm (all day Wed & Sat), with €2–3 off sushi, and full menus from €5. Plenty of veggie dishes and free green tea.

LUTTER & WEGNER

Charlottenstr. 56 ⓤ Französische Str. ☎ 030/20 29 540. ⓦ www.l-w-berlin.de. Daily 11am–3am, kitchen till 1am. MAP P.54–55, POCKET MAP C14

This refined, airy Austro-German restaurant is the finest of the *Lutter & Wagner* mini empire. It was here the wine merchant started (in 1811) – there's a high-end wine store alongside. Prices are high (set menus around €35, mains from €13.50) but that's what happens when the *New York Times* crowns your Wiener schnitzel the best outside Vienna (though the Sauerbraten is the real highlight). There's a cheaper bistro with a shorter menu and the same wine list of around 750.

VAU

Jägerstr. 54–55 ⓤ Hausvogteiplatz
☎ 030/20 29 730, ⓦ www.vau-berlin.de.
Mon–Sat noon–2.30pm & 7–10.30pm.
MAP P.54–55, POCKET MAP D14

An acclaimed (and expensive) restaurant run by chef Kolja Kleeberg – a famous TV chef who produces fantastic, modern takes on classic international cuisine. The six-course menu costs €120, three-course lunches are €85, and the wine list is incredible. Reservations essential.

Cafés and bars

CAFÉ EINSTEIN

Unter den Linden 42 ⓤ/Ⓢ Brandenburger
Tor ☎ 030/20 43 632. Daily 7am–10pm.
MAP P.54–55, POCKET MAP B13

The younger sibling to the famous *Einstein* (see p.138), this branch doesn't have the same panache, but it's popular with Berlin's cultural elite and serves excellent Austro-Hungarian specialities. It's also a handy spot for a coffee and cake.

CAFÉ NÖ!

Glinkastr. 23 ⓤ Französische Str. ☎ 030/20
10 871, ⓦ www.cafe-noe.de. Mon–Fri
noon–1am, Sat 7pm–1am, kitchen till
midnight. MAP P.54–55, POCKET MAP B14

This wine bar-restaurant serves very decent food for very reasonable prices. The menu includes *Flammkuchen* and the like, a huge mixed plate for two featuring almost everything on the menu is €23, and the wine list is vast enough for most tastes. Service is pleasant but not overly formal.

NEWTON BAR

Charlottenstr. 57 ⓤ Stadtmitte ☎ 030/20 61
29 99. Mon–Thurs & Sun 10am–3am, Fri &
Sat 10am–4am. MAP P.54–55, POCKET MAP C14

Dedicated to photographer

OPERNCAFÉ IN OPERNPALAIS

Helmut Newton, this classy cocktail bar, all leather chairs and oak furnishings, is popular with a mature, well-heeled crowd. The large windows look out onto Gendarmenmarkt, though since a huge Newton photograph called *Big Nudes* covers one wall, you won't be short on eye candy either way.

OPERNCAFÉ IN OPERNPALAIS

Unter den Linden 5 Ⓢ/ⓤ Friedrichstr.
☎ 030/20 26 83. MAP P.54–55, POCKET MAP D13

A little piece of Vienna in Berlin, frequented mostly by mature, cake-loving Germans, this Baroque timewarp has over fifty cakes and pastries in its repertoire. The brunches (from €14.90) are also good.

SHOCHU BAR

Behrenstr. 72 ⓤ/Ⓢ Brandenburger Tor
☎ 030/30 11 17 328, ⓦ www.shochubar.de.
Mon–Sat 6pm–2am. MAP P.54–55, POCKET MAP B14

This swanky bar offers flamboyant yet elegant cocktails made from the Japanese spirit it's named after. Japanese food is served until 11pm and there are sometimes live jazz performances. Expect to find a dressy, upmarket crowd.

TADSHIKISCHE TEESTUBE

Am Festungsgraben 1 Ⓢ/ⓤ Friedrichstr.
☎ 030/20 41 112. Mon–Fri 5pm–midnight, Sat &
Sun, 1pm–midnight. MAP P.54–55, POCKET MAP D13

It's easier to pronounce after a couple of drinks, but you won't be visiting *Tadshikische Teestube* to get drunk. With an interior from 1974 – donated for an exhibition – you'll be frequenting this delightfully kitsch Russian tearoom to try one of their 25 varieties of tea (tea ceremony €8) in the cushioned, Oriental-style space.

WINDHORST

Dorotheenstr. 65 ⓊⓈ Friedrichstr. ☎030/20 45 00 70. Mon–Fri 6pm–late, Sat 9pm–late. MAP P.54–55, POCKET MAP C13

This little cocktail haven is tucked away, and though it's not a residential area, feels like a neighbourhood spot. It's a smart, fairly simple place, but the cocktails are above average and go well with the jazz (on vinyl) that they love to play.

Clubs and venues

KOMISCHE OPER

Behrenstr. 55–57 Ⓤ Französische Str. ☎030/47 99 74 00, Ⓦwww.komische-oper-berlin.de. MAP P.54–55, POCKET MAP C13

Specializing in German opera and musicals, the Comic Opera – the smallest of Berlin's three opera houses – was built between 1891 and 1892. Since 2004 it has been operated by the Berliner Opernstiftung.

KONZERTHAUS

Gendarmenmarkt Ⓤ Französische Str. ☎030/203 09 21 01 (tickets) Ⓦwww.konzerthaus.de. MAP P.54–55, POCKET MAP C14

The concert house was built on the ruins of the national theatre by Schinkel in 1821. Since 1984 it has been the home of the Konzerthausorchester Berlin and is regarded to be amongst the best classical concert venues in the world. Daily tours are available (for example Sat 1pm; 75min, €3).

MAXIM GORKI THEATER

Am Festungsgraben 2 ⓊⓈ Friedrichstr. ☎030/20 22 10, Ⓦwww.gorki.de. MAP P.54–55, POCKET MAP D13

Named after Russian socialist-realist author Maxim Gork, this theatre, built in 1827, is one of Berlin's largest and hosts classic dramas by him plus contemporary works by the likes of Fassbinder.

STAATSOPER

Unter den Linden 7Ⓤ Französische Str. ☎030/20 35 45 55, Ⓦwww.staatsoper-berlin.de. MAP P.54–55, POCKET MAP D13

The state opera's history goes back to the eighteenth century, and it has attracted many illustrious conductors including Richard Strauss. Today it is one of the world's leading opera houses. Closed for renovation until 2013, performances take place at the Schillertheater (Bismarckstr. 110; Ⓤ Ernst-Reuter-Platz).

TAUSEND

Schiffbauerdamm 11, Albrechtstr. ⓊⓈ Friedrichstr. ☎ 030/41 71 53 96, Ⓦwww.tausendberlin.com. €10. MAP P.54–55, POCKET MAP B12

Signposted by an enormous eye that emits a golden glow over the tunnel-shaped space, this upmarket club attracts a decidedly dapper crowd – so make sure you look the part. Inside you'll find a mix of upbeat disco and 1980s nights.

KOMISCHE OPER

Alexanderplatz and the Nikolaiviertel

Alexanderplatz – or Alex, as it's colloquially known – is one of Berlin's ugliest, bleakest and best-known squares. Named in honour of a visit from Russian Czar Alexander I in 1805, by the start of the twentieth century it had become a commercial centre busy enough to rival Potsdamer Platz. Under the GDR it was a nondescript pedestrianized area and in 1989 was the site of the Peaceful Revolution, the largest demonstration in the history of East Germany. Today its grey, concrete GDR tower blocks, themselves towered over by the needle-like spire of the Fernsehturm (TV Tower), join more recent buildings like the Alexa shopping mall and the Saturn electronics store to create a thoroughly charmless transport hub. More scenic, though touristy, is the adjacent Nikolaiviertel, with its pretty old town feel and various museums, a reconstruction of the historical heart of the city that dates back to the thirteenth century.

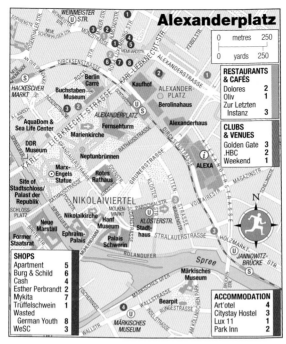

Alexanderplatz

| 0 | metres | 250 |
| 0 | yards | 250 |

RESTAURANTS & CAFÉS

Dolores	2
Oliv	1
Zur Letzten Instanz	3

CLUBS & VENUES

Golden Gate	3
.HBC	2
Weekend	1

SHOPS

Apartment	5
Burg & Schild	6
Cash	4
Esther Perbrandt	2
Mykita	7
Trüffelschwein	1
Wasted German Youth	8
WeSC	3

ACCOMMODATION

Art'otel	4
Citystay Hostel	3
Lux 11	1
Park Inn	2

FERNSEHTURM (TV TOWER)

Panoramastr. 1a ⓤ/Ⓢ Alexanderplatz
☏ 030/24 75 75 875, ⓦ www.tv-turm.de.
Daily: March–Oct 9am–midnight; Nov–Feb
10am–midnight. €11. MAP ABOVE, POCKET MAP F12

The city's most ubiquitous structure, the 368m concrete spike known as the Fernsehturm (television tower), is the building most likely to crop up in all your photographs when you get home – whether you realized you'd been photographing it or not. Built in 1969 as a broadcasting system for East Berlin, and intended as a showpiece structure for the GDR, visible in West Berlin, it has a visitor platform at 200m – a lift zooms you up in forty seconds – and a small photographic exhibition in the lobby where you can see how the tower was built (it took four years). Above the visitor platform, there's also a rotating restaurant, the *Telecafé*, that serves coffee, snacks and meals while revolving once around the tower's axis every thirty minutes. The tower receives around a million visitors a year and the queues can be long whatever the weather. You don't need a reservation for the tower, but it can be handy for the restaurant (in high season). Another option is to get a VIP ticket (adults €19.50, under 16s €11.50, available on the website in advance), which enables you to dodge the queues and has an option for a table reservation.

If the sun's out when you're out and about, take a look up at the Fernsehturm and see if you can spot the cross that's reflected across the main steel sphere: the religious symbolism caused a great deal of embarrassment for the atheist GDR government.

DDR MUSEUM

Karl-Liebknecht-Str. 1 ⓤ/Ⓢ Alexanderplatz
☎ 030/84 71 23 731 (tickets), Ⓦ www
.ddr-museum.de. Mon–Fri & Sun 10am–8pm,
Sat 10am–10pm. €6. MAP P.65, POCKET MAP E13

Located opposite the Berliner
Dom (see p.46), this collection
of memorabilia from the
Deutsche Demokratische
Republik (DDR/GDR) makes
for a fun and interactive visit.
There are screens to touch,
buttons to press, drawers to
open – even a Trabant to sit in
and a bugged apartment to
listen in on. You can inspect a
reconstruction of a GDR living
room and ponder the East
German penchant for public
nudity – little wonder it's one of
the most visited museums in
Berlin. The museum recently
doubled in size and added
several new areas, many of
them emphasizing the dark
side of GDR life – party, state,
prison – making this a much
more rounded experience than
it used to be.

ROTES RATHAUS

Rathausstr. 15 ⓤ Klosterstr.
Ⓢ/ⓤ Alexanderplatz ☎ 030/90 26 24 11.
Mon–Fri 9am–6pm. Free (ID required).
MAP P.65, POCKET MAP E13

This distinctive building gets its
name (which means red town

hall) from the red clinker brick
of its facade. The building,
inspired by Italian High
Renaissance architecture, was
erected in the 1860s. During
communist times, it was East
Berlin's town hall, when the red
in the name really came into its
own; today it's the office of the
city mayor, and is the political
centre of power in Greater
Berlin. Its neo-Renaissance
clock tower and frieze
depicting Berlin's history until
1879 in 36 terracotta plaques,
each 6m long, are its most
impressive architectural
features. At the top of the
grand stairwell is a coat-of-
arms hall and some exhibits.
The building also has a
cafeteria with low-price
lunches.

MARIENKIRCHE

Karl-Liebknecht-Str. 8 ⓤ/Ⓢ Alexanderplatz
Ⓦ www.marienkirche-berlin.de. Daily April–Oct
10am–8pm; Nov–March 10am–6pm (no visits
during services). Free. MAP P.65, POCKET MAP E12

Standing somewhat
incongruously at the edge of
Alexanderplatz and the
Marx-Engels-Forum, the
Marienkirche (church of
St Mary) – one of Berlin's oldest
churches – is the last remnant in
the area of its time. Built some

A DISPLAY IN THE DDR MUSEUM

time in the thirteenth century, its oldest part is the granite base, upon which a hall church (Hallenkirche) stands. The tower was added during the fifteenth century, and the steeple in 1790 by Carl Gotthard Langhan, architect of the Brandenburg Gate. The church escaped heavy damage during World War II and was later fully restored. Visitors today can see the *The Dance of Death* (*Totentanz*), a large fresco (2m high, 22m long), dating from about 1485, that was discovered in 1860 under layers of paint and depicts various classes of society dancing with death. Other notable artworks include a bronze baptismal font from 1437, *The Crucifixion* painted by Michael Ribestein in 1562 and an alabaster pulpit created by Andreas Schlüter in 1703, decorated with reliefs of John the Baptist and personifications of Faith, Hope and Love.

ROTES RATHAUS

BUCHSTABENMUSEUM

Karl-Liebknecht-Str. 13 (1st floor of Berlin Carré) Ⓤ/Ⓢ Alexanderplatz ☎ 0177 42 01 587, Ⓦ www.buchstabenmuseum.de. Thurs, Fri & Sat 1–3pm. Free. MAP P.65, POCKET MAP E12

Buchstaben means "letter" (as in "alphabetic character"), and this small, unique museum is dedicated solely to the preservation and protection of artisan-esque examples of lettering in the age of digitalization. Though the museum is still building its permanent collection, the assortment of old and new industrial signs is well worth navigating the slightly eccentric opening hours for. Though the museum collects lettering of any language, the ultimate goal is to honour "local colour", which museum founder Barbara Dechant feels is waning. (Note that the current

location is temporary, so check the website for opening dates and times while this is in flux).

AQUADOM AND SEA LIFE CENTER

Spandauer Str. 3 Ⓤ/Ⓢ Alexanderplatz ☎ 030/99 28 00, Ⓦ www.sealifeeurope.com. Daily 10am–7pm. €16.95. MAP P.65, POCKET MAP E13

The Sealife Center's chief claim to fame is the AquaDom – the world's largest cylindrical fish aquarium, a 25m-tall acrylic glass aquarium, with built-in transparent elevator, located right in the lobby of the adjacent *Radisson SAS* hotel. Filled with around 900,000 litres of seawater, the aquarium contains around 2600 fish, covering 56 species. The AquaDom can be visited separately, but visitors who want a broader overview of the underwater world can visit the Sealife Center first, a succession of themed tunnels that illustrate marine life from various habitats including the Spree and the Pacific Ocean. It's insightful enough and a well laid-out exhibition, though it lacks the comprehensive scope and diversity – not to mention the manatees and sharks – of the Zoo Aquarium (see p.124).

EPHRAIM-PALAIS

Poststr. 16, corner Mühlendamm
Ⓤ Klosterstr./Ⓤ/Ⓢ Alexanderplatz
Ⓣ 030/24 00 21 62 & 030/24 00 20, Ⓦ www
.stadtmuseum.de. Tues, Thurs & Sun
10am–6pm, Wed noon–8pm. €5.
MAP P.65, POCKET MAP E13

This attractive Rococo-style
residential palace, located in the
southern corner of Berlin's
Nikolaiviertel, is a replica of a
1762 original built by Veitel
Heine Ephraim, a court
jeweller. His original building
was torn down in 1936 when
the Mühlendamm was widened,
but the reconstruction has been
painstaking and the new
version is an exquisite place to
visit, with its elegantly curving,
decorated facade (complete
with cherubs), Tuscan columns,
wrought-iron balconies and an
oval staircase and ornate ceiling
crafted by Schlüter. The
associated museum contains
prints from the Stadt Museum
(city museum) collection, and
also hosts temporary
exhibitions that tend to
showcase Berlin's artistic,
cultural and political history.

MÄRKISCHES MUSEUM

Am Köllnischen Park 5
Ⓤ/Ⓢ Jannowitzbrücke Ⓣ 030/30 86 62 15,
Ⓦ www.stadtmuseum.de. Tues, Thurs & Sun
10am–6pm, Wed noon–8pm, Fri & Sat
2pm–10pm, €6, MAP P.65, POCKET MAP F14

The red-brick Märkisches
Museum, built at the turn of
the twentieth century, is the
headquarters of Berlin's City
Museum Foundation. The
museum hosts a wide array of
art-historic collections in its
atmospheric rooms – everything from medieval sculptures,
artefacts and paintings that tell
the story of Berlin from the
first settlers until now (German
text only). Thoughtfully divided
into sections of the city – Unter
den Linden, Friedrichstrasse

A DISPLAY AT THE MÄRKISCHES MUSEUM

and so on –favourites include a
working mechanical musical
instrument that's shown off
every Sunday (3pm), seven
original graffitied segments of
the Berlin Wall and a
Kaiserpanorama: a stereoscope
dating from the 1880s that
produces a fascinating 3D show
of images from nineteenth-
century Berlin. Behind the
museum is small Köllnischen
Park where you can visit the
two brown bears, Schnute, the
official Berlin city bear, and
Maxi, her daughter.

HANF MUSEUM

Mühlendamm 5 Ⓤ/Ⓢ Alexanderplatz/
Ⓤ Klosterstr. Ⓣ 030/24 24 827, Ⓦ www
.hanfmuseum.de. Tues-Fri 10am–8pm, Sat &
Sun noon–8pm, € 4.50. MAP P.65, POCKET MAP E13

The Hanf museum is 250
square metres of space devoted
exclusively to the agricultural,
manufacturing, industrial and
legal aspects of hemp – a plant
most commonly associated
with marijuana. This museum,
while slightly dingy, isn't just
for the stoners: the aim is to
give a broader overview of this
fascinating botanical treasure
and its myriad applications,
from textile and paper to
medicine and cosmetics. Texts
are in German only.

Shops

APARTMENT

Memhardstr. 8 ⓤ/ⓢ Alexanderplatz
☎ 030/28 04 22 51. Mon–Fri 11am–7pm, Sat noon–7pm. MAP P.65, POCKET MAP F12

You'll have to be careful not to walk right past what looks like an all-white art space: the goods lie downstairs (follow the spiral staircase), where you'll find jeans, jackets, shoes and accessories with a distinctly Berlin twist. For more retro styles, check out Cash around the corner.

BURG & SCHILD

Rosa-Luxemburg-Str. 3 ⓤ Rosa-Luxemburg-Platz ☎ 030/24 63 05 01. Mon–Sat 11am–8pm. MAP P.65, POCKET MAP E12

Visit an America that's long vanished by way of vintage Levis, Filson bags, Mr Freedom shirts and more, all on display in a store decorated with vintage motorbikes that generate an authentic odour of oil and tar.

CASH

Rosa-Luxemburg-Str. 11 ⓤ Weinmeisterstr. Mon–Fri 2–7pm, Sat noon–7pm. MAP P.65, POCKET MAP F12

The younger sibling of Apartment (see above), located just around the corner, Cash takes a more retro slant, selling high-end fashions as well as unbranded vintage shirts in bunker-style surroundings.

ESTHER PERBANDT

Almstadtstr. 3 ⓤ Weinmeisterstr.
☎ 030/88 53 67 91. Mon–Fri 10am–7pm, Sat noon–6pm. MAP P.65, POCKET MAP E12

A relative veteran of the Berlin fashion scene, Esther Perbandt sells rock and avant-garde styles with an audaciously gender-bending slant. Her deliberately androgynous clothing is complemented by bags, belts jewellery and more. Pricey but nice.

MYKITA

Rosa-Luxemburg-Str. 6 ⓤ/ⓢ Alexanderplatz ☎ 030/67 30 87 15. Mon–Fri 11am–6pm, Sat noon–6pm. MAP P.65, POCKET MAP F12

Sunglasses and spectacles with a stylish twist, sold in a square space with large street-facing windows. Berlin-based Mykita opened in 2003, and has achieved international prominence.

TRÜFFELSCHWEIN

Rosa-Luxemburg-Str. 21 ⓤ Rosenthaler Platz ☎ 030/70 22 12 25. Mon–Sat noon–8pm. MAP P.65, POCKET MAP F11

This pleasant, airy store sells everything from sexy shoes and trendy jumpers to belts and dapper swimwear. Labels include Original Penguin, Knowledge Cotton Apparel, Howlin' and Superga.

BURG & SCHILD

WASTED GERMAN YOUTH

Memhardstr. 1 ⓤWeinmeisterstr./
Alexanderplatz ☎0177 24 84 858. Tues–Fri
2–7pm, Sat noon–7pm. MAP P.65, POCKET MAP F12
New Zealand born designer
and artist Paul Snowden has
made a name for himself in
Berlin and beyond with his
savvy, techno-influenced
slogans written in bold
lettering. Here you'll find
T-shirts, hoodies and more.
Ravers with taste rejoice.

WESC

Münzstr. 14–16 (entrance Max-Beer-Str.)
ⓤWeinmeisterstr. ☎030/60 05 92 19.
Mon–Sat 11am–8pm. MAP P.65, POCKET MAP E12
Swedish collective WeSC –
WeAretheSuperlativeConspiracy
– cater for the skate and
snowboard community with a
broad line of clothing for men
and women, as well as shades
and other cool accessories.

Cafés and bars

DOLORES

Rosa-Luxemburg-Str. 7 ⓤRosa-Luxemburg-
Platz ☎030/28 09 95 97, ⓦwww
.dolores-online.de. Mon–Sat 11.30am–10pm,
Sun 1–10pm. MAP P.65, POCKET MAP E12
Run by Germans who spent a
considerable time in California,
Berlin's first and only burrito
shop is a basic but colourful
spot that has a Subway-style
feel with its "make-your-own"

options. There are pre-prepared
"classics" too, making it a good
spot for a cheap, filling bite
(burritos from €3.70) or
takeaway.

OLIV

Münzstr. 8 ⓤWeinmeisterstr./
Rosa-Luxemburg-Platz ☎030/89 20 65 40,
ⓦwww.oliv-cafe.de. Mon–Fri 8.30am–7pm,
Sat 9.30am–7pm, Sun 10am–6pm.
MAP P.65, POCKET MAP E12
With a modern interior, great
coffee and decent, unpretentious food (sandwiches,
quiches, soups, cakes),
newcomer *Oliv* is a pleasant
spot for breakfast or lunch, and
very conveniently located if
you're seeking respite from
boutique bashing. Cash only.

ZUR LETZTEN INSTANZ

Waisenstr. 14–16 Ⓤ Klosterstr. ☎ 030/24 25 528, Ⓦ www.zurletzteninstanz.de. Mon–Sat noon–1am. MAP P.65, POCKET MAP F13

Yes it's the oldest pub in Berlin (the building goes right back to 1561), yes the interior is textbook Alt Berlin, and yes it's a tourist haunt, but the food here – traditional dishes like pork knuckle, dumplings and Berlin meatballs – is delicious and care is taken to source ingredients from local producers. Portions are hearty and there's Pilsner on draft to wash it all down.

GOLDEN GATE

Clubs and venues

GOLDEN GATE

Dircksenstr. 77–78 Ⓤ/Ⓢ Jannowitzbrücke ☎ 030/28 29 295, Ⓦ www.goldengate-berlin .de. Wed from 10pm, Thurs–Sat from 11pm. MAP P.65, POCKET MAP J5

Lurking beneath the tracks near Jannowitzbrücke train station (close to the river Spree), this club consists of two wilfully shabby rooms kitted out in secondhand furniture and is dedicated to two- or three-day-long free-for-alls. The crowds here tend to be a dressed down, unpretentious lot who arrive well after midnight to try their luck with the difficult bouncers. Music policy is mostly house and techno but there are sometimes surprises.

.HBC

Karl-Liebknecht-Str. 9 Ⓤ/Ⓢ Alexanderplatz ☎ 030/24 34 29 20, Ⓦ www.hbc-berlin.de. Mon–Sat 7pm–2 am, Mon weekly club night 10pm–2am. MAP P.65, POCKET MAP E12

Part restaurant/bar, part exhibition hall, part music venue, part whatever else fits – this capacious, multifunctional space (1800 square metres), somewhere between retro-socialist-chic and avant-garde coolness, is housed in the former Hungarian cultural centre. It hosts anything from DJ parties to hipster fashion- and flea-markets, film shows, concerts and cultural events. The restaurant and bar have splendid views of the Fernsehturm. Check the website for what's on.

WEEKEND

Alexanderstr. 7 (12th floor) Ⓤ/Ⓢ Alexanderplatz ☎ 030/24 63 16 76. Thurs–Sat 11pm–late. €10–€12. MAP P.65, POCKET MAP F12

Accessed via a lift that shoots punters up to the top of a Communist-era tower block, this chic, spacious club has attained veteran status in the city thanks to its consistently good house and techno parties. International guests and high-profile residents play most weekends, and there's a very popular gay night on Sundays. In summer the wonderful roof terrace is a must.

Potsdamer Platz and Tiergarten

A major public transport hub and popular entertainment district, Potsdamer Platz was one of the liveliest squares in Europe during the 1920s. Reduced to rubble during the War, afterwards it became – literally – a no-man's-land, sandwiched between the different sectors. What little remained was levelled when the Berlin Wall went up in 1961. After the Wall fell, it became the largest construction site in Europe as an ambitious rebuilding programme started. Commercial, even futuristic in tone, the centrepiece today is the Sony Center, surrounded by a new U-Bahn station and a few slabs from the old Berlin Wall. Just to the west is the Kulturforum, a fine collection of cultural institutions, built in the 1960s as West Berlin's response to East Berlin's Museumsinsel, including the Gemäldegalerie, and its important collections of Old Masters. Adjacent to the Platz is Tiergarten, Berlin's oldest and most beautiful park.

SONY CENTER

Potsdamer Str. 4 ⓤ/ⓢ Potsdamer Platz ☎ 030/230 97 95, ⓦ www.sonycenter.de. Free. MAP P.74–75, POCKET MAP A15

The striking, eco-friendly, glass-and-steel Sony Center, by Helmut Jahn, opened in 2000 and cost a cool €750 million to build. The centre houses shops for everything from cosmetics and jewellery to, of course, Sony electronics, plus restaurants, a conference centre, art and film museums, cinemas, including an **IMAX**, and a **Legoland** (daily 10am–7pm; ⓦ www.legoland discoverycentre.de; €15.95).

SONY CENTER

The "Forum", the semi-enclosed roofed space between the buildings, is also used as a public space with occasional cultural and entertainment events. There's plenty to do, although the experience is generally soulless and the shopping expensive (though there is free wi-fi).

FILM AND TELEVISION MUSEUM

Potsdamer Str. 2 ⊕/Ⓢ Potsdamer Platz
☎ 030/300 90 30, Ⓦ www.deutsche
-kinemathek.de. Tues–Sun 10am–6pm, Thurs
till 8pm. €6. MAP P.74–75, POCKET MAP A15

One of the must-sees in the Sony Center is the impressively slick **Deutsche Kinemathek** museum, which collects German cinema under one roof. This "journey through film history" explores the pioneering years, silent-film divas, films from the Weimar era, cinema under the Nazis and goes right up to contemporary cinema, with rooms that cover postwar German filmmakers (1946–80) and the present (from 1981). As well as a special exhibit on Germany's biggest star, Marlene Dietrich, there's memorabilia and model film sets from key directors including Fritz Lang and an exhibit that compares East and West German television

broadcasts. The museum also organizes the retrospective section of the Berlinale film festival, and hosts special film series, exhibitions and events.

KOLLHOFF TOWER

Potsdamer Platz 1 ⊕/Ⓢ Potsdamer Platz
☎ 030/25 29 43 72, Ⓦ www.panoramapunkt
.de. Platform winter: Mon–Fri & Sun
10am–6pm, Sat 10am–8pm; summer: daily
10am–8pm, weather permitting until sunset.
€5.50. MAP P.74–75, POCKET MAP A15

Located on the northern edge of Potsdamer Platz, the 25-storey (103m), dark, peat-fired brick Kollhoff Tower is named after architect Hans Kollhoff, a member of the international team of architects (headed by Renzo Piano) that designed many of the buildings for the new Platz. The ground floor houses a number of restaurants and shops, the upper floors are used for office space and – the real highlight – the **Panorama-punkt** on the top floors, offers an open-air viewing platform, reached via Europe's fastest elevator. From the top you can see the Reichstag, Brandenburg Gate, TV Tower, Sony Center, Tiergarten and Kulturforum. Admission includes entry to an exhibition on the history of the area and there's also a café with an outdoor terrace.

DAIMLER CONTEMPORARY

Alte Potsdamer Str. 5, in Haus Huth ⓤ/Ⓢ Potzdamer Platz ☎ 030/25 94 14 20. ⓦ www.collection.daimler.com. Daily 11am–6pm. Free. MAP BELOW, POCKET MAP A15

The Daimler art collection was set up in 1977 as a space for twentieth-century art, initially mainly focused on German artists. The museum expanded in the 1990s with the inclusion of works by other European and American artists, including Andy Warhol and Jeff Koons. The impressive collection includes approximately 1800 works by international artists, showcased in rotating exhibitions across this attractive 600-square-metre space, which used to be a restaurant and storage area. Much of the collection is modernist in nature – geometric, challenging and abstract – so not one for traditionalists. As well as exhibiting its own collection, the gallery regularly puts on a variety of temporary exhibitions.

GAMÄLDEGALERIE

Matthäikirchplatz 4/6 ⓤ/Ⓢ Potsdamer Platz ☎ 030/26 62 951, ⓦ www.smb.museum/gg. Tues–Fri 10am–6pm, Sat & Sun 11am–6pm. €8. MAP BELOW, POCKET MAP E6

With a history that goes back to 1830, the Gemäldegalerie holds one of the world's most renowned collections of classical European painting. Created from the treasures of the Prussian royalty – including that of Frederick the Great – the collection used to be part of Museum Island (see p.46). The museum – and some of the works – were damaged by Allied bombing during World War II, and the artworks were then split between East

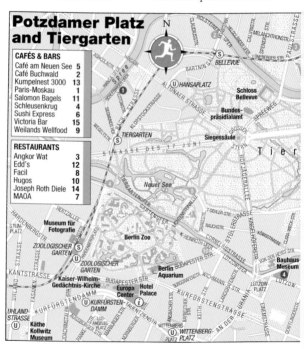

Potzdamer Platz and Tiergarten

CAFÉS & BARS	
Café am Neuen See	5
Café Buchwald	2
Kumpelnest 3000	13
Paris-Moskau	1
Salomon Bagels	11
Schleusenkrug	4
Sushi Express	6
Victoria Bar	15
Weilands Wellfood	9

RESTAURANTS	
Angkor Wat	3
Edd's	12
Facil	8
Hugos	10
Joseph Roth Diele	14
MAOA	7

THE GAMALDEGALERIE

and West during the Cold War. After the Wall fell the collection came together again here. Spread across 72 rooms, divided up by country, with sections on Italian, Flemish and Dutch works, the treasures include many highpoints of European art by including works by Bruegel, a particularly good selection by Cranach (pictured), Dürer, Raphael, Rubens, Vermeer and many others. The Rembrandt room and Caravaggio's exquisite Cupid, *Love Conquers All*, are both well worth seeking out.

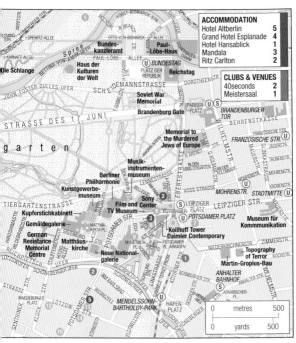

KUNSTGEWERBEMUSEUM

Matthäikirchplatz ⓤ/Ⓢ Potsdamer Platz
☎ 030/266 42 43 36, Ⓦ www.smb.museum
/kgm. Mon–Fri 10am–6pm, Sat & Sun
11am–6pm. €8; Thurs 2–6pm free.
MAP P.74–75, POCKET MAP E6

Interested in crafts? Berlin's
Museum of Decorative Arts –
one of the oldest in Germany
– boasts a collection of
decorative arts and home
furnishings that ranges from
the Middle Ages to Art
Nouveau. Over 7000 square
metres of dimly lit space, the
museum covers all major styles
and periods, including
jaw-dropping silks, tapestries,
Renaissance bronzes,
contemporary furniture,
Rococo glassware, faïence work
and porcelain, and stunning
gold and silver works. The
lower floor has a "new
collection" which places an
emphasis on the arts and crafts
of the twentieth century,
complemented by examples of
industrial products. It's unlikely
you'll need to see more fine
crafts after this, but if you do
wish to, try the second
museum out in the suburbs at
Schloss Köpenick (Schlossinsel
1 Ⓢ Köpenick; Thurs–Sun
10am–5pm; €4). The Baroque
palace houses over 500 exhibits
and is structured around a
concept called "Room Art", in
which furniture and other
interior decorations from the
Renaissance, Baroque and
Rococo periods are displayed.

KUPFERSTICHKABINETT

Matthäikirchplatz ⓤ/Ⓢ Potsdamer Platz
☎ 030/26 64 23 040, Ⓦ www.smb.museum
/kk. Tues–Fri 10am–6pm, Sat & Sun
11am–6pm. €6. MAP P.74–75, POCKET MAP E6

The Kupferstichkabinett, or
"print room", is the largest
collection of graphic art in
Germany, and one of the four
most important museums of its

DISPLAY AT THE KUNSTGEWERBEMUSEUM

kind in the world. The museum
houses over 500,000 prints and
110,000 drawings, waterco-
lours, pastels and oil sketches
from European artists from the
Middle Ages to the present, all
on paper. Major artists such as
Sandro Botticelli, Albrecht
Dürer, Rembrandt, Adolph von
Menzel, Pablo Picasso and
Andy Warhol are represented.
Due to the size and sensitivity
of the collection (being largely
on paper), there's no permanent display – visitors must
check for special exhibitions, or
request to see specific art works
via the study hall.

BERLINER PHILHARMONIE

Herbert-von-Karajan-Str. 1 ⓤ/Ⓢ Potsdamer
Platz ☎ 030/254 88 0, Ⓦ www.berliner
-philharmoniker.de. MAP P.74–75,
POCKET MAP E6

Built by architect Hans
Scharoun between 1960 and
1963, the Berliner
Philharmonie is one of the
most important concert halls in
Berlin and home to the
world-renowned Berlin
Philharmonic. The asymmet-
rical, tent-like building has an
equally distinctive pentagon-
shaped concert hall (plus a
smaller hall, Kammermusik-
saal, which seats 1180) that

enables great views from all sides. Guided tours of both the Philharmonic Hall and the Chamber Music Hall are offered daily from 1pm (☏030/25 48 81 56; €3/€2).

MUSIKINSTRUMENTEN-MUSEUM

Tiergartenstr. 1 (visitor's entrance Ben-Gurion-Str.) ⓤ/Ⓢ Potsdamer Platz ☏ 030/25 48 10, Ⓦ www.mim-berlin.de. Tues, Wed & Fri 9am–5pm, Thurs 9am–10pm, Sat & Sun 10am–5pm. €4 including audioguide.
MAP P.74–75, POCKET MAP E6

The Musikinstrumenten-Museum embraces Germany's glorious history of music with over three thousand instruments from the sixteenth to the twenty-first centuries, making it one of the country's most comprehensive collections. A large selection are on permanent display here, including a rare Stradivarius violin, Frederick the Great's flutes, a glass harmonica invented by Benjamin Franklin and – the flamboyant centrepiece – a massive Mighty Wurlitzer theatre organ once owned by the Siemens family. The museum also veers into electronic music with electric guitars, mixing stations and other experimental instruments, including the Mixturtrautonium on which Oskar Sala composed his famous soundtrack for Alfred Hitchcock's film *The Birds*.

NEUE NATIONALGALERIE

Potsdamer Str. 50 ⓤ/Ⓢ Potsdamer Platz ☏ 030/266 42 30 40, Ⓦ www.smb.museum /nng. Tues, Wed, & Fri 10am–6pm, Thurs 10am–10pm, Sat & Sun 11am–6pm. €8.
MAP P.74–75, POCKET MAP E6

The "temple of light and glass" (as it's modestly known) and its sculpture gardens were famously designed by Bauhaus affiliate Ludwig Mies van der Rohe. Opened in 1968, the museum houses an extensive collection of twentieth-century European paintings and sculptures from the nineteenth century to the 1960s, including household names like Bacon, Picasso, Klee, Dix and plenty of German art (E.L. Kirchner, Beckmann). The museum displays portions of its permanent collection on a rotating basis, so each visit is different, and a number of special exhibitions also occur throughout the year, during which the permanent collection may not be on view. There's also a café on the ground floor (10.30am–5.45pm).

MUSEUM FÜR KOMMUNIKATION

Leipziger Str. 16 ⓤ Stadtmitte ☏ 030/20 29 40, Ⓦ www.museumsstiftung.de. Tues–Fri 9am–5pm, Sat & Sun 11am–7pm. €3.
MAP P.74–75, POCKET MAP C15

Founded in 1872 as the first postal museum of the world, the Museum for Communication experienced a rebirth in 2000, as evidenced by the blue neon writing on the neo-Baroque facade and three robots in the lobby. The permanent exhibition showcases the origins, development and future perspectives of the "information society", while the computer gallery on the second floor extends the exhibition into virtual space. Highlights of the permanent exhibition are wax seals, postcards and stamps (such as the famous Blue Mauritius), telephones (including some of the first), radios, film, telegraphs and computers. The museum's interactive and lively approach makes it an ideal destination for kids, but adults will appreciate the temporary exhibitions featuring cutting-edge artists.

HAUS DER KULTUREN DER WELT

THE GERMAN RESISTANCE MEMORIAL CENTRE

Stauffenbergstr. 13–14 (entrance through the commemorative courtyard)
🚇 Mendelssohn-Bartholdy-Park ☎ 030/26 99 50 00, 🌐 www.gdw-berlin.de. Mon–Wed & Fri 9am–6pm, Thurs 9am–8pm, Sat & Sun 10am–6pm. Free. MAP P.74–75, POCKET MAP D6

Located in an historic section of the former headquarters of the Nazi army high command, the site of the assassination attempt on Adolf Hitler on July 20, 1944, the **Gedenkstätte Deutscher Widerstand** (German Resistance Memorial Centre) was set up to illustrate how people and groups took action against the Nazis between 1933 and 1945. It's part museum, part memorial, with the memorial courtyard dedicated to the conspiring German army officers who were killed after the assassination attempt. The permanent exhibition, called Resistance to National Socialism, has over five thousand photographs and documents spread across 26 topics that go beyond Nazi dissent to address the wider context of resistance, including the role of Christian beliefs in protest, opposition by young

people specifically and general defiance of wartime environments in daily life. The exhibition is mostly in German but English audioguides (and related books) are available from reception.

BAUHAUS MUSEUM

Klingelhöferstr. 14 🚇 Nollendorfplatz
☎ 030/25 40 020, 🌐 www.bauhaus.de.
Mon–Wed & Thurs–Sun 10am–5pm. Mon, Sat & Sun €7, Wed–Fri €6 (includes audio tour).
MAP P.74–75, POCKET MAP D6

Talk about dying young but leaving an attractive corpse. Germany's Bauhaus ("building house") design school may have only lasted from 1919 to 1933 but it went on to became one of the twentieth century's most influential movements – more famous outside the country than Goethe or Schiller. Founded by Walter Gropius, the movement explored the links between fine art and craftsmanship and – a bit later – art and mass production. The Bauhaus Archive and Museum, housed in a distinctive building designed by Gropius himself, is the best place to explore the breadth and depth of Bauhaus's expansive activities. Here are tubular steel furniture from Marcel Breuer, armchairs and desks from Mies van der Rohe, paintings from Itten, Schlemmer, Feininger, Albers and Klee…even dapper wallpaper and beautiful chess sets. The archive next door holds the largest Bauhaus resource in the world, while the museum shop stocks an impressive range of high-quality reproductions, and there's an adjoining café.

HAUS DER KULTUREN DER WELT

John-Foster-Dulles-Allee 10 ①/⑤ Bundestag ☎ 030/397 870, ⓦ www.hkw.de. Daily 10am–7pm. Exhibitions: Mon & Wed–Sun 11am–7pm. MAP P.74–75, POCKET MAP E5

Known as the "pregnant oyster" because of its distinctively curvaceous facade, the House of World Cultures hosts exhibitions with a focus on artistic and cultural movements in non-European cultures. Formerly known as the Kongresshalle conference hall, the building, designed in 1957 by US architect Hugh Stubbins Jr, was a gift from the United States (John F. Kennedy spoke here during his 1963 visit to West Berlin). In 1980 the roof collapsed, injuring many people (and killing one) and was rebuilt in its original style in 1987. The building's maze of rooms include an exhibition hall, auditorium for concerts and theatre and a congress hall, and it is an ideal location for the colourful variety of events held here throughout the year. The eclectic and globally minded spread of events range from educational programmes to exhibitions, music, performing arts, literature festivals and more.

THE TIERGARTEN

MAP P.74–75, POCKET MAP 05

Full of paths, forested areas, lakes and meadows, the luscious and vast Tiergarten park – bisected by Strasse des 17 Juni – began its life as the preferred hunting ground for the electors of Brandenburg. Designed in its current form in 1830 by landscape architect Peter Joseph Lenne, it is now one of the most relaxing spots in Berlin, is dotted with a couple of interesting attractions, with the Siegessäule (see p.80) its focal point.

CYCLISTS IN THE TIERGARTEN

THE SIEGESSÄULE

SIEGESSÄULE

Grosser Stern 1 ⓤ Hansaplatz ⓌＷＷＷ
.monument-tales.de. Winter: Mon–Fri
10am–5pm, Sat & Sun 10am–5.30pm;
summer: Mon–Fri 9.30am–5.30pm, Sat & Sun
10am–7pm. €2.20. MAP P.74–75, POCKET MAP D5

You can't miss the huge victory
column at the centre of the
"Grosser Stern" (great star)
roundabout in the Tiergarten.
The cocksure monument is
otherwise known as the tricky
to pronounce Siegessäule, built
from 1864 to 1873 after a
design by Johann Heinrich
Stack to commemorate the
Prussian victory in the
Prusso-Danish war of 1864. It's
69m (25ft) tall, weighs 35 tons
and features a *Goddess of
Victory* on top, added later after
further Prussian victories in
wars against Austria and
France. At the base you can see
bas-reliefs of battles and at the
top there's an observatory,
which gives great views of the
Reichstag, the Brandenburg
Gate and the Fernsehturm, but
you have to climb the 285 steps
to access it. There's also a small
café, souvenir shop and small
exhibition connecting the
column with the events in
German history that it
represents.

SCHLOSS BELLEVUE

Spreeweg 1 ⓤ Hansaplatz. Closed to the
public. MAP P.74–75, POCKET MAP D5

Situated on an area of twenty
hectares (about 50 acres) beside
the River Spree, Schloss
Bellevue was built for Prince
August Ferdinand of Prussia,
the younger brother of
Frederick II of Prussia. The
sparkling white home was
designed by architect Philipp
Daniel Boumann and has the
distinction of being the first
Neoclassical building
constructed in Germany. It was
uninhabited in the nineteenth
century and used by various
institutions such as a museum
of ethnography in the 1930s. In
1938, the building was
converted into a guesthouse of
the government and the
entrance to the palace was
redesigned. Severely damaged in
World War II, it was renovated
during 1954–59 and set up as
the official residence of the
federal president in Berlin. The
main sights include a ballroom
designed by Carl Gotthard
Langhans, the huge lawn behind
the palace and the modern
building to the south – known
as the "presidential egg" due to
its oval shape. The palace is
currently closed to visitors.

JOSEPH ROTH DIELE

Restaurants

ANGKOR WAT

Paulstr. 22 Ⓤ/Ⓢ Hauptbahnhof ☎ 030/39
33 922, Ⓦ www.kambodschareise.de. Mon–Fri
6pm–midnight, Sat & Sun noon–midnight.
MAP P.74–75, POCKET MAP D4

This cavernous restaurant
serves a mean Cambodian
fondue. The friendly service
makes up for the exotic decor,
and if you don't like frying
your own meat the menu
extends to other Cambodian
classics with plenty of spices
and creamy coconut.

EDD'S

Lützowstr. 81 Ⓤ Kurfürstenstr. ☎ 030/215 52
94, Ⓦ www.edds-thairestaurant.de. Mon–Fri
11.30am–3pm & 6pm–midnight, Sat 5pm–
midnight, Sun 2pm–midnight.
MAP P.74–75, POCKET MAP E7

Edd and his wife present
well-balanced, spicy Thai food
(the banana blossom salad is a
signature dish) in an elegant
– largely wood – space free of
kitsch. It's expensive for Thai
food (€15.50–€25 mains) but
popular, so make a reservation.

FACIL

Mandala Hotel, Potsdamer Str. 3 Ⓤ/
Ⓢ Potsdamer Platz ☎ 030/59 005 ext. 1234,
Ⓦ www.facil.de. Mon–Fri noon–3pm &
7–11pm, closed Sat & Sun.
MAP P.74–75, POCKET MAP A15

Michael Kempf's restaurant in
the *Mandala Hotel* not only
offers amazing food but also
splendid views from its
fifth-floor dining room,
surrounded by a lush bamboo
garden. Popular with business
types, politicos and serious
foodies, Kempf's Michelin-
starred, fish-heavy menu has
become justly famous. Dinner
is €16–55 per course; try a
lunch reservation for
something slightly cheaper
(€18–39 per course).

HUGOS

Hotel InterContinental, Budapester Str. 2
Ⓤ Wittenbergplatz ☎ 030/26 02 12 63,
Ⓦ www.hugos-restaurant.de. Mon–Sat
6–10.30pm, closed mid-July to mid-Aug.
MAP P.74–75, POCKET MAP C6

In a gorgeously appointed
room at the top of the *Hotel
InterContinental*, superstar chef
Thomas Kammeier creates
Michelin-starred "New
German–Mediterranean" food
that you can sample – for a
price – while enjoying the
restaurant's panoramic views
(mains €44–€52).

JOSEPH ROTH DIELE

Potsdamer Str. 75 Ⓤ Kurfürstenstr.
☎ 030/26 36 98 84, Ⓦ www.joseph-roth-diele
.de. Mon–Fri 10am–midnight, Sat 6pm–
midnight. MAP P.74–75, POCKET MAP E7

A splash of charm and colour
on nondescript Potsdamer
Strasse, this quirky restaurant
pays homage to the life and
work of inter-war Jewish
writer Joseph Roth. The daily
specials are very reasonable
(€3.95–€8), though the food is
far from high end. Nonetheless
it's a charming place to eat and
popular with a wide range of
people at lunchtimes.

MAOA

Leipziger Platz 8 Ⓤ/Ⓢ Potsdamer Platz
☎ 030/22 48 80 87, Ⓦ www.maoa.de.
Mon–Sat 5pm–1am, Sun 11.30am–1am.
MAP P.74–75, POCKET MAP A15

MAOA, which stands for
Modern Art of Asia, sounds
like a museum but is actually
a Mongolian barbecue
featuring exotic dishes with
ingredients like ostrich,
crocodile, and other
off-the-wall but delicious
meats – all in a sleek, minimal
Asian-style interior. Choose
either one item a la carte
(€16.90) or help yourself
buffet-style (€23.70)

Cafés and bars

CAFÉ AM NEUEN SEE

Lichtensteinallee 2 ⓤ Zoologischer Garten
☎ 30/25 44 93 00, ⓦ www.cafe-am-neuen-see
.de, Daily 9am–midnight. MAP P.74–75, POCKET MAP C6

A fantastic stop off on any tour of the Tiergarten, this old school beer garden with modern restaurant serves great coffee and draught beers, has pizza and pasta dishes (€10) and a fuller menu inside. It's a beautiful location, right on the lake (the Neuen See), and there are even rowing boats for rent.

CAFÉ BUCHWALD

Bartningallee 29 ⓤ Hansaplatz ☎ 030/39 15
931, ⓦ www.konditorei-buchwald.de. Mon–Sat
9am–6pm. MAP P.74–75, POCKET MAP C4

Take a short stroll down a pleasant path from Schloss Bellevue to find *Café Buchwald*, which has been standing here for 130 years. Not just standing but selling some of the best cakes and tarts in town – they used to supply the court and still sell such delicious confections as the home-made *Baumkuchen*. There are a few seats in the charming little front garden.

KUMPELNEST 3000

Lützowstr. 23 ⓤ Kurfürstenstr. ☎ 030/26 16
91 8, ⓦ www.kumpelnest3000.com. Mon–
Thurs & Sun 5pm–5am, Fri & Sat 5pm–late.
MAP P.74–75, POCKET MAP E7

Hard to believe that this charming den of iniquity is only a few minutes' stroll from Potsdamer Platz. With its deliberately tacky decor, loyal mixed/gay crowd and anything goes atmosphere, especially at weekends, it's a good place if you're in the area and looking for the lure of the mirrored discoball rather than the commercial glare of the Platz.

PARIS-MOSKAU

Alt-Moabit 141 ⓤ/Ⓢ Hauptbahnhof
☎ 030/39 42 081, ⓦ www.paris-moskau.de.
MAP P.74–75, POCKET MAP E4

This curious mix of old Berlin and contemporary elegance is set in a nineteenth-century rail signalman's house (it's named after the Paris-Moscow line) and serves hearty dishes like deer and rabbit, fish dishes and vegetarian lasagne with beetroot and chestnuts (€39–65). It's all backed up by a great wine list.

SALOMON BAGELS

Alte Potsdamer Str. 7 ⓤ/Ⓢ Potsdamer
Platz ☎ 030/25 29 76 26, ⓦ www
.salomon-bagels.de. Mon–Sat 9am–10pm,
Sun 10am–8pm. MAP P.74–75, POCKET MAP A15

Bagels, bagels, bagels. And sandwiches. And excellent cakes, like their New York-style cheesecake. Located in a mall, this shop does takeaways, but there are sofas too – a good spot for a cheap snack ($5–10).

SCHLEUSENKRUG

Müller-Breslau-Str. corner Unterschleuse
ⓤ/Ⓢ Zoologischer Garten ☎ 030/31 39 909,
ⓦ www.schleusenkrug.de, Daily: summer
10am–1am; winter 10am–6pm.
MAP P.74–75, POCKET MAP B6

CAFÉ BUCHWALD

A classic Berlin beer garden, *Schleusenkrug* is a fine place to tuck into a glass of beer and an organic *Wurst*, enjoy a coffee while watching the boats cruise down the canal, or enjoy the live music they have from time to time in the summer.

SUSHI EXPRESS

Potsdamer Platz 2 ⓤ/Ⓢ Potsdamer Platz
☎ 030/25 75 18 63, ⓦ www.sushi-expressberlin
.de. Mon–Sat 11.30am–10pm, Sun 2–10pm.
MAP P.74–75, POCKET MAP A15

It's a bit of a hassle to find, but *Sushi Express* – located in the Sony Center courtyard in a passage to the S-Bahn – is worthwhile for a decent range of conveyor-belt sushi, especially when half-price offers are on (Mon–Fri noon–6pm). Hot dishes and lunchboxes also available, though it's usually packed at lunchtimes. Main courses €5.

VICTORIA BAR

Potsdamer Str. 102 ⓤ Kurfürstenstr.
☎ 030/25 75 99 77, ⓦ www.victoriabar.de.
Mon–Thurs & Sun 6.30pm–3am, Fri & Sat
6.30pm–4am. MAP P.74–75, POCKET MAP E7

This much-loved cocktail bar is great for a low-key and decently mixed drink in the week or a livelier atmosphere at weekends. The long bar, subdued lighting and discreet but upbeat music create a decent buzz.

WEILANDS WELLFOOD

Marlene-Dietrich-Platz 1 ⓤ/Ⓢ Potsdamer
Platz ☎ 030/25 89 97 17, ⓦ www
.weilands-wellfood.de. Daily 10am–1am.
MAP P.74–75, POCKET MAP A15

Right by a pond near bustling Potsdamer Platz, this health-conscious, fast-food style store sells food low in calories and high in vitamins: couscous, salads, curries and sandwiches stacked with fresh ingredients. Popular with local workers at lunchtimes.

BOATS BY CAFÉ AM NEUEN SEE

Clubs and venues

40SECONDS

Potsdamer Str. 58 ⓤ/Ⓢ Potsdamer Platz
☎ 030/89 06 420, ⓦ www.40seconds.de. Fri–Sat
11pm–late. €10. MAP P.74–75, POCKET MAP E6

Named after the amount of time it takes for the elevator to whisk you up to the top floor, this part futurist, part 1980s throwback bar gives great views over Potsdamer Platz. There are three lounge areas, lit by Verner Panton lamps, and balconies for summer. The music is standard r'n'b, house and electronic, and the mood is glamorous.

MEISTERSAAL

Köthener Str. 38 ⓤ/Ⓢ Potsdamer Platz
☎ 030/32 59 99 710, ⓦ www
.meistersaal-berlin.de. MAP P.74–75, POCKET MAP F6

This 100-year-old music venue and recording studios has drawn major artists from Kurt Tucholsky and David Bowie to U2 and Herbert Grönemeyer. Built in 1913 in what was once Berlin's music quarter, the building fell into disrepair after World War II. Since then, though, the Meistersaal has become Berlin's version of London's Abbey Road, world-renowned for its excellent acoustics.

Prenzlauer Berg

Built in the nineteenth century as a working-class district, Prenzlauer Berg's fortunes have seesawed over the subsequent century and a half. Having survived the War relatively intact, the area was neglected by the GDR, becoming a ghetto of rebellion as intellectuals, punks and bohemians took up residence in its crumbling tenements. Merciless post-Wall gentrification has transformed the district yet again. Today's refurbished buildings and handsome, cobbled streets create an attractive Alt Berlin atmosphere beloved by wealthy creative types and middle-class families, who gravitate towards leafy, laid-back squares like Helmholtzplatz and Kollwitzplatz. While low on major sights, the district has a few intriguing buildings worth seeking out – Rykestrasse's synagogue and the distinctive watertower near Knaackstrasse for example – though most come to browse the upscale boutiques along Kastanienallee, hang out in the independent bars and cafés, or visit the atmospheric Sunday flea market at Mauerpark.

GEDENKSTÄTTE BERLINER MAUER

Bernauer Str. 111/119 ⓤ Bernauer Str./ Ⓢ Nordbahnhof ⓣ 030/467 98 66 66, ⓦ www .berliner-mauer-dokumentationszentrum.de. April–Oct Tues–Sun 9.30am–7pm; Nov–March Tues–Sun 9.30am–6pm. Free. MAP P.86–87, POCKET MAP G2

Based slightly away from the tourist centre, so avoiding the crowds that throng Checkpoint Charlie, the Berlin Wall Memorial takes a more academic and sober look at Germany's division. A section of the former border strip is the

STALL AT MAUERPARK FLEA MARKET

focus for the **memorial**, while an outdoor exhibition on the former death-strip shows the history of Bernauer Strasse and the wall itself. Stretching 1.4km up to the Mauerpark, it includes traces of border obstacles that retain the appearance of the Wall as it would have been at the time.

The **museum** opposite documents the lives of those attempting to escape the dictatorship (the most famous and successful escape tunnels were dug near here) and the resistance efforts – sometimes fatal – organized by those living nearby. There's also a separate exhibition on the division of the U-Bahn and S-Bahn lines displayed in the adjacent **Nordbahnhof** station (open during station opening hours). The memorial on the former border strip is open all year round, and prayer services for the victims of the Berlin Wall are held in the **chapel** from Tuesday to Friday at noon.

MAUERPARK FLOHMARKT

Bernauer Str. 63–64 ⓤ Bernauer Str. ☎ 0176 292 50 021, ⓦ www.mauerparkmarkt.de. Sun: winter 8am–6pm; summer 8am–8pm. Free. MAP P.86–87, POCKET MAP H2

One of Berlin's best loved flea markets, Mauerpark is an institution in the city, popular every Sunday with hungover students, bargain hunters, families and bemused-looking, shade-wearing clubbers who come to scan the food stalls, clothes shops and nostalgic junk that seems to extend forever. You can find everything here from bike parts and badges, 1950s cutlery sets and faded jigsaws, new and vintage clothes, GDR memorabilia, cats on strings, banana telephones and record players, bibles and lots of vinyl and CDs. As with most flea markets, there's a decent amount of what might uncharitably be called "junk" but also some genuine antiques. Adjacent to the market you'll find the actual **Mauerpark**, a strip of landscaped green that was once the site of a stretch of Berlin Wall and the associated death-strip, loomed over by the Friedrich-Ludwig-Jahn-Sport-park and the Max-Schmeling-Halle. When the weather's warm check out the weekly karaoke session in the "bearpit", which attracts massive crowds between 1.30pm and 5pm.

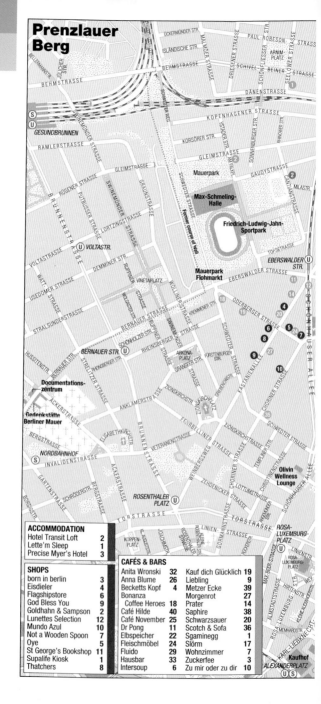

Prenzlauer Berg

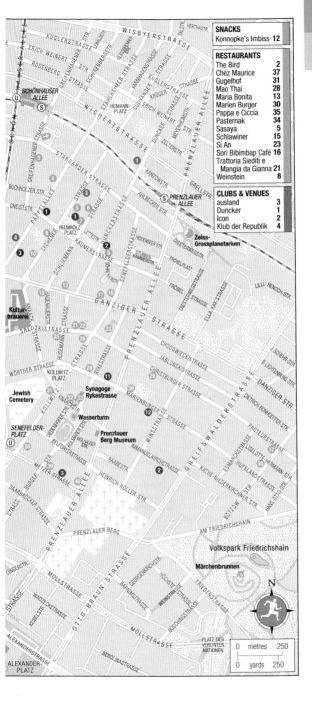

SNACKS

Konnopke's Imbiss	12

RESTAURANTS

The Bird	2
Chez Maurice	37
Gugelhof	31
Mao Thai	28
Maria Bonita	13
Marien Burger	30
Pappa e Ciccia	35
Pasternak	34
Sasaya	5
Schlawiner	15
Si An	23
Sori Bibimbap Café	16
Trattoria Siediti e Mangia da Gianna	21
Weinstein	8

CLUBS & VENUES

ausland	3
Duncker	1
Icon	2
Klub der Republik	4

KOLLWITZPLATZ

Kollwitzplatz ⓤ Eberswalder Str./ Senefelderplatz. MAP P.86–87, POCKET MAP J2

Kollwitzplatz is one of Prenzlauer Berg's best-known and most attractive squares. It was named after artist Käthe Kollwitz (1867–1945), who lived in the area at the turn of the twentieth century (a simple plaque commemorates her former home on Kollwitzstr.) and whose squat, serious-looking **sculpture** is one of the main features of the square. From the appearance of the lavishly restored facades it is hard to tell that Kollwitzplatz was once one of Berlin's poorest areas, but Kollwitz's work (see p.128) reveals the area to have once been home to the city's more impoverished and downtrodden citizens. This was one of the first areas to be gentrified when the Wall fell in 1989 and today symbolizes Prenzlauer Berg's yuppie status as well as its bias towards families (some call this part of the city Pramzlauerberg). It's a lovely place to come for a stroll – three **playgrounds** and a leafy **park** lie within the square and endless restaurants, cafés and smart boutiques are scattered around its perimeter. Saturdays are especially popular thanks to the extensive **farmers' market** that takes over three of its four streets, offering everything from organic meat and fish, fruit and veg, sweets and coffee and clothes. A smaller (and less crowded) organic market also takes place on Thursdays. In summer especially the fun carries on till late at night.

JEWISH CEMETERY

Schönhauser Allee 23–25 ⓤ Senefelderplatz. Mon–Thurs 8am–4pm, Fri 8am–1pm. ☎ 030/441 98 24. Free. MAP P.86–87, POCKET MAP J2

A short hop from the Senefelderplatz U-Bahn, Prenzlauer Berg's small but charming Jewish Cemetery (Jüdischer Friedhof) was built to cater for the overspill from the one on Mitte's Grosse Hamburger Strasse. It was mostly used between 1827 and 1880, at a time when the Jewish population in this area was thriving, and holds approximately 22,000 graves and almost a thousand hereditary family plots, including the graves of painter Max Liebermann, the publisher Leopold Ullstein, the composer Giacomo Meyerbeer and German-Jewish banker Joseph Mendelssohn (son of the influential philosopher Moses Mendelssohn). Sadly many gravestones, the original cemetery entrance and mourning chapel were

TABLE TENNIS PLAYERS ON KOLLWITZPLATZ

destroyed during World War II and subsequent anti-Semitic vandalism – and many graves are still in a dilapidated state, some riddled with bullet holes. The cemetery was rebuilt in the 1960s, and the adjacent lapidarium – on the site of the former mourning hall – was opened in 2004 as a place to preserve and protect sixty of the most valuable stones, as well as to display panels on Jewish culture and Jewish mourning rituals. Note that men are obliged to cover their heads to visit the cemetery: hats can be borrowed from the lapidarium but visitors are urged to bring their own.

SYNAGOGE RYKESTRASSE

Rykestr. 53 Ⓤ Senefelderstr. ☎ 030/44 85 298, Ⓦ www.synagoge-rykestrasse.de. Open for services only. Fri: Nov–March 6pm; April–Oct 7pm; Sat 9.30am. MAP P.86–87, POCKET MAP J2

Built by Johann Hoeniger at the turn of the twentieth century, this gorgeous Neoclassical synagogue (inaugurated in 1904) is one of Germany's oldest and biggest – and one of Berlin's loveliest. The building survived *Kristallnacht* in 1938 as it was located between "Aryan" apartment buildings, although precious Torah scrolls were damaged and rabbis and congregation members were deported to Sachsenhausen (see p.140). The synagogue was also used as stables during the war, but was finally restored to its former glory by architects Ruth Golan and Kay Zareh in 2007, who used black-and-white photographs and a €4-million budget to lavishly recreate the remarkable original. Unfortunately the synagogue has stopped offering guided tours so visits are restricted to prayer services.

THE WASSERTURM

Corner of Knaackstr. & Rykestr. Ⓤ Eberswalder Str./Senefelderplatz. MAP P.86–87, POCKET MAP J2

Designed by Henry Gill, constructed by the English Waterworks Company and finished in 1877, the 30m-high cylindrical brick water tower, known as "Dicker Hermann", has become one of Prenzlauer Berg's unofficial symbols. One of the oldest of its kind in the city, it was one of the first places to provide running water in the country, and remained in use until the 1950s. Its engine house was used as an unofficial prison by the SA in 1933–45 – 28 bodies were later found in the underground pipe network, and a commemorative plaque stands outside on Knaack-strasse. During GDR times the tower was used to store canned fish, which could apparently be smelled across the whole neighbourhood. The building was then abandoned and became a "playground" for local kids. Today the refurbished tower is home to much-coveted cake-wedge shaped apartments (formerly belonging to the tower's operators), while the underground reservoir space is home to sporadic art and music events (see Ⓦ www.singuhr.de).

OLIVIN WELLNESS LOUNGE

Schönhauser Allee 177 Ⓤ Senefelderplatz ☎ 030/44 04 25 00, Ⓦ www.olivin-berlin.com. Daily: autumn/winter noon–midnight; summer 5pm–midnight. MAP P.86–87, POCKET MAP J3

With its exposed brick walls, saunas and an excellent bamboo garden this Finnish sauna is a great way to unwind whatever the season. Special offers are available in winter and massages start at a very reasonable €45 an hour. Thursdays are women only.

KULTURBRAUEREI

Schönhauser Allee 36 (entrance in Sredzkistr.) ⊕ Eberswalder Str. or trams #20, #50, #53. ☎ 030/44 35 260, ⓦ www .kulturbrauerei-berlin.de. Mon–Sat 9am–7pm. Free for main complex, price varies for specific venues. MAP P.86–87, POCKET MAP J2

This lovely, sprawling red-and-yellow brick complex dates back to 1842, when it was a small brewery and pub. It was taken over in 1853 by famous brewer Schultheiss, who expanded it to its current size. Since the late 1990s it's been one of Prenzlauer Berg's major commercial hubs: 25,000 square metres of office space, music halls, bars, restaurants, clubs and an eight-theatre, 1500-capacity cinema (Kino in der KulturBrauerei; ☎ 018 05 11 88 11, ⓦ www.cinestar.de). Despite its prowess on paper, it's a fairly soulless place, out of synch with the rest of Prenzlauer Berg's more independent cultural scene – although the Scandinavian Christmas Market is worth a visit, and the Kesselhaus concert hall hosts some decent indie rock and pop shows. The venue also offers guided cycle tours from March till November (☎ 030/43 73 99 99, ⓦ www.berlinonbike.de).

PRENZLAUER BERG MUSEUM

Prenzlauer Allee 227–228 ⊕ Senefelderplatz. Mon–Fri 9am–6pm. ☎ 030/42 40 10 97. Free. MAP P.86–87, POCKET MAP J3

Spread across the first floor of a former school, this small but lively museum documents the history of the district and its mainly poor working-class inhabitants from the nineteenth century to today. The permanent exhibition consists mainly of photos and text (German only) displayed along school-like corridors, though a couple of large rooms and a separate building across the courtyard are occasionally given over to more modern, multimedia exhibitions on themes such as life in Prenzlauer Berg before, during and after the Wall and the evolution of lesbian, gay and transgender life in the area.

ZEISS-GROSSPLANETARIUM

Prenzlauer Allee 80 ⑤ Prenzlauer Allee ☎ 030/42 18 450. Tues–Thurs 9am–noon, Fri 6–9.30pm, Sat 2.30pm–9pm, Sun 1.30–9pm. €5. MAP P.86–87, POCKET MAP K1

A massive silver golf-ball-esque building set back from bustling Prenzlauer Allee, the Zeiss Planetarium was built in 1987. At the time, it was one of Europe's largest and most modern stellar theatres, with a giant silver dome measuring 23m across. Today its auditorium, with artificial projection of the starry skies into the roof, is host to astronomical, film and music programmes that impress with their cutting-edge prowess, and are also entertaining and educational. The "Wonders of the Cosmos" astronomical show can be booked in advance in English and Russian, and the planetarium is open later on Friday and Saturday evenings for special events.

Shops

BORN IN BERLIN

Pappelallee 9 Ⓤ Eberswalder Str. ☎ 030/47 37 43 41. Mon–Fri noon–7pm, Sat noon–6pm. MAP P.86–87, POCKET MAP J1

Actually born in Turin, but this sister shop nonetheless sells edgy, industrial cuts – all handmade – that suit the city perfectly. Made from wools, linens and cottons, there are innovative collections for men and women, as well as some fantastic kids clothes and bags.

EISDIELER

Kastanienallee 12 Ⓤ Eberswalder Str. ☎ 030/28 39 12 91. Mon–Sat 10am–8pm. MAP P.86–87, POCKET MAP J2

Eisdieler stocks its own custom clothing (hoodies, sneakers, T-shirts) as well as selected brands (Le Coq Sportif, Spring Court, Schmoove), plus an impressive range of vintage shades from makes like Cartier, Porsche and Ray Ban.

FLAGSHIPSTORE

Oderberger Str. 53 Ⓤ Eberswalder Str. ☎ 030/43 73 53 27. Mon–Sat noon–8pm. MAP P.86–87, POCKET MAP H2

Representing dozens of Berlin's fashion labels and international designers, Flagshipstore offers a vast range of urban clothing and accessories (for women and men), plus shoes, magazines and more.

GOD BLESS YOU

Kastanienallee 31 Ⓤ Eberswalder Str. ☎ 030/29 66 68 80. Mon–Sat 11am–8pm. MAP P.86–87, POCKET MAP H2

Quirky dressers will adore this store, which stocks unusual street designs for men and women as well as iron-on-patches (guitars, grenades) so you can customize your own clothing.

STREET ART AT EISDIELER

GOLDHAHN UND SAMPSON

Dunckerstr. 9 Ⓤ Eberswalder Str. ☎ 030/41 19 83 66. Mon–Sat 8am–8pm. MAP P.86–87, POCKET MAP J1

A foodies' paradise that houses a vast spread of herbs, spices and other tasty delicacies from all over the world, plus cookbooks and kitchen utensils. It holds regular wine tasting and cooking courses.

LUNETTES SELECTION

Marienburger Str. 11 Ⓤ Senefelderplatz ☎ 030/34 08 27 89. Mon–Fri noon–8pm, Sat noon–6pm. MAP P.86–87, POCKET MAP K2

Vintage eyewear fanatics will adore this small space, which stocks original frames from brands like Alain Mikli and Christian Dior, as well as in-house designs by Uta Geyer.

MUNDO AZUL

Choriner Str. 49 Ⓤ Senefelderplatz ☎ 030/49 85 38 34. May–Sept Mon 10am–6pm, Tues–Fri 10am–7pm, Sat 10am–4pm; Oct–April Mon 10am–6pm, Tues–Fri 10am–7pm, Sat 11am–6pm. MAP P.86–87, POCKET MAP J2

"Blue world" is a children's bookstore that stocks beautiful books in French, Spanish, German and English, and also runs events and workshops. A must for visiting parents.

NOT A WOODEN SPOON

Oderberger Str. 2 ⓤ Eberswalder Str. Mon–Sat 10am–6pm. MAP P.86–87, POCKET MAP J2

British carpenter/designer Michael Ferguson makes eco-furnishings from discarded furniture, window frames and doors, transforming the city's flotsam and jetsam into attractive cabinets, chairs and more. Commissions undertaken.

OYE

Oderberger Str. 4 ⓤ Eberswalder Str. ☎ 030/66 64 78 21. Mon–Fri 1pm–8pm, Sat noon–8pm. MAP P.86–87, POCKET MAP J2

Originally catering for collectors of Latin, soul and funk vinyl, Oye now covers an impressive range of styles, from Afrobeat and blip-hop to Berlin club staples like house and techno.

ST GEORGE'S BOOKSHOP

Wörther Str. 27 ⓤ Eberswalder Str. ☎ 030/81 79 83 33. Mon–Fri 11am–8pm, Sat 11am–7pm. MAP P.86–87, POCKET MAP J2

Founded in 2003 by British twins Paul and Daniel, this delightful bookstore sells a fine selection of new and used English-language books. There's a sofa to chill on, free wi-fi and they'll buy your used books.

OYE

SUPALIFE KIOSK

Raumerstr. 40 ⓤ Eberswalder Str. ☎ 030/44 67 88 26. Mon–Sat noon–7pm. MAP P.86–87, POCKET MAP J1

This small boutique sells the wares of Berlin urban artists, from comics and fanzines to silkscreen prints and paintings. They're well connected to some of the city's best-known artists so expect special one-offs too.

THATCHERS

Kastanienallee 21 ⓤ Eberswalder Str. ☎ 030/24 62 77 51. Mon–Fri 11am–7pm, Sat noon–6pm. MAP P.86–87, POCKET MAP H2

Upmarket fashion store for women who like their dresses, skirts and shirts classy and sexy without ever being over the top. A perfect place to pick up sensual evening dresses or sophisticated club wear.

Restaurants

THE BIRD

Am Falkplatz 5 ⓤ/Ⓢ Schönhauser Allee ☎ 030/51 05 32 83. Mon–Sat 6pm–late, Sun noon–late. Cash only. MAP P.86–87, POCKET MAP H1

This no-nonsense New York-style steakhouse is famed for its large and tasty burgers, spicy chicken wings and casual ambience. With the neon bar, exposed brickwork and US accents it's a bit like being on the set of *Cheers*. A great place to fill up cheaply and sip on a cold beer.

CHEZ MAURICE

Bötzowstr. 39 Ⓢ Greifswalder Str. ☎ 030/42 50 506, ⓦ www.chez-maurice.com. Daily from 6pm, Tues–Sat also noon–4pm. MAP P.86–87, POCKET MAP L3

One of the finer dining spots in the quietly upmarket Bötzowviertel, *Maurice* is an intimate, rustic place offering high-quality seasonal French dishes – they'll even take

ka gai, spring rolls, glass noodle salads – make this a popular place.

MARIA BONITA

Danziger Str. 33 ⓤ Eberswalder Str. ☎ 0176 70 17 94 61, ⓦ www.maria-bonita.com. Daily noon–11pm. MAP P.86-87, POCKET MAP J2

Tucked away amidst the slew of Imbisses and kebab shops that make up much of this part of Danziger Str., *Maria Bonita* stands out for its above-average street-style Mexican food. You couldn't swing an enchilada inside, but the burritos, tacos and quesadillas – and the guacamole for that matter – are well worth trying.

MARIEN BURGER

Marienburger Str. 47 ⓤ Senefelderplatz ☎ 030/30 34 05 15, ⓦ www .marienburger-berlin.de, Daily 11am–10pm. MAP P.86-87, POCKET MAP K2

This diminutive but buzzy burger hangout lures locals back again and again with huge, delicious beef, chicken, fish or vegetable burgers (the Marienburger is almost too big to eat in one sitting). Organic options also available.

PAPPA E CICCIA

Schwedter Str. 18 ⓤ Senefelderplatz ☎ 030/61 62 08 01, ⓦ www.pappaeciccia.de. Mon–Thurs 9.30am–midnight, Fri 9.30am–1am, Sat 11am–1am, Sun 11am–11pm. MAP P.86-87, POCKET MAP H2

Bored of the usual Berlin brunch formula? Check out Sundays at this smart-casual Italian restaurant, where chefs dole out freshly baked lasagne and salmon, tomato and mozzarella and other scrumptious dishes, and diners gather on the long communal tables outside. It's all organic and there are decent vegetarian and vegan options. Ice cream, cakes and more on offer at the adjacent organic deli.

requests with enough notice - and an expansive wine list (over 200 from France alone). The *plat du jour* specials (noon –3.30pm) are good value: two courses €10, three courses €15.

GUGELHOF

Knaackstr. 37, cnr Kollwitzplatz ⓤ Senefelderplatz /Eberswalder Str. ☎ 030/44 29 229, ⓦ www.gugelhof.com. Mon–Fri 4pm–1am Sat & Sun 10am–1am. MAP P.86-87, POCKET MAP J2

A Kollwitzplatz classic, *Gugelhof* has been serving consistently good Alsatian food since the Wall fell, and counts Bill Clinton amongst its many dignified diners. It's a surprisingly down-to-earth place, with friendly staff and robust yet refined cuisine that includes *Flammkuchen* (*tarte flambee*) and pork knuckle. Reservations recommended.

MAO THAI

Wörther Str. 30 ⓤ Eberswalder Str. ☎ 030/44 19 261, ⓦ www.maothai.de, Daily noon–midnight. MAP P.86-87, POCKET MAP J2

Don't be put off by the beaming Buddhas in the window – there's a refreshing lack of garish decoration inside this reliable neighbourhood Thai restaurant. Decent service and a tasty range of classics – *tom*

PASTERNAK

Knaackstr. 22–24 ⓾ Senefelderplatz ☎ 030/44 13 399, ⓦ www.restaurant-pasternak.de, Daily 9am–1am. MAP P.86–87, POCKET MAP J2

This long-standing Russian/Jewish restaurant, named after the author of *Doctor Zhivago*, is best known for its incredible Sunday brunch (10am–4pm, €12.40): a regal spread of blini, caviar, fish and much more; it's so popular you'll need to wake up early to find a seat (no reservations). Evenings feature live piano music and fixed price menus.

SASAYA

Lychener Str. 50 Ⓢ/⓾ Schönhauser Allee ☎ 030/44 71 77 21, Mon, Tues & Thurs–Sun noon–3pm & 6–10pm. MAP P.86–87, POCKET MAP J1

Bucking the trend for catch-all pan-Asian menus, *Sasaya* focuses on serving traditional and innovative Japanese food. The quality and freshness of the ingredients is high, the food is delicious and service is swift, making this a serious contender for best sushi spot in the city.

SCHLAWINER

Hagenauer Str. 9 ⓾ Eberswalder Str. ☎ 030/44 03 70 59. Daily from 6pm. MAP P.86–87, POCKET MAP J2

Schlawiner is a new Austrian spot whose simple, unfussy interior – just a few simple wooden tables and some black and white photos on the walls – disguises the fact that the Austrian chef serves up the best Wiener Schnitzel in the neighbourhood. Daily specials are chalked up on the blackboard behind the bar. Mains from €8.

SI AN

Rykestr. 36 ⓾ Eberswalder Str. ☎ 030/40 50 57 75. ⓦ www.sian-berlin.de, Daily noon–midnight. MAP P.86–87, POCKET MAP K2

One of the most popular Vietnamese spots in the area. The interior is cosy, subtly upscale yet traditional (oak tables, handmade lamps) and the menu, while small, changes twice weekly and is generally fresh (all dishes are guaranteed glutamate-free). In summer sit outside by the immaculately landscaped street garden.

SORI BIBIMBAP CAFÉ

Senefelderstr. 34 ⓾ Eberswalder Str. ☎ 030/50 18 68 39. Daily noon–3pm & 6–10pm. MAP P.86–87, POCKET MAP K2

Blink and you'll miss this infinitesimal and incredibly cute Korean restaurant, which has just four or five tables and dishes up excellent home-made food. The small menu includes fantastic bibimbap with veggie, tofu, beef and organic veal options (€8–12).

TRATTORIA SIEDITI E MANGIA DA GIANNA

Sredzki Str. 43, ⓾ Eberswalder Str. ☎ 030/83 10 94 60. Mon–Fri 4.30pm–midnight, Sat noon–3pm & 4.30pm–midnight. Cash only. MAP P.86–87, POCKET MAP J2

Nearby *Trattoria Papparazzi* gets all the heat, but this smaller Italian serves superior food – simple, home-style Italian, made with freshly prepared ingredients – and has a more intimate atmosphere. Its handful of tables are spread over two tiers inside, but you can also sit right out on the pavement in summer. Pasta dishes from €7.50.

WEINSTEIN

Lychener Str. 33 ⓾ Eberswalder Str. ☎ 030/44 11 842, ⓦ www.weinstein.eu. Mon–Sat 5pm–2am, Sun 6pm–2am; kitchen 6–11.30pm. MAP P.86–87, POCKET MAP J1

This intimate wine bar and restaurant, all sturdy wooden tables and wine barrel decoration, is a bit of a local secret. It serves up food as traditional as the interior, but has a strong emphasis on local produce and German wines, as well as imported high-quality products like French cheeses and Iberian ham. Mains start at €8.50, and from Monday to Wednesday you can get a selection of eight small courses for €38.

Snacks

KONNOPKE'S IMBISS

Below ⓊEberswalder Str. ☎030/44 27 765. ⓌWww.konnopke-imbiss.de. Mon–Fri 5.30am–7pm, Sat 11.30am–7pm. MAP P.86–87, POCKET MAP J1

This legendary stand has been serving up Berlin street snacks – *Currywurst, pommes frites, Bockwurst* – since 1930. Incredibly it's been run by the same family all that time and remains one of the best places in the area for a quick bite.

Cafés and bars

ANITA WRONSKI

Knaackstr. 26–28 ⓊSenefelderplatz ☎030/44 28 483. Daily 9am–2am. MAP P.86–87, POCKET MAP J2

Located opposite the Wasserturm, *Anita Wronski* has two levels of wooden tables and chairs and a welcoming, established feel. It serves very good breakfasts and brunches, and while busy at weekends is usually quiet enough through the week to enjoy a good newspaper or book in peace.

ANNA BLUME

Kollwitzstr. 83 ⓊEberswalder Str. ☎030/44 04 87 49. ⓌWww.cafe-anna-blume.de. Daily 8am–2am. MAP P.86–87, POCKET MAP J2

Part flower shop, part café and part bakery, this Art Deco classic – named after a Kurt Schwitters poem, whose lines

are elegantly inscribed on the walls inside – is one of the area's best known cafés. Slide into one of the red leather banquets and sample one of their superb cakes, or come early at the weekend and try a refined tiered breakfast platter.

BECKETTS KOPF

Pappelallee 64 Ⓤ/ⓈSchönhauser Allee ☎016 22 37 94 18. Tues–Sun 8pm–4am. MAP P.86–87, POCKET MAP J1

It's easy to walk straight past this deliberately clandestine cocktail bar – but you'd be missing out. Look out for the glowering head of Mr Beckett staring at you from the darkness, and enter to find a sophisticated and intimate space with one of the best cocktail lists in town.

BONANZA COFFEE HEROES

Oderberger Str. 35 ⓊBernauer Str./ Eberswalder Str. ☎017 81 44 11 23, ⓌWww .bonanzacoffee.de. Mon–Fri 8.30am–7pm, Sat & Sun 10am–7pm. MAP P.86–87, POCKET MAP H2

Coffee connoisseurs flock to tiny *Bonanza* to sample the wares of their famed baristas: perfect lattes and flat whites knocked up on a fancy Synesso Cyncra machine (one of only three in Europe). Staff are cool but friendly.

BRUNCH AT ANNA BLUME

CAFÉ HILDE

Metzer Str. 22 ⓤ Senefelderplatz ☎ 030/04 05 04 172, ⓦ www.hilde-berlin.com. Mon–Fri 9am–11pm, Sat & Sun 9.30am–11pm.
MAP P.86–87, POCKET MAP J3

This sizeable café on the corner of busy Prenzlauer Allee is a lovely spot to unwind, with books and magazines to read during the day, home-made cakes and lunches, plus film screenings and book readings in the evenings. They also serve up a hearty Irish breakfast at weekends.

CAFÉ NOVEMBER

Husemannstr. 15 ⓤ Senefelderplatz/ Eberswalder Str. ☎ 030/44 28 425, ⓦ www .cafe-november.de. Mon–Sat 9am–2am, Sun 10am–2am. MAP P.86–87, POCKET MAP J2

Café November is an appealing, gay-friendly but mixed café that sells good cakes and schnitzels, as well as a decent range of teas and coffees. There's a breakfast buffet until 3pm on Saturdays and 4pm on Sundays, free wi-fi and the outside patio is great in the summer.

DR PONG

Eberswalder Str. 21 ⓤ Eberswalder Str. ⓦ www.drpong.net. Mon–Sat 8pm–late, Sun 2pm–late. MAP P.86–87, POCKET MAP J2

Like table tennis? Love beer? Then *Dr Pong* is for you. The action here revolves – literally – around the ping-pong table in the middle of the main room. Rent a bat (or bring your own) and join the crowd as they move slowly around the table, bats in one hand, beer bottles in the other, playing a communal game. DJs grace the sound system from time to time, though be warned the bar is on the tourist beer crawl route and can get suddenly very packed.

ELBSPEICHER

Sredzkistr. 41 ⓤ Eberswalder Str. ☎ 030/52 68 26 02, ⓦ www.elbspeicherb.de. Mon–Fri 8am–7pm, Sat & Sun 10am–7pm.
MAP P.86–87, POCKET MAP J2

Specializing in Hamburg "Elbgold" roasts, this coffee hub has a battleship grey espresso bar downstairs and elegant, spacious rooms and areas upstairs in which you can sample the world-class beans and try the home-made cookies, cakes and ciabattas.

FLEISCHMÖBEL

Oderberger Str. 2 ⓤ Eberswalder Str. Mon–Fri noon–open end, Sat & Sun 11am– open end. MAP P.86–87, POCKET MAP J2

"Meat furniture" is a much less menacing establishment than its name and beaten-up facade suggests – in fact it's completely harmless, drawing a friendly, bubbly crowd of locals who come for coffees and people watching in the day and beer and wine at night.

FLUIDO

Christburger Str. 6 ⓤ Senefelderplatz/ Ⓢ Greifswalder Str. ☎ 030/44 04 39 02. Mon–Thurs 8pm–2am, Fri & Sat 8pm–4am. MAP P.86–87, POCKET MAP K2

Far from the madding crowds, this off-the-beaten-track cocktail bar makes a perfect destination if you're looking for an intimate chat in a refined environment. Leather seats, dim lighting and high-quality cocktails are all conducive to a pleasant evening.

HAUSBAR

Rykestr. 54 ⓤ Senefelderplatz ☎ 030/44 04 76 06. Daily 7pm–5am. MAP P.86–87, POCKET MAP J2

It might be small, but this unpretentious, dimly lit bar, right across from the Wasserturm and a couple of doors down from the synagogue, is a great deal of fun on the right nights – and a great spot if you're seeking some late night drinking action in the area.

INTERSOUP

Schliemannstr. 31 ⓤ/ⓢ Schönhauser Allee ☎ 0151 29 11 18 98. Mon–Fri 6pm–3am, Sat & Sun 6pm–5am. MAP P.86–87, POCKET MAP J1

This *gemütlich* (cosy) den of shabby chic has crafted a natty little niche for itself as one of the few bars in the area regularly promoting local and international DJs (upstairs) and bands (downstairs). It's a comfortable spot for a drink any evening, but weekends are always buoyant.

KAUF DICH GLÜCKLICH

Oderberger Str. 44 ⓤ Bernauer Str./ Eberswalder Str. ☎ 030/44 35 21 82, ⓦ www .kaufdichgluecklich.de. Mon–Fri noon–1am, Sat & Sun 10am–1am. MAP P.86–87, POCKET MAP H2

Come here for waffles, ice cream – and a spot of cutely kitsch capitalism. "buy yourself happy" is an irrepressibly cheerful place where you can not only get great coffee and sweet treats, but also buy any of the second-hand furniture – tables, chairs, lamps, sunglasses – you see around you.

LIEBLING

Raumerstr. 36 ⓢ Prenzlauer Allee/ ⓤ Eberswalder Str. ☎ 030/41 19 82 09. ⓦ www.cafe-liebling.de. Mon 9am–1pm, Tues Sun 9am–1am, Wed 9am–2am, Thurs 9am–2pm, Fri 9am–3am, Sat 9am–3.30am. MAP P.86–87, POCKET MAP J1

There's no sign on this café/bar, but you'll find it right on the corner of Dunckerstr. and Raumerstr. Inside is a subtly cool interior, great cakes and decent lunch options (paninis, soups, quiches). The good wine and beer, and the *au courant* music on the system, makes it popular in the evenings too.

METZER ECKE

Metzer Str. 33 ⓤ Eberswalder Str. ☎ 030/44 27 656, ⓦ www.metzer-eck.de. Mon–Fri 4pm–1am, Sat & Sun 6pm–1am. MAP P.86–87, POCKET MAP F10

The oldest pub in Prenzlauer Berg (1913) inevitably packs plenty of old-school charm. It's faded slightly since its days as a major meeting point for Prenzlauer Berg's more bohemian contingent in the GDR, but still serves a decent Pilsner and *Lecker Bolettes* (meatballs) and *Bockwurst*.

MORGENROT

Kastanienallee 85 ⓤ Eberswalder Str. ☎ 030/44 31 78 44, ⓦ www.cafe-morgenrot .de, Tues–Thurs noon–1am, Fri & Sat 11am–3am, Sun 11am–midnight. MAP P.86–87, POCKET MAP H2

Kastanienallee's best-known alternative café is located right next to an immense squat (one of the last in the area). Despite the anti-capitalist slogans and punk aura, it's a friendly, open place that serves up a good weekend breakfast (vegetarian) for which you pay between €4 and €7, depending on your income.

FLEISCHMÖBEL

PRATER

service, average food and a smoky, plain interior. Still, it has a certain Berlin-esque atmosphere that makes it decidedly popular.

SCOTCH & SOFA

Kollwitzstr. 18 Ⓤ Senefelderplatz
☎ 030/44 04 23 71. Daily 2pm–open end.
MAP P.86–87, POCKET MAP F10

This highly agreeable, quietly hip neighbourhood bar is a fine spot for sinking into a granny-style sofa, sipping on a decently made cocktail and having a tête à tête. They always play interesting music – everything from Elvis to rap – and smokers and ping-pong fans can indulge their passions downstairs.

PRATER

Kastanienallee 7–9 Ⓤ Eberswalder Str.
☎ 030/44 85 688, Ⓦ www.pratergarten.de.
Mon–Sat 6–11pm, Sun noon–11pm.
MAP P.86–87, POCKET MAP J2

Dating back to 1837, *Prater* is the city's oldest beer garden and remains a fantastic place for a taste of traditional Berlin boozing, especially during summer when people swarm around the long tables and snack kiosks. During winter, it's all about feasting on home-made Berlin cuisine inside the classic interior.

SAPHIRE

Bötzowstr. 31 Ⓢ Greifswalder Str. ☎ 030/25 56 21 58, Ⓦ www.saphirebar.de. Mon–Thurs & Sun 8pm–2am, Fri & Sat 8pm–4am.
MAP P.86–87, POCKET MAP L3

The Saphire Bar mixes together its whisky and cocktail bar credentials as well as it mixes its drinks, with two elegant lounges to enjoy a cultivated yet unpretentious evening in.

SCHWARZSAUER

Kastanienallee 13 Ⓤ Eberswalder Str.
☎ 030/448 56 33, Ⓦ www.schwarzsauer.com.
Daily 9am–6am. MAP P.86–87, POCKET MAP J2

"Black and Sour" lives up to its name by offering moody

SGAMINEGG

Seelower Str. 2 Ⓤ/Ⓢ Schönhauser Allee
☎ 030/44 73 15 25, Ⓦ www.sgaminegg.de.
Mon–Fri 8.30am–7pm, Sat 10am–6pm.
MAP P.86–87, POCKET MAP J1

There are a dearth of decent cafés north of Stargarderstrasse, but *Sgaminegg* is an absolute treasure thanks to delicious coffees, home-made lunches – couscous, lentil and south German dishes – and a little shop that sells local produce.

SLÖRM

Danziger Str. 53 Ⓤ Eberswalder Str./
Ⓢ Prenzlauer Allee ☎ 030/70 08 36 87,
Ⓦ www.sloerm.net. Mon–Sat 8am–6pm.
MAP P.86–87, POCKET MAP J2

Real parrots out back, hip-hop on rotation and a collection of comfy, old furniture, *Slörm* is unique even by Prenzlauer Berg's café standards. The coffees are excellent too, as are the inventive fruit juices, which come with b-boy titles like Nas and MC Hammer.

WOHNZIMMER

Lettestr. 6 Ⓤ Eberswalder Str. ☎ 030/44 55 458, Ⓦ www.wohnzimmer-bar.de. Daily 9am–4am. MAP P.86–87, POCKET MAP J1

This retro, elegant "living room" – formerly a corner pub – is a local institution. One of the first spots to champion flea-market chic, it serves as both a daytime café and amiable bar later on. At weekends a cocktail bar magically pops up between its two rooms.

ZUCKERFEE

Greifenhagener Str. 15 Ⓤ/Ⓢ Schönhauser Allee ☎ 030/52 68 61 44, Ⓦ www .zuckerfee-berlin.de. Tues–Sun 10am–6pm. MAP P.86–87, POCKET MAP J1

"Sugar Plum Fairy" is an apposite name for this delightful, fairy-tale place, tucked away on a quiet street. The immaculate interior – all Victorian dolls and tasteful ornamentation – reflects the menu, which features delicious waffles, cakes and uniquely presented breakfasts and lunches (book ahead at weekends).

ZU MIR ODER ZU DIR

Lychener Str. 15 Ⓤ Eberswalder Str. ☎ 0176 24 41 29 40, Ⓦ www.zumiroderzudir.com. Daily from 8pm. MAP P.86–87, POCKET MAP J1

One of the hipper bars north of Danziger, the coquettishly titled "your place or mine?" boasts a vaguely decadent lounge-bar feel. sassily soundtracked by DJs spinning house, funk, electro and soul.

Clubs and venues

AUSLAND

Lychener Str. 60 Ⓢ Prenzlauer Allee ☎ 030/44 77 008, Ⓦ www.ausland-berlin.de,. MAP P.86–87, POCKET MAP J1

One for the experimentalists, *Ausland* is a non-profit club committed to promoting music, performance and related public and non-public events. You can find anything from free jazz and sound art gigs to movies and installations, all of which take place in an undecorated bunker in front of an apartment block. Door fees go directly to the artists.

DUNCKER

Dunckerstr. 64 Ⓢ Prenzlauer Allee ☎ 030/445 95 09, Ⓦ www.dunckerclub.de. Mon 9pm–late, Tues, Thurs & Sun 10pm–late, Fri & Sat 11pm–late. €2.50–4, free Thurs. MAP P.86–87, POCKET MAP K1

Duncker touches the musical parts other Prenzlauer Berg clubs don't reach, thanks to a mix of new wave and indie nights and particularly its weekly "Dark Mondays" – one of the city's few dedicated goth/industrial nights. Aptly enough it's located in a striking neo-Gothic church.

ICON

Cantianstr. 15 Ⓤ Eberswalder Str. ☎ 030/32 29 70 520, Ⓦ www.iconberlin.de. Tues 11pm–late, Fri & Sat 11.30pm–late. €3–€10. MAP P.86–87, POCKET MAP J1

This basement club is one of Berlin's premier drum'n'bass venues, though it occasionally expands into beats, breaks, dirty house and hip-hop. The crowd is young and energetic and the lighting and sound system are high quality.

KLUB DER REPUBLIK

Pappelallee 81 Ⓤ Eberswalder Str. Ⓦ www .myspace.com/klubderrepublik. Daily from 10pm. MAP P.86–87, POCKET MAP J1

Look out for the distinctive gold-rimmed windows, then duck behind the dilapidated facade and head up the metal staircase. Pay the bouncer €1 and you'll find yourself in a stylish bar filled with furnishings allegedly salvaged from the GDR's Palast der Republik. Bridging the gap between student bar and club, *KDR* plays upbeat music from retro funk to techno.

Friedrichshain

Though part of an ensemble of former East inner-city areas, Friedrichshain has developed a slightly differently mien than that of neighbouring Mitte and Prenzlauer Berg. A magnet for lefties, anarchists and students, it has managed to resist the same levels of gentrification thanks to an organized squatter scene, activist demos and the occasional car-burning frenzy. That said, its defiantly unkempt environs have succumbed to an invasion of bars and cafés around Boxhagener Platz, and an encroaching media presence along the river. It's most popular for bar-hopping, clubbing and cheap midnight snacking, but, the area does offer some heavyweight public monuments, the world-famous East Side Gallery and the imposing Karl-Marx-Allee among them. The area is also home to – indeed named after – the lovely, sprawling Volkspark Friedrichshain.

VOLKSPARK FRIEDRICHSHAIN

🚇 Strausberger Platz /Weberwiese.
MAP P.102–103, POCKET MAP K3

Established 150 years ago to commemorate the centenary of Frederick the Great's accession to the throne, Volkspark Friedrichshain is one of Berlin's oldest parks. Casually straddling the boroughs of Prenzlauer Berg and Friedrichshain, it's a sprawling place featuring lots of recreational opportunities (tennis courts, volleyball nets and climbing walls) and a wealth of impressive monuments. Highlights include the **Märchenbrunnen**, a neo-Baroque fountain built at the turn of the twentieth century, memorials to Frederick the Great, the German anti-fascist groups of World War II and a **peace bell** given to East Berlin by Japan. The park's two main hills (the 78m Grosse Bunkerberg and the 48m Kleine Bunkerberg) were constructed with rubble from the war. The park is also home to a café, *Café Schönbrunn*, and an open-air cinema (summer only).

CAFÉ SYBILLE ON KARL-MARX-ALLEE

EAST SIDE GALLERY

Mühlenstr. 1 🚇 Warschauer Str. 📞 030/25 17 159, 🌐 www.eastsidegallery-berlin.com. Open 24hr. MAP P.102–103, POCKET MAP L6

This 1.3km-long section of the Berlin Wall by the Spree is purportedly the largest

open-air gallery in the world and one of the city's best-known landmarks. Painted in 1990 (on the east side) when the Wall fell, the gallery features works from over a hundred artists from all over the world. Over the years it has fallen victim to vandalism and erosion, hence a decision to repaint it in 2009 – in time for the twentieth anniversary of the fall of the Wall. The original artists were invited back to repaint their pieces, but the decision caused controversy and many refused. The re-painting went ahead anyway.

KARL-MARX-ALLEE

Ⓤ Frankfurter Tor/Strausberger Platz.
MAP P.102–103, POCKET MAP L5

The monumental Karl-Marx-Allee, as the name suggests, is a thoroughly communist phenomenon. Built between 1952 and 1960, the imposing 89m-wide, 2km-long street – book-ended by German architect Hermann Hensel-mann's tiered "wedding cake" towers at Frankfurter Tor and Strausberger Platz – was originally named Grosse Frankfurter Strasse and later Stalinallee. The idea was to build luxurious apartments for workers (they were inevitably

doled out to party officials) as well as a leisure area featuring shops, restaurants, cafés and the still-standing Kino International, made famous by the film *Good Bye Lenin!*. On June 17, 1953, the street was the focus of worker demonstrations against the government that sparked a national uprising, but that were put down by Soviet forces (at least 125 people died). Since reunification most of the buildings have been restored and the apartments converted into upmarket flats and offices. The vast dimensions of the street and its run of blocky Soviet architecture make it a fantastic place for a stroll. Stop off at *Café Sybille* (see p.105), which hosts a small but insightful museum on the street's history.

BOXHAGENER PLATZ MARKET

Boxhagener Platz Ⓤ Samariterstr. Ⓦ www
.boxhagenerplatz.de. Farmers' market: Sat
8am–1.30pm. Flea market: Sun 10am–6pm.
MAP P.102–103, POCKET MAP A17

The flea market at Boxhagener Platz is a popular way for locals and tourists alike to spend a Sunday. While not as large as Mauerpark (see p.85), you can find vinyl, vintage fashion, old crockery and more.

OBERBAUMBRÜCKE

⓪ Warschauer Str. MAP P.102–103, POCKET MAP M7

This attractive, Spree-spanning landmark connects the districts of Friedrichshain and Kreuzberg, today officially part of the same borough but previously divided by the Berlin Wall. The double-decker bridge (and its name) dates back to the eighteenth century when it was originally constructed – from wood – and acted as a gateway to the city. A new version opened in 1896, designed by architect Otto Stahn in brick gothic style. In 1945 the bridge was partly destroyed by the Wehrmacht to stop the Red Army crossing it, and afterwards ended up straddling the American and Soviet sectors. When the Berlin Wall went up in 1961 the bridge became part of East Berlin's border with West Berlin; when

it fell in 1989, the bridge was restored to its former appearance with a new steel middle section designed by Spanish architect Santiago Calatrava. Today the bridge stands as a symbol of unity between Friedrichshain and Kreuzberg (and is the site of an friendly "water battle" in summer). Look out for the neon *Stone Paper Scissors* installation by Thorsten Goldberg – a political statement about the apparent arbitrariness of decisions to grant immigration or asylum status.

STASI MUSEUM

Ruschestr. 103, Haus 22, Lichtenberg ⓪ Magdalenenstr. ☏ 030/55 368 54, ⓦ www.stasimuseum.de. Mon–Fri 11am–6pm, Sat & Sun 2–6pm. €5 (reductions for groups). MAP P.102–103, POCKET MAP M5

East Germany's State Security Service – Stasi – struck terror

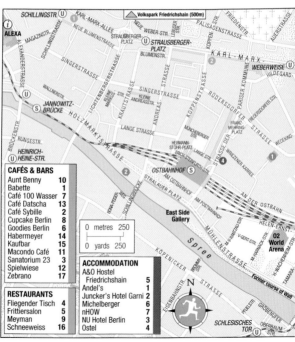

into East Germans, using dark and dastardly spying methods to unveil any potential signs of rebellion. This museum – in Lichtenberg, just east of Friedrichshain – used to be the Stasi headquarters: it was stormed and taken over when the Wall fell by an indignant group of people, many of whose lives had been affected by years of abuse, and members of this group still run the museum today. The main building of the campus (Haus 1, which housed the Minister of State Security among others), is currently under renovation so the museum is temporarily housed in a smaller building Haus 22 (the guesthouse and conference room). Visitors can see Stasi chief Erich Mielke's ridiculously immense desk (and equally large number of telephones),

OBERBAUMBRÜCKE

the complex filing system that includes samples of body odours, and around 185km of files. Tours in English, German and Swedish are available if requested in advance, and can take place outside of normal operating hours.

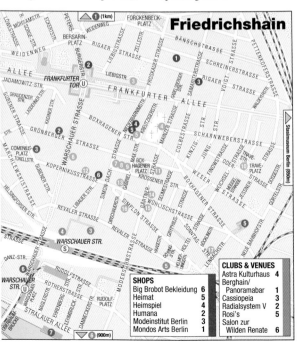

SHOPS

Big Brobot Bekleidung	6
Heimat	5
Heimspiel	4
Humana	2
Modeinstitut Berlin	3
Mondos Arts Berlin	1

CLUBS & VENUES

Astra Kulturhaus	4
Berghain/ Panoramabar	1
Cassiopeia	3
Radialsystem V	2
Rosi's	5
Salon zur Wilden Renate	6

Shops

BIG BROBOT BEKLEIDUNG

Kopernikusstr. 19 Ⓤ Frankfurter Tor
☎ 030/74 07 83 88. Mon–Fri 11am–8pm, Sat
11am–6pm. MAP P.102–103, POCKET MAP A16
Lively, friendly and vaguely
trashy store where you can
browse books, games, shoes,
postcards, art and streetwear.

HEIMAT

Niederbarnimstr. 17 Ⓤ Samariterstr.
☎ 030/74 69 99 14. Mon–Fri noon–8pm,
Sat noon–7pm. MAP P.102–103, POCKET MAP A16
Specializes in stylish T-shirts,
as well as chic bags and cool
accessories. Robots, bicycles,
strange animals and other
hipster designs make
appearances on almost
every item.

HEIMSPIEL

Niederbarnimstr. 18 Ⓤ Samariterstr.
☎ 030/20 68 78 70. Mon–Fri 11am–8pm, Sat
11am–6pm. MAP P.102–103, POCKET MAP A16
This cute little store sells an
assortment of trendy women's
clothing, kitsch Berlin-themed
postcards and games and
locally produced artworks.

HUMANA

Frankfurter Tor 3 Ⓤ Frankfurter Tor
☎ 030/42 22 017. Mon–Sat 10am–8pm.
MAP P.102–103, POCKET MAP A16
This immense five-storey
warehouse, part of a grand
Soviet palazzo, brims with
secondhand clothes. The
top floor has the best
vintage gear.

MODEINSTITUT BERLIN

Samariterstr. 8 Ⓤ Samariterstr. ☎ 030/42
019 088. Mon–Sat noon–7pm. MAP P.102–103,
POCKET MAP B16
An Aladdin's Cave of vintage
clothes, accessories, bags,
colourful shoes, disco lamps,
leather jackets, rare magazines
and old books.

MONDOS ARTS BERLIN

Schreinerstr. 6 Ⓤ Samariterstr. ☎ 030/42 02
02 25. Mon–Fri 10am–7pm, Sat 11am–5pm.
MAP P.102–103, POCKET MAP B16
Small, dusty shop committed to
all things former East –
T-shirts with communist
slogans, Ossi cigarettes, classic
films and even kids' stuff.

Restaurants

FLIEGENDER TISCH

Mainzer Str. 10 Ⓤ Samariterstr. ☎ 030/29 77
64 89. Mon–Fri & Sun noon–midnight, Sat
5pm–midnight. MAP P.102–103, POCKET MAP B16
"The flying table" is a small,
cosy place with just a few
wooden tables. It's justly
popular thanks to tasty Italian
staples like thin-crust pizza and
risotto for decent prices (€6–7).

FRITTIERSALON

Boxhagener Str. 104 Ⓤ Samariterstr.
☎ 030/25 93 39 06, Ⓦ www.frittiersalon.de.
Mon–Thurs 5pm–midnight, Fri–Sun 1pm–
midnight. MAP P.102–103, POCKET MAP A16
With a name that won't appeal
to healthy eaters, the "deep
fried salon" actually serves
delicious organic burgers and
Bratwurst. There's always a
burger-of-the-week deal, plus
vegetarian and vegan options.

MEYMAN

Krossener Str. 11A ⓤ Samariterstr. ☎ 016 38 06 16 36. Mon–Thurs & Sun noon–2am, Fri & Sat noon–3am. MAP P.102–103, POCKET MAP A17

This unassuming restaurant is great for late night cravings or for a break between bar hops. They specialize in tasty Moroccan and Arabic dishes along with pizza. Ingredients are fresh, prices are reasonable (€3–7 for a main), and there's usually a table free.

SCHNEEWEISS

Simplonstr. 16 ⓤ Warschauer Str. ☎ 030/29 04 97 04, ⓦ www.schneeweiss-berlin.de. Mon–Fri 6pm–1am. Sat & Sun 10am–1am. MAP P.102–103, POCKET MAP A17

One of Friedrichshain's few upmarket restaurants, "Snow White" is an understated place with a minimalist design and a menu that it describes as "Alpine" – Italian, Austrian and south German recipes such as schnitzel and pasta. There's also a decent Sunday brunch, fireplace lounge and a low-key bar vibe come evening.

Cafés and bars

AUNT BENNY

Oderstr. 7 ⓤ Samariterstr. ☎ 030/66 40 53 00. Mon–Fri 8.30am–7.30pm, Sat & Sun 10am–7pm. MAP P.102–103, POCKET MAP B17

Run by a German-Canadian team, *Aunt Benny* is a modern welcoming café. The range of teas and coffees is good, there's bagels, daily soups and other breakfast and lunch options available, plus free wi-fi and homemade baked treats.

BABETTE

Karl-Marx-Allee 36 ⓤ Schillingstr. ☎ 01763 83 88 943, ⓦ www.barbabette.com. Daily from 6pm. MAP P.102–103, POCKET MAP K4

Formerly *KMA*, *Babette* resides in a glass box of a building that was once a cosmetics shop. At night, the only identifying marker is the warm glow of the cube's interior lights. The ground floor is open and sparsely furnished, while the former treatment rooms upstairs occasionally have live music and private dinners.

CAFÉ 100 WASSER

Simon-Dach-Str. 39 ⓤ Frankfurter Tor ☎ 030/29 00 13 56, ⓦ www.cafe-100-wasser .de. Daily 9am–late. MAP P.102–103, POCKET MAP A17

Named after the Austrian artist Hundertwasser, *100 Wasser* has a fittingly colourful interior of yellow walls and a red-brick bar. It's an unpretentious place, with a hearty menu of burgers, pizza and flans. The weekend all-you-can-eat brunch buffet (Sat €7.90, Sun €9.50; 9am–4pm) is deservedly popular.

CAFÉ DATSCHA

Gabriel-Max-Str. 1 ⓤ Samariterstr. ☎ 030/70 08 67 35, ⓦ www.cafe-datscha.de. Daily from 10am. MAP P.102–103, POCKET MAP A17

Built in the style of a traditional Russian home – wood furniture, tall ceilings – albeit a fairly smart one, *Datscha* offers a rich spread of Russian and Ukrainian dishes like borscht, blini and *solyanka* (a spicy, sour soup). There's a daily changing lunch menu (€6) and Sunday brunch (10am–3pm; €9.80).

CAFÉ SYBILLE

Karl-Marx-Allee 72 ⓤ Strausberger Platz ☎ 030/29 35 22 03, ⓦ www.cafe-sibylle.de. Mon–Fri 10am–8pm, Sat & Sun 11am–8pm. MAP P.102–103, POCKET MAP L5

It's worth a stop at *Café Sybille* not just for the ice cream, cakes and coffee, but because it also hosts a small museum about the history of Karl-Marx-Allee, with propaganda posters, socialist statues and other exhibits to browse while your drinks are made.

CUPCAKE BERLIN

Krossener Str. 12 ⓤ Samariterstr. ☎ 030/25 76 86 87. Mon & Tues 1–7pm, Wed–Sun noon–7pm. MAP 102–103, POCKET MAP A17

The city's first outlet dedicated to cupcakes, all home-made by American owner, Dawn, for sale in a café that's every bit as sweet and retro as her cakes. Vegan cupcakes, brownies, fantastic New York cheesecake and pecan pie are also available (all around €2.50).

GOODIES BERLIN

Warschauer Str. 69 ⓤ Frankfurter Tor ☎ 0179 73 80 813. Mon–Fri 7am–8pm, Sat & Sun 9am–8pm. MAP 102–103, POCKET MAP A17

Goodies is a tiny but wholesome café that serves home-made baked goods, sandwiches and bagels. The organic soup changes daily and there's a small but varied selection of salads and vegan options. Free wi-fi, and a children's area. Cash only.

HABERMEYER

Gärtnerstr. 6 ⓤ Samariterstr. ☎ 030/29 77 18 87. Daily 7pm–late. MAP 102–103, POCKET MAP A17

This low-key, dive-style hangout is a Friedrichshain classic. Slightly off the main path, it features dark lighting, table football and pinball machines, a miscellany of seating and DJs playing Northern soul, rock and techno. Best late on weekends.

KAUFBAR

Gärtnerstr. 4 ⓤ Samariterstr. ☎ 030/29 77 88 25. Tues & Wed 3pm–1am, Thurs–Mon 10am–1am. MAP 102–103, POCKET MAP A17

This neighbourhood favourite enjoys a unique charm that goes beyond its gimmick – that everything from the chairs to the artwork is for sale. Its appeal lies in its breezy café ambience; it's a great spot to play games, read a book or drink tea or wine. Light snacks

(salads, soups) are available and a garden opens in summer.

MACONDO CAFÉ

Gärtnerstr. 14 ⓤ Samariterstr. ☎ 0151 10 73 88 29. Mon–Fri 3pm–late, Sat & Sun 10am–late. MAP 102–103, POCKET MAP A17

Kitted out with fraying vintage furniture, this local chill-out spot offers a good selection of books and board games and a great atmosphere for lounging. Serves brunch at weekends.

SANATORIUM 23

Frankfurter Allee 23 ⓤ Frankfurter Tor ☎ 030/42 02 11 93. Daily from 4pm. MAP 102–103, POCKET MAP A16

Set in a Soviet-style building, *Sanatorium* is a fun hangout with red-and-white leather beds separated by see-through curtains, Swiss red crosses hanging on the ceilings, DJ sets (electro and techno mainly) and the odd art exhibition.

SPIELWIESE

Kopernikusstr. 24 ⓤ Warschauer Str. ☎ 030/28 03 40 88. Mon, Thurs, Fri & Sat 2pm–midnight, Tues 2–7pm, Sun 2–9pm. MAP 102–103, POCKET MAP A17

Advertising itself as a "game library", this café stocks over 1200 games, from chess to Risk. For a small fee (€0.50–3), you

CUPCAKE BERLIN

can play games in the café or rent them (€1–3 per day) to take home. A great place to lose yourself for a couple of hours.

ZEBRANO

Sonntagstr. 8 ⓤ Samariterstr. ☎ 030/29 36 58 74. Daily 10am–late. MAP 102–103, POCKET MAP B17

Located on the lovely "Sunday Street", *Zebrano* is a fairly hip neighbourhood bar with a good selection of draught beers, a great cocktail menu (happy hour daily 7–9pm) and decent breakfasts (daily 10am–4pm; €2.20–€6.90).

Clubs and venues

ASTRA KULTURHAUS

Revaler Str. 99 ⓤ/Ⓢ Warschauer Str. ☎ 030/20 05 67 67, ⓦ www.astra-berlin.de. MAP 102–103, POCKET MAP A17

Owned by *Lido* (see p.123), *Astra* is a force to be reckoned with on Berlin's live music scene with shows from local and international artists like La Roux and Ben Harper.

BERGHAIN/PANORAMABAR

Am Wriezener Bahnhof Ⓢ Ostbahnhof ☎ 030/29 36 02 10, ⓦ www.berghain.de. Fri & Sat midnight–late. €10–15. MAP 102–103, POCKET MAP L6

A strong contender for best club in the city, if not the world, this former power station attracts techno fans from all over the globe for its fantastic sound system, purist music policy and awe-inspiring industrial interior. The best time to arrive is after 5am on Saturday morning; the club runs till Sunday evening.

CASSIOPEIA

Revaler Str. 99 ⓤ Warschauer Str. ☎ 030/47 38 59 49, ⓦ www.cassiopeia-berlin.de. MAP 102–103, POCKET MAP A17

Cassiopeia was renovated from an urban dump into an imaginative concrete playground. The sprawling space has several club areas, an exhibition venue, huge indoor skate park, beer garden and the highest climbing tower in Berlin. Music veers from hip-hop and techno DJ sets to live funk and reggae and there's an open-air cinema in summer.

RADIALSYSTEM V

Holzmarktstr. 33 Ⓢ Ostbahnhof ☎ 030/28 87 885, ⓦ www.radialsystem.de, MAP 102–103, POCKET MAP K6

This sprawling space, housed in a former pumping station on the Spree, was retrofitted and reopened as a space for the arts in 2006, with a glass extension added. As well as visual and performing arts exhibitions, it hosts events ranging from opera concerts to relaxed jam sessions, which are often geared towards children and families.

ROSI'S

Revaler Str. 29 ⓤ Warschauer Str. ⓦ www.rosis-berlin.de. Daily from 10pm. MAP 102–103, POCKET MAP B17

Nothing more – or less – than a derelict industrial shack, decorated with second-hand furniture, graffiti and ping pong tables, *Rosi's* puts on some very decent indie, punk and electronic nights. Best in summer when the yard is open for barbecues or the occasional market on Sundays.

SALON ZUR WILDEN RENATE

Alt-Stralau 70 Ⓢ Treptower Park ⓦ www .renate.cc. MAP 102–103, POCKET MAP M7

Located near the train tracks that run towards Treptower Park, *Renate* is an artist-run event space in a semi-derelict house with a couple of bars, a ping pong table and flamboyant decor that changes with each party. The music is good and the crowd is mixed.

West Kreuzberg

The western section of Kreuzberg is centred on the main streets of Gneisenaustrasse and Bergmannstrasse, and pretty Viktoriapark. Once one of the poorest areas in Berlin, it's now one of its most bourgeois and bohemian and lies in sharp contrast to the more scruffy, multicultural part of the district to the east. Indeed, walking along café and boutique-lined streets like Bergmannstrasse you're reminded of the gentrified environs of Prenzlauer Berg. At the end of this street is Viktoriapark, whose iron cross monument gives the district its name, and nearby is Chamissoplatz, which hosts a popular organic farmers' market every Saturday morning.

CHECKPOINT CHARLIE / HAUS AM CHECKPOINT CHARLIE

Friedrichstr. 210 ⓤ Kochstr. ☎ 030/253 72 50, ⓦ www.mauermuseum.de. Daily 9 am–10pm €12.50. MAP OPPOSITE, POCKET MAP C15

"Checkpoint C" (or "Checkpoint Charlie" as it was called by the Western Allies) was the best-known Berlin Wall crossing point between East Berlin and West Berlin during the Cold War. Today it's one of the key places to learn about life in Berlin during the division. The museum – founded in 1962 by Dr Rainer Hildebrandt – is marked by the well-known "YOU ARE NOW LEAVING THE AMERICAN SECTOR" sign that remains outside the building alongside stone-faced (mock) guards, and a replica of the checkpoint (the original is in the Allied Museum in Dahlem). One of the most visited museums in Berlin, its exhibitions are focused mostly on the creative ways East Berliners tried to escape – hot-air balloons, vehicles with special concealments, even a one-man submarine. There are also related exhibits on the concept of freedom and non-violent protest in general, including the Charter 77 typewriter and Mahatma Gandhi's diary.

CHECKPOINT CHARLIE

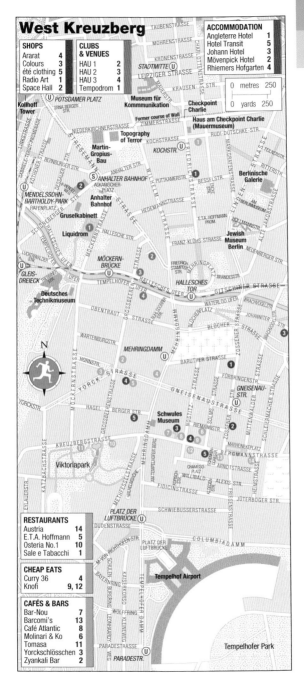

TOPOGRAPHY OF TERROR

Niederkirchnerstr. 8 / ⑤ Potsdamer Platz
① 030/25 45 09 50, ⓦ www.topographie.de.
Daily 10am–8pm. Free. MAP P.109, POCKET MAP F6

From 1933 to 1945, the headquarters of the Gestapo, their "house prison" and the Reich Security main office, as well as other SS offices, stood on this site, making it one of the most notorious locations of Nazi brutality. It's now called the Topography of Terror (Topographie des Terrors) documentation centre, and though many of the buildings were destroyed in World War II, visitors can walk around the largely open-air museum, where exhibits display the history of the site, and explore the events of the Holocaust and Nuremburg Trials. A documentation centre focuses on the central institutions of the SS and police in the Third Reich and their crimes. The displays are graphic, so families visiting with children should exercise caution.

MARTIN-GROPIUS-BAU

Niederkirchnerstr. 7 ① / ⑤ Potsdamer Platz
① 030/25 48 60, ⓦ www.gropiusbau.de. Free.
MAP P.109, POCKET MAP F6

Envisioned as an applied arts museum, the stunning Martin-Gropius-Bau has evolved into one of Berlin's major contemporary art venues. The ornate, Renaissance-style building was badly damaged during World War II, and rebuilt in 1966. It draws big-name international displays on art and history, such as exhibitions on Mexico's pyramids and retrospectives of Frieda Kahlo.

ANHALTER BAHNHOF

Askanischer Platz 6 ① Mendelssohn-
Bartholdy-Park ① 030/ 50 58 68 30. Free.
MAP P.109, POCKET MAP F7

This haunting landmark is a remnant of the Anhalter Bahnhof, once one of Berlin's busiest railway stations. The terminus opened in 1841 but its notoriety stems from World War II when it was one of the three stations used to deport Jews to Theresienstadt (or Terezín), and from there to the death camps. Nearly 10,000 Jews were deported from here, usually in groups of fifty to a hundred; the last train left on March 27, 1945. Though badly damaged in World War II, it was only closed in 1952. Today, all that remains is a portion of the entrance facade and a commemorative plaque, though an S-Bahn station shares its name.

DEUTSCHES TECHNIKMUSEUM

Trebbiner Str. 9 ① Gleisdreieck ① 030/90 25 40,
ⓦ www.sdtb.de. Tues–Fri 9am–5.30pm, Sat &
Sun 10am–6pm. €4.50. MAP P.109, POCKET MAP F7

Opened in 1982 in the former goods depot of the Anhalter Bahnhof, the German Technology Museum presents a comprehensive – some might say overwhelming – overview of technology created in Germany. The vast collection includes trains and planes, as well as computers, radios, cameras and more. There's a

BERLINISCHE GALERIE

DEUTSCHES TECHNIKMUSEUM

strong emphasis on rail, with trains from 1835 to the present day, but there are also maritime and aviation halls and exhibits on technology from the industrial revolution to the computer and space age, and on the development of the pharmaceutical and chemical industry and its impact on everyday life. A new exhibition on the history of mobility is housed in the annexe on Ladestrasse. Though much of the museum is based on viewing life-sized reproductions and actual machines, there's a building, the Science Center Spectrum annexe at Möckernstrasse 26, dedicated to interactive exhibits.

JEWISH MUSEUM BERLIN

Lindenstr. 9–14 Ⓤ Hallesches Tor/Kochstr. ☎ 030/25 99 33 00, Ⓦ www.jmberlin.de. Mon 10am–10pm, Tues–Sun 10am –8pm. €5. MAP P.109, POCKET MAP G7

Daniel Libeskind's Jewish Museum (Jüdisches Museum) is a must-see in Berlin, both historically and architecturally. The stark, zinc-covered building has been thoughtfully designed, with each element symbolizing various aspects of the historical Jewish experience. The process of moving through the building – which really is a work of art – is an experience in itself. The

building has five vertical voids, walls of dark concrete and several additional, symbolic elements. Displays cover over two thousand years of Jewish history. Guided tours are available and the restaurant serving Jewish and Mediterranean cuisine (though not kosher) is very good.

BERLINISCHE GALERIE

Alte Jakobstr. 124–128 Ⓤ Hallesches Tor/ Kochstr. ☎ 030/78 90 26 00, Ⓦ www .berlinischegalerie.de. Mon & Wed–Sun 10am–6pm. €8, free first Mon of the month; combined ticket with Jewish museum available. MAP P.109, POCKET MAP H7

Founded in 1975 as a private institution, the Berlinische Galerie was once part of the Martin-Gropius-Bau before moving to its current premises in 2004. Its mission is to showcase art made in Berlin, bringing together fine art, photography and architecture. The permanent exhibition includes works from 1870 to the present day, spanning major movements such as the Secessionists, Fluxus, Dada and the Expressionists, with works by Max Liebermann, Otto Dix, Georg Grosz and Hannah Höch. A spacious hall also hosts temporary exhibitions and there are tours, occasional lectures and film screenings.

SCHWULES MUSEUM

Mehringdamm 61 ⓤ Mehringdamm
ⓣ 030/69 31 17 2, ⓦ www.schwulesmuseum
.de. €5. Mon, Wed–Fri & Sun 2–6pm, Sat
2–7pm. MAP P.109, POCKET MAP G8

Located close to several gay
bars, this museum – which
celebrated its 25th anniversary
in 2011 – provides one of the
world's most comprehensive
accounts of LGBT culture. The
permanent exhibition covers
the history of gay Berlin, from
the nineteenth century to the
famous golden 1920s and then
Nazi persecution, to today.
There's also an archive, library
and temporary exhibits.

GRUSELKABINETT

Schöneberger Str. 23 A ⓤ Mendelssohn-
Bartholdy-Park ⓣ 030/26 55 55 46, ⓦ www
.gruselkabinett-berlin.de. Mon 10am–3pm,
Tues, Thurs, Fri & Sun 10am–7pm, Sat
noon–8pm. €9. MAP P.109, POCKET MAP F7

The Gruselkabinett, which
means "horror cabinet", is a
strange mix of historical and
playful. The former air-raid
shelter was part of a network of
World War II bunkers. It now
houses a small museum of
sorts, which includes artefacts
such as recordings of Allied
bombings, and personal effects
from people who used the
bunkers. The maze is creepy in
its own right, but the addition
of monsters and skeletons and
piped screams make the
horrors more present than past.

TEMPELHOFER PARK

Columbiadamm 192 ⓤ Südstern. Daily
6am–9.30pm. Free. MAP P.109, POCKET MAP G9

The largest park in continental
Europe, Tempelhofer Park was
once the site of Tempelhof
airport, an immense building
created by the Nazis – the
terminal was designed to
resemble an eagle in flight. It
became most famous, however,
as the place where the Berlin
Airlift took place in 1948–49.
While the former airport
buildings are fenced off, you
can still see them, and the
sheer size of the outlying area
– nearly four square kilometres
– gives an idea of the
astounding scale of the airport.
The wide-open space doesn't
boast any actual attractions but
does provide a great place to go
cycling, walking, roller-skating
– or enjoy a picnic.

LIQUIDROM

Möckernstr. 10 ⓤ Möckernbrücke ⓣ 030/25
80 07 820, ⓦ www.liquidrom-berlin.de.
Sun–Thurs 10am–midnight, Fri & Sat
10am–1am. MAP P.109, POCKET MAP F7

Upping the ante for relaxation
in Berlin, this designer spa
features saunas, a food bar,
slightly cramped chill out areas
and a large, domed flotation
pool where you can drift and
listen to soft electronic music,
sometimes mixed live by DJs.
A range of massage treatments
are also available.

CYCLISTS IN TEMPELHOFER PARK

Shops

ARARAT

Bergmannstr. 9 ⓤGneisenaustr. ☎030/69 49 532. Mon–Sat 10am–8pm. MAP P.109, POCKET MAP G9

Sells postcards, cards and a wealth of gimmicky gifts. It's easy to lose yourself here; over the road, another branch sells picture frames and artworks.

COLOURS

Bergmannstr. 102 ⓤMehringdamm ☎030/69 43 348. Mon–Fri 11am–8pm, Sat 10am–4pm. MAP P.109, POCKET MAP G9

Colours is a retro fan's paradise with secondhand clothes spanning the 1960s to 1980s, but particularly good on the 1970s, as well as new designs.

ETÉ CLOTHING

Bergmannstr. 18 ⓤGneisenaustr. ☎030/32 89 55 43. Mon–Sat 11am–8pm. MAP P.109, POCKET MAP G9

With shirts and hoodies from trusted brands like Cheap Monday, RVLT, Volcom and Mazine, and a good range of sneakers, this is a good stop for skatewear in Kreuzberg.

RADIO ART

Zossener Str. 2 ⓤMehringdamm ☎030/69 39 43 5. Thurs & Fri noon–6pm, Sat 10am–1pm. MAP P.109, POCKET MAP G8

A fantastic and visually satisfying shop for radio lovers, with shelves brimming with vintage (and some modern) radio sets and record players.

SPACE HALL

Zossener Str. 33 & 35 ⓤGneisenaustr. ☎030/530 88 718. Mon–Sat 11am–8pm. No 35 Thurs & Fri till 10pm. MAP P.109, POCKET MAP G8

This two-store, multi-roomed record shop is one of the best stocked in the city, with a large CD collection at no. 33 (rock, pop, electronic, rap) and DJ-friendly vinyl at no. 35.

RADIO ART

Restaurants

AUSTRIA

Bergmannstr. 30, on Marheineke Platz ⓤGneisenaustr. ☎ 030/69 44 440. Daily 6pm–1am. MAP P.109, POCKET MAP G9

In a hunting lodge-style interior with wood furniture and antlers, *Austria* serves classic Austrian dishes made with organic ingredients. The huge schnitzel is justly famous (mains €13.50–€17.50).

E.T.A HOFFMANN

Yorckstr. 83 ⓤMehringdamm ☎030/78 09 88 09, ⓦwww.restaurant-e-t-a-hoffmann.de, Mon & Wed–Sun 5–11pm. MAP P.109, POCKET MAP G8

An upmarket bistro overseen by Thomas Kurt, who serves rich European dishes like entrecote with braised cabbage and red wine shallots (€28) and scallops with foie gras (€21), or set menu for €42. The interior is classic and comfortable, and there's a lovely courtyard.

OSTERIA NO. 1

Kreuzbergstr. 71 ⓤMehringdamm ☎030/78 69 162, ⓦwww.osteria-uno.de. Daily noon–2am. MAP P.109, POCKET MAP F9

Run by Fabio Angilè, this popular café/restaurant offers some of the best Italian food in Kreuzberg. The interior is simple yet classic and prices are reasonable (mains €8.50–€17), especially the lunchtime deals.

SALE E TABACCHI

Rudi-Dutschke-Str. 23 ⓤ Kochstr.
☎ 030/25 21 155, ⓦ www.sale-e-tabacchi.de.
Mon–Fri 9am–2am, Sat & Sun 10am–2am.
MAP P.109, POCKET MAP G6

Located towards the Mitte end of Kreuzberg, "Salt and Tobacco" has a more classic feel than most restaurants in the area. It's known for its excellent seafood dishes (tuna €11.50, sea bass €19) and impressive list of Italian wines. The interior is large and airy and there's a garden out back.

Cheap eats

CURRY 36

Mehringdamm 36 ⓤ Mehringdamm ☎ 030/25 17 368. Mon–Fri 9am–4pm, Sat 10am–4pm, Sun 11am–3pm. MAP P.109, POCKET MAP G8

Everyone in Berlin has a favourite place to eat *Currywurst* – sausage doused in curry sauce – but *Curry 36* is cited more often than most (along with *Konnopke's*, see p.95); its popularity alone guarantees it's a buzzy place to grab a snack (around €2).

KNOFI

Bergmannstr. 11 & 98 ⓤ Gneisenaustr.
☎ 030/69 56 43 59. Daily 7am–midnight.
MAP P.109, POCKET MAP G9

There are two *Knofis* opposite each other. At no. 11 you'll find a small deli-style restaurant serving tasty Turkish food like stuffed vine leaves, hummus and more (mixed platter €6). Over the road is a Turkish deli.

Cafés and bars

BAR-NOU

Bergmannstr. 104 ⓤ Mehringdamm
☎ 030/74 07 30 50, ⓦ www.bar-nou.com.
Daily 8pm–4am. MAP P.109, POCKET MAP G9

You'll find this discreet cocktail bar down in a Bergmannstrasse basement. Expect red lighting, stylish decor and very good drinks served by friendly staff. A consistently good spot for a sophisticated tête-à-tête.

BARCOMI'S

Bergmannstr. 21 ⓤ Gneisenaustr. ☎ 030/69 48 138. Mon–Sat 8am–9pm, Sun 9am–9pm.
MAP P.109, POCKET MAP G9

Not quite as cosy as its Mitte branch (see p.41), but you can find excellent quality coffee – *Barcomi's* roasts its thirteen coffee varieties here, hence the decorative coffee sacks and delicious odour – as well as handmade breads and pastries.

CAFÉ ATLANTIC

Bergmannstr. 100 ⓤ Gneisenaustr. ☎ 030 /69 19 29 2. Mon–Thurs & Sun 9am–1am, Fri & Sat 9am–2am. MAP P.109, POCKET MAP G9

This large, classic-feeling café, with its colourful paintings in the back room and bar stools in the front, serves an abundant weekend breakfast (eleven ways to have your eggs scrambled, from €5.90) till 5pm, and has daily lunch specials and dinner options too.

MOLINARI & KO

Riemannstr. 13 ⓤ Gneisenaustr. ☎ 030/69 13 903. Mon–Fri 8am–1pm, Sat & Sun

CURRY 36

CAFÉ ATLANTIC

9am–1pm. MAP P.109, POCKET MAP G9

This Italian café/bar/restaurant is hidden away on a residential street. It's a welcoming place with a predominantly wooden interior, friendly staff and menu of breakfast and snacks, pasta and pizza. A decent wine and beer selection make it good for evenings too.

TOMASA

Kreuzbergstr. 62 ⓤ Mehringdamm ☎ 030/81 00 98 85, Ⓦ www.tomasa.de. Sun–Thurs 9am–1am, Fri & Sat 9am–2am. MAP P.109, POCKET MAP F9

This old-school villa, on the edge of Viktoriapark, is a particularly pleasant place for a relaxed breakfast or lunch. The classic interior, good, seasonal menu (from tapas to pasta and Asian dishes) and friendly service attract a mixed clientele, families included. Business lunches are available daily (noon–3pm) from €5.

YORCKSCHLÖSSCHEN

Yorckstr. 15 ⓤ Mehringdamm ☎ 030/21 58 070, Ⓦ www.yorckschloesschen.de. Mon–Sat: winter 5pm–3am; summer 10am–3am. Sun 10am–3am all year. MAP P.109, POCKET MAP F8

This place has been a Kreuzberg institution for over a hundred years, though it doesn't seem to have been updated since the 1970s. The menu is mostly basic and local – meatballs and *Leberkäse* (meatloaf) – and the service gruff, but the tree-shaded garden is a very pleasant place to eat. Live jazz, blues and country bands play most days (Wed–Sat 9pm, Sun 2pm).

ZYANKALI BAR

Grossbeerenstr. 64 ⓤ Mehringdamm ☎ 030/25 16 333, Ⓦ www.zyankali.de. Daily 8pm–late. MAP P.109, POCKET MAP F8

There's no place quite like this in Berlin: a chemist-themed bar that's brimming with its own weird science. Glass-topped coffins with fake skeletons serve as tables; drinks (there are over 200 cocktails) contain some very interesting ingredients, sometimes homemade and served in laboratory glasses. Movie-themed nights take place in the back room.

Clubs and venues

HEBBEL AM UFER

HAU 1 Stresemannstr. 29; HAU 2 Hallesches Ufer 32; HAU 3 Tempelhofer Ufer 10 ⓤ Hallesches Tor ☎ 030/25 90 04 27, Ⓦ www .hebbel-am-ufer.de. MAP P.109, POCKET MAP G7

Three neighbouring venues – Hebbel-Theater (HAU 1), Theater am Halleschen Ufer (HAU 2) and the small Theater am Ufer (HAU 3) – are the places for groundbreaking theatre, the occasional concert and more.

TEMPODROM

Möckernstr. 10 ⓤ Möckernbrücke ☎ 030/74 73 70, Ⓦ www.tempodrom.de. MAP P.109, POCKET MAP F7

A giant tent-like arena in the heart of Berlin, Tempodrom puts on concerts, shows, plays, galas, conferences, fashion shows – you name it, Tempodrom's hosted it.

East Kreuzberg

An isolated section of West Berlin throughout the Cold War,
Kreuzberg has since grown into one of Berlin's most colourful
districts – a magnet for left-wing anarchists, gays, Turkish
immigrants (it's sometimes called Little Istanbul) and,
increasingly, hipsters and tourists. Despite being a coherent
borough (nowadays part of Kreuzberg-Friedrichshain), Kreuzberg
is still largely considered two distinct halves roughly coterminous
with the former postal codes: SO 36 and SW 61 in the eastern and
western sides respectively. Much of the eastern part of Kreuzberg
abutted the wall on the West side and was strongly associated
with Berlin's squatter and anarchist scenes. Though the area
has gentrified somewhat since those heady days, it maintains a
grungy, vibrant feel that spreads out from Schlesisches Tor down
to Kottbusser Tor and beyond, fuelled by an ever-expanding series
of excellent independent bars, clubs and restaurants.

East Kreuzberg

| 0 metres 250 |
| 0 yards 250 |

RESTAURANTS
Baraka	10
Defne	17
Hartmanns	21
Henne	1
Kimchi Princess	12
Le Cochon Bourgeois	22
Rosa Caleta	4

CHEAP EATS
Babanbè	2
Maroush	6
Musashi	18
Ron Telesky	20

CAFÉS & BARS
Ankerklause	16
Barbie Deinhoff	11
Bateau Ivre	7
Café Matilda	19
Club der Visionaere	15
Das Hotel	14
Luzia	3
Möbel-Olfe	9
Roses	8
Tiki Heart	13
Würgeengel	5

MUSEUM DER DINGE

Oranienstr. 25 ⓤ Kottbusser Tor ☏ 030/92 10 63 11, ⓦ www.museumderdinge.de. Mon & Fri–Sun noon–7pm. €4. MAP BELOW. POCKET MAP J7

A museum dedicated to the somewhat ambiguous culture of "things" could have gone either way. In fact it succeeds by presenting an interesting array of implements – around 25,000 to be precise, as well as 30,000 documents. Everyday houseware, furniture and knick-knacks are mixed with the unusual, spanning the nineteenth century to the present day. Located on the top floor of a Kreuzberg apartment block, the museum is a design-fiend's dream, with exhibits including Manoli ashtrays and Art Deco fondue sets and World War II memorabilia, all inside a room that's modern and well

DISPLAY IN THE MUSEUM DER DINGE

organized. One of the latest attractions is the modular "Frankfurt Kitchen" designed by Viennese architect Margarete Schütte-Lihotzky in 1926 – the model for the fitted kitchen of today. The main exhibition text is in German, but a brochure in English is available from the counter.

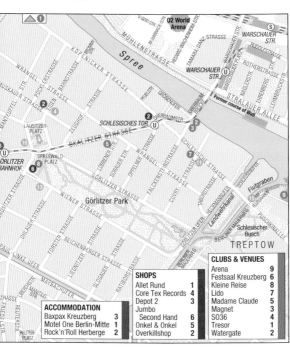

ACCOMMODATION

Baxpax Kreuzberg	3
Motel One Berlin-Mitte	1
Rock'n'Roll Herberge	2

SHOPS

Allet Rund	1
Core Tex Records	4
Depot 2	3
Jumbo Second Hand	6
Onkel & Onkel	5
Overkillshop	2

CLUBS & VENUES

Arena	9
Festsaal Kreuzberg	6
Kleine Reise	8
Lido	7
Madame Claude	5
Magnet	3
SO36	4
Tresor	1
Watergate	2

Shops

ALLET RUND

Dresdener Str. 16 Ⓤ Kottbusser Tor
☎ 0163 44 07 289. Tues–Fri noon–7pm, Sat noon–5pm. MAP P.116–117, POCKET MAP J7

Joachin Semrau offers designs for slightly bigger sizes (42–60). Everything is fairtrade and one piece, the fabrics are European and the clothes are made right here in Kreuzberg.

CORE TEX RECORDS

Oranienstr. 3 Ⓤ Görlitzer Bahnhof ☎ 030/61 28 00 50. Mon–Fri 11am–7pm, Sat 11am–4pm. MAP P.116–117, POCKET MAP K7

The best place in the city to stock up on punk or hardcore music, as well as related T-shirts, accessories and books.

DEPOT 2

Oranienstr. 9 Ⓤ Görlitzer Bahnhof
☎ 030/61 14 655. Mon–Sat 11am–8pm.
MAP P.116–117, POCKET MAP K7

An ice-cool assortment of street-oriented fashions, including Vans and other stylish footwear.

JUMBO SECOND HAND

Wiener Str. 63 Ⓤ Görlitzer Bahnhof. Mon–Sat 11am–7.30pm. MAP P.116–117, POCKET MAP K7

It's all about quantity over quality at this second-hand store, with a bewildering amount of clothes, from dresses to bags, sunglasses and more. It can be a little overpriced and it's worth trying to bargain.

ONKEL & ONKEL

Oranienstr. 195 Ⓤ Kottbusser Tor
☎ 030/61 07 39 57. Mon–Sat 10am–6pm.
MAP P.116–117, POCKET MAP K7

A magazine shop that specializes in graphic design, photography and street-art books, Onkel & Onkel also publishes its own titles, all in a library-esque atmosphere.

OVERKILLSHOP

Kopenicker Str. 195a Ⓤ Schlesisches Tor
☎ 030/69 50 61 26. Mon–Sat 11am–8pm.
MAP P.116–117, POCKET MAP L7

A must-visit spot for fans of street art and graffiti or if you're hunting for that limited edition pair of Adidas. Stocks most of the best international brands, one-off models and graffiti related books and magazines.

Restaurants

BARAKA

Lausitzer Platz 6 Ⓤ Görlitzer Bahnhof
☎ 030/61 26 330, Ⓦ www.baraka-berlin.de.
Mon–Thurs 11am–midnight, Fri & Sat 11am–1am. MAP P.116–117, POCKET MAP K7

North African food fans will adore *Baraka*. The decor is authentic without slipping into kitsch (although the back room comes close) and the food – tagines, chicken skewers, schwarma – is some of the best in town, and at decent prices (mains €5–12). The mixed plate for two is immense.

DEFNE

Planufer 92 Ⓤ Kottbusser Tor/Schönleinstr.
☎ 030/81 79 71 11, Ⓦ www.defne-restaurant.de.
Daily: April–Sept 4pm–1am; Oct–March 5pm–1am (kitchen till midnight all year).
MAP P.116–117, POCKET MAP J8

CORE TEX RECORDS

Defne serves up a great menu of Turkish/Mediterranean food from fresh ingredients. Classics include "Imam Fainted" (aubergines with pine nuts, peppers and tomato-herb sauce, €8.60) or lamb skewers (€11.90). The interior is simple and spacious; the terrace, overlooking the Landwehr-kanal, is lovely in summer.

HARTMANNS

Fichtestr. 31 ⓤ Südstern ☎ 030/61 20 10 03, ⓦ www.hartmanns-restaurant.de. Mon–Sat 6pm–midnight. MAP P.116–117, POCKET MAP J8

Chef Stefan Hartmann creates innovative French-Mediterra-nean cuisine that's devilishly divine and rich – think goose liver, pork chops and quail – in a setting that's at once romantic and tasteful. Three- to seven-course menus (€47–€76) or a la carte (mains €29–€32).

HENNE

Leuschnerdamm 25 ☎ 030/61 47 73 0, ⓦ www.henne-berlin.de. Tues–Sat 7pm–1am, Sun 5pm–1am. MAP P.116–117, POCKET MAP J7

Most books will tell you the only thing served here is half a chicken. Not so: there's also *Berliner Boulette* (meatballs), though the chicken's the star. A glorious, milk-roasted half chicken to be precise (€6.50) which blends perfectly with the cabbage and potato salad sides. Reservations essential.

KIMCHI PRINCESS

Skalitzer Str. 36 ☎ 0163 45 80 203, ⓦ www .kimchiprincess.com. Tues–Sun 6pm–1am. MAP P.116–117, POCKET MAP K7

Part of a trend for cool Korean eateries in Berlin, *Kimchi Princess* is one of the better ones. Simple wooden pallets serve as seating, the interior is spacious and staff are as cool as the clientele. There's *bibimbap* and more on the menu but the Korean barbecue is the thing to

KIMCHI PRINCESS

go for (from €15.50). Afterwards, check out *Soju Bar* upstairs, accessed via *Angry Chicken* around the corner.

LE COCHON BOURGEOIS

Fichtestr. 24 ⓤ Südstern ☎ 030/69 30 101, ⓦ www.lecochon.de. Daily 6pm–late. MAP P.116–117, POCKET MAP J9

One of the more romantic places to dine in Kreuzberg, located in an elegant old house, the restaurant offers high-end French cuisine – oysters, frog's legs, juicy steaks – but not much for vegetarians. There are fixed-price menus (from €40) and a la carte options too. Reservations necessary.

ROSA CALETA

Muskauer Str. 9 ⓤ Görlitzer Bahnhof ☎ 01778 902 704, ⓦ www.rosacaleta.com. Tues–Sat 6pm–1am, Sun 2pm–1am MAP P.116–117, POCKET MAP K7

This Jamaican/European fusion restaurant has created quite a buzz in a city hopelessly devoid of Caribbean cuisine. There's plenty of Jerk-style food on the menu, but also dishes like oven-roast pork fillet, mango-ginger lentil salad and tofu and vegetable stew (mains from €8). It also functions as an art space and hosts DJ parties.

Cheap eats

BABANBÈ

Oranienplatz 2 ⓤ Görlitzer Bahnhof ⓦ www
.babanbe.tumblr.com. Mon-Sat noon-8pm.
MAP P.116-117, POCKET MAP J7

This chic, glass-walled fast-food
joint is run by Germans, but
once you've tasted their *banh
mi* (Vietnamese sandwiches)
– fluffy white bread buns filled
with fresh vegetables and
flavoursome meats – you'll
think they hail from Saigon.
Though this is the speciality,
the menu also features *pho bo*
(noodle soup) and more.

MAROUSH

Adalbertstr. 93 ⓤ Kottbusser Tor ⓣ 030/69
53 61 71, ⓦ www.maroush-berlin.de. Daily
11am-2am. MAP P.116-117, POCKET MAP J7

With a cosy dining area,
authentically Middle Eastern
decor and tasty sandwiches,
kebabs, falafels and fresh
salads, this small Lebanese
restaurant is one of the better
of its type. Vegetarian options
also available.

MUSASHI

Kottbusser Damm 102 ⓤ Schönleinstr.
ⓣ 030/69 32 042. Mon-Fri & Sun
noon-10.30pm, Sat 2-10pm. MAP P.116-117,
POCKET MAP J8

This tiny spot serves up decent
sushi in a refreshingly
designer-free space, decorated
with posters of sumo wrestlers
and populated with just a few
bar tables. The Japanese chefs
prepare fresh, tasty makis and
inside-out rolls for very good
prices (€6.50 for a set menu).

RON TELESKY

Dieffenbachstr. 62 ⓤ Schönleinstr. ⓣ 030/61
62 11 11. Mon-Fri noon-10pm, Sat & Sun
3-10pm. MAP P.116-117, POCKET MAP J8

Canadian pizza served from a
canoe – how can you say no?
Especially when the pizza
toppings include walnut,
mango, feta and maple syrup.
Aside from the canoe (outside)
the interior features national
emblems like a moose head.
Vegan options available.

Cafés and bars

ANKERKLAUSE

Kottbusser Damm 104 ⓤ Kottbusser Tor
ⓣ 030/41 71 75 12. Tues-Sun 10am-4am,
Mon 4pm-4am. MAP P.116-117, POCKET MAP J8

Situated by Maybachufer, next
to the Turkish vegetable market
(Tues & Fri), *Ankerklause* is a
popular café during the day,
with a decent range of snacks
(and seats out front and a
terrace overlooking the water
out back). Later, there's
something of the alternative
scene about it when the jukebox
plays rock'n'roll classics.

BARBIE DEINHOFF

Schlesische Str. 16 ⓤ Schlesisches Tor
ⓦ www.barbiedeinhoff.de. Mon-Fri 6pm-6am.
Sat & Sun 4pm-6am. MAP P.116-117, POCKET MAP L7

This colourful dive bar is a lot
of fun, attracting a heady mix of
transvestites, gay men and
curious onlookers. The decor
runs from deliberately kitsch to
the colourfully futuristic and
there are regular DJs,

MAROUSH

happenings and art events. A fun place to get comprehensively trashed (two-for-one happy hour Mon–Fri 6–9pm, Sat & Sun from 4pm) – or to recover, with "Sunday Hangover Cures", disguised as *Beverly Hills 90210* episodes from 4pm.

BATEAU IVRE

Oranienstr. 18 Ⓤ Görlitzer Bahnhof ☎ 030/61 40 36 59. Daily 9am–3am, kitchen till 4pm (except tapas). MAP P.116–117, POCKET MAP K7

Probably the best café/bar on lively Oranienstrasse, *Bateau Ivre* feels like it's been there forever, eschewing the trends for something much more timeless. The classic long bar puts out macchiatos, soups and chilli con carne during the day and wines, beer and cocktails at night. You're lucky if you get a seat outside; head to the raised back area for more intimacy.

CAFE MATILDA

Graeferstr. 12 Ⓤ Schönleinstr. ☎ 030/81 79 72 88. Daily 9am–2am. MAP P.116–117, POCKET MAP J8

Choose from one of the tables in the front or grab a comfy sofa in the back room. There are several good breakfast options as well as yummy sandwiches, coffee and cakes. The owners play soul and funk vinyl during the day, there are DJs at weekends, and regular bingo and crime TV nights.

CLUB DER VISIONAERE

Am Flutgraben 1 Ⓤ Schlesisches Tor ☎ 030/69 51 89 42 ⓦ www.clubdervisionaere .com. May–Sept Mon–Fri 2pm–late, Sat & Sun noon–late. Food served daily 6pm–1am. Admission €1–5 MAP P.116–117, POCKET MAP M8

Just beyond the Kreuzberg/Treptow border, this legendary summer-only techno bar enjoys a unique setting on the intersection of the Spree and Flutgraben canal. The bar and

DJ booth is in an old ceramic-tiled boathouse, and punters stand (and dance) on the floating docks outside. It's minimal techno all the way and a fantastically upbeat place.

DAS HOTEL

Mariannenstr. 26a Ⓤ Kottbusser Tor ☎ 030/84 11 84 33. Daily 2pm–open end. MAP P.116–117, POCKET MAP J8

Located on a residential street near the Paul-Linke-Ufer, *Das Hotel* is a split-level spot where crowds gather to drink, chat and watch the odd documentary on TV. Recently expanded to three areas, it features a main bar, the odd DJ playing Latin and 1960s music and a rustic bar with a more relaxed vibe with wooden tables and candlelight.

LUZIA

Oranienstr. 34 Ⓤ Kottbusser Tor ☎ 030/61 10 74 69. Daily 10am–3am. MAP P.116–117, POCKET MAP J7

Oranienstrasse's key hipster hangout, *Luzia* is styled in the manner of an industrial loft, with exposed brickwork, velvet armchairs, wall paintings by street artists, rough wallpaper and a bizarre upstairs space that you have to climb a ladder to get to. Decent drinks and cocktails mean it's buzzing most nights.

MÖBEL-OLFE

Reichenberger Str. 177 Ⓤ Kottbusser Tor ☎ 030/23 27 46 90. Tues–Sun 6pm–late. MAP P.116–117, POCKET MAP J7

Sandwiched between a string of Turkish snack bars in a run-down building behind Kottbusser Tor, this unusual, smoky, local bar attracts gays, hipsters, ageing drunks and more. There are regular DJ nights but it's more about experiencing the diversity of the Kreuzberg crowds.

ROSES

Oranienstr. 187 ⓤ Kottbusser Tor/Görlitzer Bahnhof ☎ 030/61 56 570. Daily 10pm–5am. MAP P.116–117, POCKET MAP K7

A legendary gay hangout, *Roses* provides a welcoming bosom for all manner of sexual orientations to crowd around. The kitsch decor mirrors the clientele and the fun vibe well. Sunday is the main day – and the "gayest" – but women are welcome anytime.

TIKI HEART

Wiener Str. 20 ⓤ Görlitzer Bahnhof ☎ 030/61 07 47 03, ⓦ www.tikiheart.de. Mon–Fri 11am–late, Sat & Sun 10am–late. MAP P.116–117, POCKET MAP K8

Berlin's only Hawaiian-rockabilly themed joint is renowned for its unapologetically kitsch interior and innovative menu. The breakfasts, served till 5pm, feature items like the "Oi-Fast" – a heady mix of scrambled eggs and chorizo (€7). There are veggie burgers and – one for the serious rockers – a Lemmy burger grilled in whisky. Strong cocktails are served and the *Wild at Heart* club next door roars into action with regular rock, punk, metal and surf nights.

ROSES

WÜRGEENGEL

Dresdener Str. 122 ⓤ Kottbusser Tor ☎ 030/61 55 560, Daily 7pm–late. MAP P.116–117, POCKET MAP J7

One of the best bars in Kreuzberg, "the exterminating angel" has red walls, great tapas, decadent decor and an extensive cocktail and wine list. The feel is timeless, though with a trendy clientele.

Clubs and venues

ARENA

Eichenstr. 4 ⓤ Treptower Park ☎ 030/533 20 30, ⓦ www.arena-berlin.de. Around €10. MAP P.116–117, POCKET MAP M8

This huge area next to the Spree between Schlesisches Tor and Treptower Park encompasses the *Arena Club*, *Glashaus*, the actual Arena, the *Badeschiff* and the *Hoppetosse*. There are frequent electronic dance parties at *Arena Club*, sometimes the *Hoppetosse* café (on a boat) can turn into a club and at Arena itself you can catch rock and metal shows.

FESTSAAL KREUZBERG

Skalitzer Str. 130 ⓤ Kottbusser Tor ☎ 030/61 65 60 03, ⓦ www.festsaal -kreuzberg.de. MAP P.116–117, POCKET MAP J7

This relatively refined venue has a regular programme of literary and cultural events, but the beautiful main hall (a former ballroom) is also used for gigs and DJ shows. There are two tiny cellar rooms used for parties and events, usually of an experimental nature.

KLEINE REISE

Spreewaldplatz 8 ⓤ Görlitzer Bahnhof ⓦ www .kr-club.com. Fri & Sat from 11pm, sometimes Sun & Thurs. P.116–117, POCKET MAP K7

This dedicated haven for electronic music lovers is located in a former bathhouse and comprises a series of rooms with classic Berlin styling – an inconspicuous entrance and DIY bar areas. The music is house, techno and electro and the crowd young and up for it. The owners also run the hostel next door.

LIDO

Cuvrystr. 7 Ⓤ Schlesisches Tor ☎ 030/69 56 68 40, Ⓦ www.lido-berlin.de. Fri & Sat 10pm–late. €5–€9. MAP P.116–117, POCKET MAP L7

An old-school club in a former theatre that's been going for over ten years, *Lido* is known for championing new music, and is home to a younger indie crowd, with the occasional techno or house event. The club also has a courtyard with canopy that makes it suitable for winter throw-downs.

MADAME CLAUDE

Lübbener Str.19 Ⓤ Görlitzer Bahnhof ☎ 030/84 11 08 61, Ⓦ www.madameclaude .de. Daily 7pm–late. P.116–117, POCKET MAP L7

This student hangout has shows five days a week, ranging from indie-rock and experimental to folk. Be prepared to feel slightly unsettled by the decor, which is upside down and on the ceiling. Pay what you want for entrance.

MAGNET

Falckensteinstr. 48 Ⓤ/Ⓢ Schlesisches Tor/ Warschauerstr. Ⓦ www.magnet-club.de, Mon– Sat 10pm–late. MAP P.116–117, POCKET MAP L7

Formerly a Prenzlauer Berg rock'n'roll mainstay, *Magnet* moved to more suitably grungy Kreuzberg in 2010. It hosts regular DJ parties and live shows, ranging from pop to rock and from metal to electro.

S036

Oranienstr. 190 Ⓤ Görlitzer Bahnhof ☎ 030/61 40 13 06, Ⓦ www.so36.de. Usually from 11pm. €3–10. MAP P.116–117, POCKET MAP K7

One of the city's most legendary clubs, *SO36*, named

after the area's postcode, has its roots in punk, post-punk and alternative music – a string of musical heroes who've played here, including Iggy Pop, David Bowie and Einstürzende Neubauten, mean it's something of a Berlin *CBGBs*. Nowadays it hosts alternative and electronic shows, including monthly parties like Gayhane, a Turkish "homoriental" party, and "Ich bin ein Berliner", where you can catch an exquisite array of Berlin-based artists playing everything from garage to synth-pop.

TRESOR

Köpenicker Str. 70 Ⓤ/Ⓢ Ostbahnhof/ Jannowitzbrücke. Wed, Fri & Sat midnight–late. Admission varies. MAP P.116–117, POCKET MAP J6

Housed in what was the main central-heating power station for East Berlin, the colossal location of this third incarnation of *Tresor* is breathtaking. (The first, which closed in 2005, was one of the most groundbreaking clubs in the city.) Only a tiny portion of its 28,000 square metres is in use, but the club is sizeable enough with three different rooms dedicated to cutting-edge, muscular techno played by a rotating roster of international DJs.

WATERGATE

Falckensteinstr. 49 Ⓤ Schlesisches Tor ☎ 030/61 28 03 96. Wed, Fri & Sat 11pm– late, occasional Tues & Thurs events. €6–€15. MAP P.116–117, POCKET MAP L7

This slick, split-level club is located right on the Spree and enjoys a killer combination of panoramic windows, excellent sound system and constant flow of renowned DJs. Music is electro, house and minimal techno. Expect to see Berlin residents like Richie Hawtin and Booka Shade too.

123

Charlottenburg

Part of the four boroughs that make up City West (along with Wilmersdorf, Schöneberg and Tiergarten) Charlottenburg has long been the beating heart of West Berlin and remains so today. Known for its wealthy residents and expensive shops, it's generally dismissed by the more boho east, and has much more in common with cities like London, Paris or Milan. The area's main artery, Kurfürstendamm (Ku'damm as it's colloquially known), which takes its name from the former Kurfürsten (Electors) of the Holy Roman Empire, is one of the most famous avenues in the city. It's often described as the city's Champs-Élysées, but the abundance of shops and relative dearth of impressive architecture makes it feel more like Oxford Street. However, many of the streets that run between Ku'damm and Kantstrasse have a charm of their own, with a wealth of independent cafés, bars, restaurants, bookstores and boutiques. The area is also home to some of the city's major sights such as Berlin's zoo and aquarium, Schloss Charlottenburg, the Kaiser Wilhelm Memorial Church and the Käthe Kollwitz Museum.

BERLIN ZOO

Hardenbergplatz 8 Ⓤ/Ⓢ Zoologischer Garten ☎ 030/25 40 10, Ⓦ www.zoo-berlin .de. Daily: mid-March to mid-Sept 9am–7pm; mid-Sept to mid-Oct 9am–6pm; mid-Oct to mid-March 9am–5pm. €12, zoo

BERLIN AQUARIUM

& aquarium €18. Family tickets available. MAP P.126–127, POCKET MAP B6

Berlin's zoo is Germany's oldest and one of the world's most popular, attracting (along with the adjacent aquarium) three million visitors in 2009. It opened in 1844 with animals donated by the royal family. Though by the zoo was decimated during World War II, when thousands of animals died, leaving only 91 remaining, it recovered, and now houses over 15,000 animals spanning 1400 species. The birdhouse, with 550 species, is a definite highlight. Famous zoo residents include Bao Bao, a giant panda.

BERLIN AQUARIUM

Budapester Str. 32 Ⓤ/Ⓢ Zoologischer Garten ☎ 030/254 01, Ⓦ www.zoo-berlin.de. Daily 9am–6pm. €12. MAP P.126–127, POCKET MAP C6

Situated next to the zoo (separate entrance), the city's impressive aquarium holds the title for world's most biodiverse collection. From jellyfish to crocodiles and other reptiles and tropical fish, the aquarium has over nine thousand creatures on three floors. Built in 1913, the aquarium has retained its old-fashioned appearance albeit incorporating modern elements. Take a walk on the bridge spanning the reptile pit and check out the new glass-roofed "Hippoquarium".

MUSEUM FÜR FOTOGRAFIE

Jebensstr. 2 ⓤ/Ⓢ Zoologischer Garten ☏ 030/26 64 24 242, Ⓦ www.smb.museum /mf. Tues, Wed & Fri–Sun 10am–6pm, Thurs 10am–10pm. €8. MAP P.126–127, POCKET MAP B6

The Museum of Photography is a relative newcomer to the Berlin museum scene. It opened in 2004 in a former casino building, and has quickly risen in popularity, drawing about 700,000 visitors a year. The city's largest museum dedicated to photography, it covers 2000 square metres and houses a thousand images by famous *Vogue* photographer Helmut Newton, who donated the collection months before he died. Newton's provocative black-and-white photographs made him famous in the world of fashion photography and beyond, and his work is shown on a rotating basis in addition to exhibits of other photographers.

CAMERA WORK

Kantstr. 149 ⓤ Uhlandstr. ☏ 030/31 00 776, Ⓦ www.camerawork.de. Tues–Sat 11am–6pm. Free. MAP P.126–127, POCKET MAP A6

Named after the famous photography journal of the same name, Camera Work is an upscale gallery where all the photographs are for sale. It also acts as a museum where you're welcome to browse – perfect for those on a budget. On display you'll generally find photographs from famous fashion and art luminaries such as Man Ray, Irving Penn, Horst P. Horst, Peter Lindbergh, Peter Beard, Richard Avedon, Diane Arbus and Helmut Newton as well as works by up-and-coming artists. Prints and books are also available.

Charlottenburg

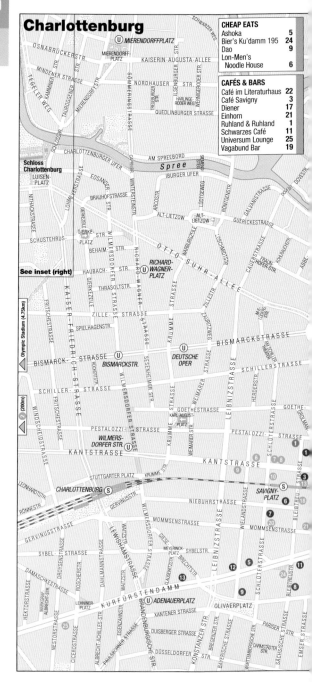

CHEAP EATS

Ashoka	5
Bier's Ku'damm 195	24
Dao	9
Lon-Men's Noodle House	6

CAFÉS & BARS

Café im Literaturhaus	22
Café Savigny	3
Diener	17
Einhorn	21
Ruhland & Ruhland	1
Schwarzes Café	11
Universum Lounge	25
Vagabund Bar	19

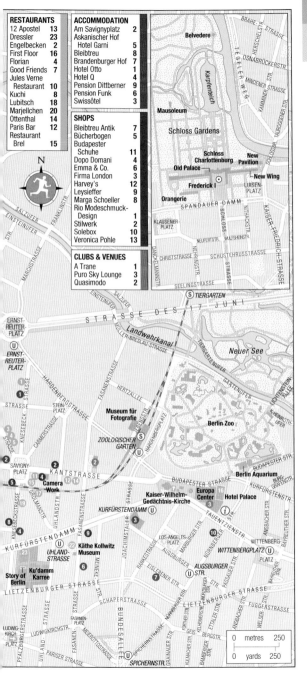

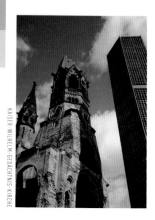

KAISER-WILHELM-GEDÄCHTNIS-KIRCHE

KAISER-WILHELM-GEDÄCHTNIS-KIRCHE

Breitscheidplatz Ⓤ Kurfürstendamm
☎ 030/2 18 50 23, Ⓦ www
.gedaechtniskirche-berlin.de. Daily 9am–7pm.
Guided tours: Mon–Sat 1.15pm, 2pm & 3pm,
Mon, Fri & Sat also 10.15am, 11am & noon;
Sun noon, 1pm, 2pm & 3pm. Church and tours
free. MAP P.126–127, POCKET MAP B7

The Kaiser Wilhelm Memorial
Church, built between 1891
and 1895 in neo-Romanesque
style by architect Franz
Schwechten, was commissioned
by Kaiser Wilhelm II and
served as a symbol of Prussian
unity. Nearly destroyed during
a World War II air raid, all that
remains are the ruins of the
spire and entrance hall. A new
structure was built in 1961, and
the stunning, blue stained-glass
windows fitted in concrete
bricks contrast memorably with
the haunting skeleton of the
old. The base of the old spire
and entrance hall is now a
memorial hall, with exhibits
documenting the old church
through photos and artefacts
that survived the bombing.

KÄTHE KOLLWITZ MUSEUM

Fasanenstr. 24 Ⓤ Uhlandstr. ☎ 030/88 25
210, Ⓦ www.kaethe-kollwitz.de. Daily
11am–6pm. €6. MAP P.126–127, POCKET MAP B7
German artist Käthe Kollwitz's

work was greatly influenced by
the loss of her son in World
War I and her grandson in
World War II. She was a
pacifist who lived in Berlin for
fifty years, and was the first
woman elected to the Prussian
Academy of the Arts but
resigned her post in 1933 in
protest at Hitler's rise to power.
Kollwitz's works were banned
by the Nazis. Many of her
pieces are powerful reminders
of some of the most painful
aspects of her life. Works on
display here include dour
self-portraits, plaintively titled
sketches, woodcuts, litho-
graphs, war protest posters, and
sculptures. The building itself is
the oldest private home on
Fasanenstrasse, built in 1871
and restored in the 1980s.

STORY OF BERLIN

Kurfürstendamm 207–208 Ⓤ Uhlandstr.
☎ 030/887 20 100, Ⓦ www.story-of-berlin.de.
Daily 10am–8pm, last admission 6pm. €10.
MAP P.126–127, POCKET MAP A7

More than just a museum, the
Story of Berlin aims to
transport visitors to each of the
eight centuries of Berlin's
history through multimedia
displays that include photos,
films and interactive exhibits. It
follow the history of the city
from its founding in 1237, to
the Thirty Years' War, Frederick
the Great's reign, the 1920s,
World War II, the Cold War,
and the fall of the Wall. Also
included is a guided tour of an
atomic bomb shelter on the
site. Tours in English at noon,
2pm, 4pm and 6pm.

SCHLOSS CHARLOTTENBURG

Spandauer Damm 10–22 Ⓤ Sophie-Charlotte-
Platz/ Richard-Wagner-Platz ☎ 030/32 0 911,
Ⓦ www.spsg.de. Old Palace Tues–Sun: April–
Oct 10am–6pm; Nov–March 10am–5pm.
€12. New Wing Mon & Wed–Sun: April–Oct
10am–6pm; Nov–March 10am–5pm, €6.

Belvedere April–Oct Tues–Sun 10am–6pm; Nov–March Sat & Sun noon–4pm, €3. Mausoleum April–Oct Tues–Sun 10am–6pm. New Pavilion reopens Dec 2011: Tues–Sun 10am–5pm €4. Combined ticket €15. MAP P.126–127, POCKET MAP A4

As you walk through Schloss Charlottenburg, you'll be in no doubt as to why its builder, Frederick I, was known as an extravagant spender who nearly bankrupted the state. The former Elector of Brandenburg who named himself king of Prussia in 1701, had this ornate Baroque palace built as a summer home for his wife, Sophie Charlotte, in 1695. It started as a relatively modest dwelling but ballooned to its present palatial status with additions throughout the 1700s. Majestic rooms, art and plenty of porcelain characterize the interiors. In fact, the art in the palace constitutes the largest collection of eighteenth-century French paintings outside of France. There's a separate entrance fee for each of the three main buildings; The **Old Palace** features Baroque rooms, royal apartments, Chinese and Japanese porcelain and silverware chambers; the **New Wing** is more Rococo with an array of refined furniture in apartments built by Frederick the Great; and the Schinkel-built **New Pavilion** features a collection of arts and crafts. Visitors can also visit the **Mausoleum**, which contains the graves of, and memorials to, members of the Hohenzollern family, and the **Belvedere**, which displays a collection of Berlin porcelain. The reconstructed **Orangerie** is also open for concerts and the gardens are open and free. Guided tours are offered of the historic apartments and chapel.

OLYMPIC STADIUM

Olympischer Platz 3 Ⓢ Olympiastadion ⓣ 030/306 88 100, Ⓦ www.olympiastadion -berlin.de. Daily 9am–6pm, 7pm or 8pm, except on event days, check in advance. €4. Guided tours available. MAP P.126–127, POCKET MAP A6

Berlin's Olympic stadium, built for the 1936 Summer Olympics (immortalized in the film *Olympia* by Leni Riefenstahl), is one of the last surviving remnants of Nazi architecture in Berlin. Occupied by the British military following the war and used by them until 1994, the stadium is now used for concerts and events and also as the official ground of Hertha BSC, Berlin's most famous football club. It was renovated for the 2006 World Cup and now has the highest all-seated capacity in Germany (74,228). The stadium remains an impressive place to visit.

SCHLOSS CHARLOTTENBURG

Shops

BLEIBTREU ANTIK

Schlüterstr. 54 Ⓢ Savignyplatz ☎ 030/88
212. Mon–Fri noon–7pm, Sat 11am–3pm.
MAP P.126–127, POCKET MAP A7

This well-established shop offers
a great selection of antiques
from 1900 to the 1960s,
including glassware, lamps,
furniture and especially stylish
1960s and 1970s jewellery.

BÜCHERBOGEN

Stadtbahnbogen 593 Ⓢ Savignyplatz
☎ 030/31 86 59 11. Mon–Fri 10am–8pm, Sat
10am–6pm. MAP P.126–127, POCKET MAP A7

You could spend hours
browsing the aisles of this
famed art book store located
beneath Savignyplatz S-Bahn.
You'll find plenty of English-
language books in the design,
architecture, art and theatre
sections, though nothing in the
literature section sadly.

BUDAPESTER SCHUHE

Kurfürstendamm 199 Ⓤ Uhlandstr. ☎ 030/88
62 42 06. Mon–Fri 10am–7pm, Sat
10am–6pm. MAP P.126–127, POCKET MAP A7

A spacious and well-stocked
shoe shop whose wares run the
gamut from reasonably priced
leather classics to designer
models from Prada and Tod's.

BÜCHERBOGEN

DOPO DOMANI

Kantstr. 148 Ⓢ Savignyplatz ☎ 030/88 22
242. Mon–Fri 10.30am–7pm, Sat 10am–6pm.
MAP P.126–127, POCKET MAP A6

Three glorious floors of swanky
designer furnishings, mostly
Italian but featuring samples
from around the world. Sofas,
bookshelves and lamps, all with
a reassuringly hefty price tag.

EMMA & CO

Niebuhrstr. 2 Ⓢ Savignyplatz ☎ 030/88 67 67
87. Mon–Fri 11am–7pm, Sat 11am–4pm.
MAP P.126–127, POCKET MAP A7

Lovingly decorated store that
has a relaxed atmosphere and
attentive staff. They carry
alternative wooden toys as well
as the classic brands for
children and babywear.

FIRMA LONDON

Bleibtreustr. 50 Ⓢ Savignyplatz ☎ 030/83 21
08 93. Tues–Fri 11am–7pm, Sat 11am–5pm.
MAP P.126–127, POCKET MAP A6

Run by former Stella
McCartney designer Sandra
Tietje and gallerist Florian von
Holstein, this place is not for
the financially faint-hearted
– but it does stock some
drop-dead gorgeous vintage
furniture and accessories.

HARVEY'S

Kurfürstendamm 56 Ⓤ Adenauerplatz
☎ 030/88 33 803. Mon–Fri 10am–8pm, Sat
10am–7pm. MAP P.126–127, POCKET MAP A7

A wonderland of men's
designer clothes from designers
such as Martin Margiela,
Comme des Garçons, and Yohji
Yamamoto to name just a few.

LEYSIEFFER

Kurfürstendamm 218 Ⓤ Uhlandstr. ☎ 030/88
57 480. Mon–Fri 9am–7pm, Sat 10am–5pm.
MAP P.126–127, POCKET MAP B7

This Ku'damm branch of the
famed German chocolateria
does a brisk trade. Aside from
the usual sweet goodies, there's

DOPO DOMANI

also a small coffee bar, useful if you're looking for a break from all the shopping.

MARGA SCHOELLER

Knesebeckstr. 33 ⓤ Uhlandstr. ☎ 030/88 11 112. Mon–Wed 9.30am–7pm, Thurs & Fri 9.30am–8pm, Sat 9.30am–6pm.
MAP P.126–127, POCKET MAP A7

Opened in 1929 by the eponymous Frau Schoeller, this bookstore is one of the longest running in Europe, and was once a focal point for West Berlin's postwar literary scene. Schoeller's son now runs the store, which continues to sell a fantastic range of German- and English-language books on poetry, theatre and philosophy as well as fiction, history, biographies – and plenty of tomes about Berlin and Germany.

RIO MODESCHMUCK-DESIGN

Bleibtreustr. 52 Ⓢ Savignyplatz ☎ 030/31 33 152. Mon–Wed & Fri 11am–6.30pm, Thurs 11am–7pm, Sat 11am–6pm. MAP P.126–127, POCKET MAP A6

Former rebel-child designer Barbara Kranz opened her jewellery store back in 1984 – she calls her creations "after 5pm" jewellery due to their natural evening-wear flamboyance and glamour.

STILWERK

Kantstr. 17 Ⓢ Savignyplatz ☎ 030/31 51 50. Mon–Fri 10am–8pm, Sat 10am–6pm.
MAP P.126–127, POCKET MAP A6

Swanky designer mall, located near Zoologischer Garten, comprising shops dedicated to home decoration, jewellery and fashion. Expect high-end stores like Bang & Olufsen, with one or two cheaper options as well. There's a café and even a babysitting service for those who want to dump the kids.

SOLEBOX

Nürnbergerstr. 16 ⓤ Wittenbergplatz
☎ 030/91 20 66 90. Mon–Sat noon–8pm.
MAP P.126–127, POCKET MAP C7

A spacious shrine to streetwear, stocking Reebok, Converse, Ellesse, Adidas sneakers plus T-shirts and hoodies.

VERONICA POHLE

Kurfürstendamm 64 ⓤ Adenauerplatz
☎ 030/88 33 731. Mon–Fri 10.30am–6.30pm, Sat 10.30am–6pm. MAP P.126–127, POCKET MAP A7

Over 200 square metres filled with designer garments from Alexander McQueen to Zinga Cashmere. Besides basics, bags and jewellery there's a wide array of dresses.

Restaurants

12 APOSTEL

Bleibtreustr. 49 Ⓢ Savignyplatz ☎ 030/31 21 433, ⓦ www.12-apostel.de. Daily 8am–1am.
MAP P.126–127, POCKET MAP A6

A smart, Baroque-style interior (check the kitsch religious frescoes) and generously sized thin pizzas mark this place out. They're slightly on the expensive side – around € 11.50 – but specials on the weekly changing menu start at €6.50. The Sunday brunch buffet is €18 but comes with a glass of sparkling wine and a hot drink.

DRESSLER

Kurfürstendamm 207–208 Ⓤ Uhlandstr. ☎ 030/88 33 53 0, Ⓦ www.restaurant -dressler.de. Daily 8am–1am, (kitchen till midnight). MAP P.126–127, POCKET MAP A7

This German take on a French brasserie enjoys something of a timewarp ambience thanks to its Art Nouveau interior, formal but friendly service and very good seasonal food. The main dining area might be a bit stiff for some, but the small front bar is perfect for a quick coffee or lunch if you're on Ku'damm.

ENGELBECKEN

Witzlebenstr. 31 Ⓤ Sophie-Charlotte-Platz ☎ 030/61 52 810, Ⓦ www.engelbecken.de. Mon–Fri 5pm–1am, Sat 4pm–1am, Sun noon–1am. MAP P.126–127, POCKET MAP A6

A high-quality restaurant that serves Bavarian and Alpine cuisine – schnitzel, goulash – with an emphasis on organic products and home-made sauces. The park-facing terrace is nice in the summer.

FIRST FLOOR

Hotel Palace, Budapester Str. 45 Ⓤ Kurfürstendamm ☎ 030/25 02 10 20, Ⓦ firstfloor.hotel-palace.biz. Mon–Fri noon–3pm & 6.30–11pm, Sat & Sun 6.30–11pm. MAP P.126–127, POCKET MAP C7

Matthias Diether is the mastermind behind one of Berlin's most celebrated restaurants. His inventive French/European menu is seasonal and changes regularly, and though not cheap (mains €24–€54) you get your money's worth. The menus are four, six or eight courses (€109–€149), and there's a two- or four-course lunch menu (€28/€56).

FLORIAN

Grolmanstr. 52 Ⓢ Savignyplatz ☎ 030/313 91 84, Ⓦ www.restaurant-florian.de. Daily 6pm–3am. MAP P.126–127, POCKET MAP A6

The two female chefs who run *Florian*, on an upmarket residential street, have been in charge for 25 years, serving fine south German food. The dishes are hearty and innovative, the interior coolly bland and the service excellent. Typical dishes include sour kidneys from the daily changing menu (mains €14.50–€24.50).

GOOD FRIENDS

Kantstr. 30 Ⓢ Savignyplatz ☎ 030/31 32 659, Ⓦ www.restaurant-goodfriends.de. Daily noon–2am. MAP P.126–127, POCKET MAP A6

Possibly the best-known Cantonese restaurant in town, though don't expect anything fancy, or even extravagantly Chinese in terms of decor. It's a large, minimal place, with dishes from €6.80 at lunch and €9.80 in the evening. Aside from the classics they serve jellyfish and spiced paunch – not for the faint hearted.

JULES VERNE RESTAURANT

Schlüterstr. 61 Ⓢ Savignyplatz ☎ 030/31 80 94 10, Ⓦ www.jules-verne-berlin.de. Daily 9am–1am, kitchen till 11.45pm. MAP P.126–127, POCKET MAP A6

The interior feels classic French but the menu is aptly global, ranging from *Flammkuchen* (tarte flambée) and schnitzel to couscous and satay. Lunchtime deals change weekly.

KUCHI

Kantstr. 30 Ⓢ Savignyplatz ☎ 030/31 50 78 15, Ⓦ www.kuchi.de. Daily noon–midnight. MAP P.126–127, POCKET MAP A6

With a sister restaurant in Mitte (see p.40), this place sells the same range of innovative sushi, sashimi, yakitori, as well as some Thai, Chinese and Korean recipes. Busy at peak times so it's best to reserve a table. Happy hour from 5pm includes noodle soups for €6 and sushi for €7.

lend this place an unfussy, classic feel that ties in well with the Austrian cuisine – which is simple yet some of the best in the area. Organic ingredients feature on the menu, which includes fish dishes, risotto and a famed Wiener schnitzel. Good Austrian wine list too.

PARIS BAR

Kantstr. 152 ⑤/Ⓤ Zoologischer Garten ☎ 030/313 80 52, Ⓦ www.parisbar.net. Daily noon–2am. MAP P.126–127, POCKET MAP B6

There's still something tangibly bohemian about the *Paris Bar*, once one of the centres of West Berlin's art scene until the Wall fell and the East took over. Interesting artworks vie for your attention and the decidedly average food takes second place to the social networking action. Lunch is around €10, dinner €17–€28.

RESTAURANT BREL

Savignyplatz 1 ⑤ Savignyplatz ☎ 030/31 80 00 20, Ⓦ www.cafebrel.de. Daily 9am–1am. MAP P.126–127, POCKET MAP A6

This well-established bistro has a comfortable, friendly but sophisticated feel, with a long wooden bar, black-and-white photos and grand piano. It's matched by excellent French food and wines; try the three-course lunch menu for just €9.

Cheap eats

ASHOKA

Grolmanstr. 51 ⑤ Savignyplatz ☎ 030/31 01 58 06. Daily 11am–midnight. MAP P.126–127, POCKET MAP A6

Ashok Sharma opened this restaurant in 1975 as he was missing the food from his home in Punjab. It offers well-priced, decent quality food (curries around €8.50) in a small Imbiss-style place. Vegetarian options and friendly staff.

LUBITSCH

Bleibtreustr. 47 ⑤ Savignyplatz ☎ 030/882 37 56, Ⓦ www.restaurant-lubitsch.de. Mon–Fri 10am–late (kitchen till 11pm), Sun 6pm–late. MAP P.126–127, POCKET MAP A6

Named after German film director Ernst Lubitsch, this place has a wonderfully old school Berlin feel to it. The food is generous and hearty – dumplings, schnitzel, cucumber salad – and though the ambience is vaguely formal it's also a friendly place. A daily lunch dish is available for €5; three-course lunches for €10.

MARJELLCHEN

Mommsenstr. 9 ⑤ Savignyplatz ☎ 030/88 32 676, Ⓦ www.marjellchen-berlin.de. Daily 5pm–midnight. MAP P.126–127, POCKET MAP A7

It's obvious from the window displays – books, photos and other paraphernalia – that this is a timewarp kind of place. Indeed, *Marjellchen* specializes in cuisine from East Prussia, Pomerania and Silesia, all served up in a cosy, traditional atmosphere. Portions are generous and service is friendly (mains €12.50–€20.20).

OTTENTHAL

Kantstr. 153 ⑤ Savignyplatz ☎ 030/313 31 62, Ⓦ www.ottenthal.com, Daily 6pm–1am. MAP P.126–127, POCKET MAP B6

White-clothed tables and relatively sparse white walls

BIER'S KU'DAMM 195

Kurfürstendamm 195 ⓤ Uhlandstr. ☎030/881
89 42. Mon–Fri 11am–5am, Sat 11am–6pm,
Sun noon–5pm. MAP P.126–127, POCKET MAP A7

One of several spots claimed
as the "best in Berlin" for
Currywurst. It also serves meat
skewers and meatballs, and is
generally busy all night; if you
feel like splashing out ask for
champagne with your Wurst.

DAO

Kantstr. 133 Ⓢ Savignyplatz ☎030/37 59
14 14, Ⓦ www.dao-restaurant.de. Daily noon–
midnight. MAP P.126–127, POCKET MAP A6

Opened by a Berliner and his
Thai wife Dao in the 1970s, this
Thai spot serves tasty dishes
that brim with flavour.
Alongside pad Thai (€8.90) and
fish and duck dishes (up to
€18) there are specials like
"Bloodnoodlesoup".

LON-MEN'S NOODLE HOUSE

Kantstr. 33 Ⓢ Savignyplatz ☎030/31 51 96 78.
Daily noon–midnight. MAP P.126–127, POCKET MAP A6

A relaxed, tiny Taiwanese
noodle shop run by friendly
grandmas who make mean
dumplings and noodle soups
(small and large portions
available). Try the "Chinese
Maultaschen" – fried
ravioli-style pasta packets filled
with pork and vegetables
(€5–6). Ask for the home-made
noodles (not on the menu).

CAFÉ IM LITERATURHAUS

Cafés and bars

CAFÉ IM LITERATURHAUS

Fasanenstr. 23 ⓤ Uhlandstr. ☎030/88 25
414, Ⓦ www.literaturhaus-berlin.de. Daily
9.30am–1am. MAP P.126–127, POCKET MAP B7

Café im Literaturhaus is every
bit as classic and elegant as the
name suggests. The spacious
interior or beautiful summer
garden are great spots for coffee
and cake, lunch or dinner: the
organic menu changes weekly
(€5.30 soup, €24.50 steak) and
has vegetarian options.

CAFÉ SAVIGNY

Grolmanstr. 53 Ⓢ Savignyplatz ☎030/44 70 83
86. Daily 9am–1am. MAP P.126–127, POCKET MAP A6

A small, classic spot that's been
serving great breakfasts and
coffee for over a decade.
Lunches start at €5.50 (soups)
with hearty Burgundy stew for
€13.50. Service is good and it's
also nice for an evening drink.

DIENER

Grolmanstr. 47 Ⓢ Savignyplatz ☎030/88 15
329, Ⓦ www.diener-tattersall.de. Daily
6pm–3am. MAP P.126–127, POCKET MAP A6

This Berlin ale house is a local
institution – not only because it
was opened in 1954 by former
German heavyweight boxer
Franz Diener, but because it
serves dishes like *Königsberger
Klopse* (meatballs in white
sauce with capers, €9.20) and
has an atmosphere as old
school as the menu.

EINHORN

Mommsenstr. 2 Ⓢ Savignyplatz ☎030/88 14
241, Ⓦ www.einhornonline.de. Daily Mon–Fri
10am–5pm. MAP P.126–127, POCKET MAP A7

A great place if you're seeking a
tasty veggie lunch. There's a
buffet selection including
antipasti and and dishes like
lentils with goat's cheese. Priced
by weight (€1.50/100g), except
for daily specials.

a futuristic feel. The menu includes pumpkin soup and burgers (mains €15–32) and the cocktails are well mixed.

VAGABUND BAR

Knesebeckstr. 77 ⓤ Uhlandstr. ☎ 030/88 11 506, ⓦ www.vagabund-berlin.de. MAP P.126-127, POCKET MAP A7

This popular gay bar opened in 1968 but has recently had a facelift. It gets crowded after 3am and has an anything goes, trashy aesthetic – very flirty, very fun, and not only for men.

Clubs and venues

A TRANE

Bleibtreustr. 1 Ⓢ Savignyplatz ☎ 030/313 25 50, ⓦ www.a-trane.de. Daily from 9pm, music from around 10pm. MAP P.126-127, POCKET MAP A6

Good jazz and decent cocktails in a classic jazz-style interior (small and smoky). Often hosts major international acts.

PURO SKY LOUNGE

Tauentzienstr. 9–11 ⓤ Kurfürstendamm ☎ 030/26 36 78 75, ⓦ www.puro-berlin.de. Tues–Sat 8pm–close. MAP P.126-127, POCKET MAP C7

Ensconced on the twentieth floor of the ugly Europa Center, the *Puro Sky Lounge* is filled with eye candy thanks to the beautiful people who flock here for the jaw-dropping views. What it lacks in musical edge – think 1980s classics– it makes up for with an upbeat crowd.

RUHLAND & RUHLAND

Knesebeckstr. 5 ⓤ Ernst-Reuter-Platz ☎ 030/80 92 34 24, ⓦ www.ruhland-ruhland .de. Mon–Fri 9am–7pm, Sat 10am–7pm. MAP P.126-127, POCKET MAP A6

Immaculate, whitewashed walls and an open kitchen gives this deli a distinctively New York feel. The food is sourced locally and ranges from delicious strudel to cinnamon-scented sauerkraut, plus salads and sandwiches.

SCHWARZES CAFÉ

Kantstr. 148 Ⓢ Savignyplatz ☎ 030/31 38 038. Daily 24hr. MAP P.126-127, POCKET MAP A6

The slightly ragged charm of the "Black Café" makes it feel like it would be better placed in the east. The downstairs is small and intimate, but upstairs the large, airy room has a relaxed, convivial vibe. Food is served 24 hours, including breakfasts (from €4.50) – but this is a night-owl place really.

UNIVERSUM LOUNGE

Kurfürstendamm 153 ⓤ Adenauerplatz ☎ 030/89 06 49 95, ⓦ www.universumlounge .com. MAP P.126-127, POCKET MAP A7

Located in the stunning Bauhaus-era Universum Cinema, this place is an oddity even by Berlin standards. A curved main bar decorated in golds and browns and lunar-themed wallpaper lend it

QUASIMODO

Kantstr. 12A ⓤ Savignyplatz ☎ 030/31 28 086, ⓦ www.quasimodo.de. MAP P.126-127, POCKET MAP B6

A classic jazz bar, *Quasimodo* (underneath the Delphi Cinema) features black-and-white photos, low ceilings and intimate tables. Aside from jazz there's funk, blues and Latin and the odd international star.

Schöneberg

Famous during the 1920s as the centre of Berlin's decadent nightlife scene and again in the 1970s when it was home to David Bowie during his dissipated sojourn in the city, Schöneberg's star waned in the 1990s as the cool kids moved east. But while East Berlin has become increasingly slick and unaffordable, this part of town has – as they say – kept it real. Nowadays the hipsters are heading back, attracted by the still-low rents and the burgeoning gallery scene in Potsdamer Strasse, and it maintains its reputation as the pinkest borough in Berlin, especially around Nollendorfplatz. It's also long-been a popular spot for writers – Christopher Isherwood had his digs in Nollendorfstrasse back in the day, and a new generation of writers including Helen DeWitt and Ida Hattemer-Higgins today call the neighbourhood home. Though it lacks any major sights, the charming Winterfeldtplatz hosts a highly popular farmers' market (Sat 8am–4pm).

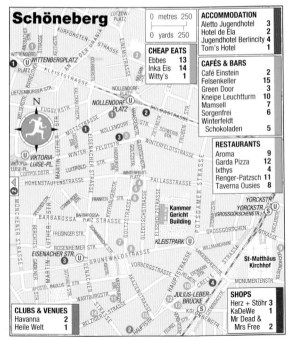

Schöneberg

| 0 metres | 250 |
| 0 yards | 250 |

ACCOMMODATION
Aletto Jugendhotel 3
Hotel de Ela 2
Jugendhotel Berlincity 4
Tom's Hotel 1

CHEAP EATS
Ebbes 13
Inka Eis 14
Witty's 1

CAFÉS & BARS
Café Einstein 2
Felsenkeller 15
Green Door 3
Kneipe Leuchtturm 10
Mamsell 7
Sorgenfrei 6
Winterfeldt
  Schokoladen 5

RESTAURANTS
Aroma 9
Garda Pizza 12
Ixthys 4
Renger-Patzsch 11
Taverna Ousies 8

SHOPS
Herz + Stöhr 3
KaDeWe 1
Mr Dead &
  Mrs Free 2

CLUBS & VENUES
Havanna 2
Heile Welt 1

Shops

HERZ + STÖHR

Winterfeldtstr. 52 ⓤ Nollendorfplatz
☎ 030/216 44 25. Mon–Fri 11am–7pm, Sat
11am–4pm. MAP OPPOSITE, POCKET MAP D8

Intelligent, elegant designs
from this German fashion duo
– the dresses and suits are
grown-up but not dowdy, and
everything can be altered to fit.

KADEWE

Tauentzienstr. 21–24 ⓤ Wittenbergplatz
☎ 030/212 10, ⓦ www.kadewe.de. Mon–Thurs
10am–8pm, Fri 10am–9pm, Sat 9am–8pm.
MAP OPPOSITE, POCKET MAP C7

If you're tired of Berlin's austere
side, check out KaDeWe
(Kaufhaus Des Westerns), a
temple to conspicuous
consumption. The largest
department store in continental
Europe, it sports designer gear
alongside some surprisingly
affordable accessories and
homewares. The legendary
sixth-floor food hall will leave
all but the most jaded of
foodies starry-eyed.

MR DEAD & MRS FREE

Bülowstr. 5 ⓤ Nollendorfplatz ☎ 030/215
14 49. Mon–Fri noon–7pm, Sat 11am–4pm.
MAP OPPOSITE, POCKET MAP D7

A dusty little legend of a music
shop crammed full of
everything from the latest
imports to rare vintage albums.

Restaurants

AROMA

Hochkirchstr. 8 Ⓢ/ⓤ Yorckstr. ☎ 030/782 58
21, ⓦ www.cafe-aroma.de. Mon–Fri from 6pm,
Sat from 3pm, Sun brunch 11am–2pm, from
2pm a la carte. MAP OPPOSITE, POCKET MAP E9

Tucked into a sleepy residential
street, this rustic Italian gem is
the unofficial headquarters for
Berlin's slow food movement.

The antipasti spread at Sunday
brunch (€12) is legendary,
while dried cod with polenta
(€7.50) and squid with baby
chard (€15.50) satisfy the
dinner crowd. The terrace is a
peaceful haven in summer.

GARDA PIZZA

Crellestr. 48 Ⓢ Julius-Leber-Brücke ☎ 030/78
09 79 70. Daily 11.30am–9pm; Dec–Feb closed
Sun. MAP OPPOSITE, POCKET MAP D9

Locals flock to *Garda Pizza* for
their trays of thin-crust
Roman-style focaccia. Their
most popular slice combines
fresh aubergine, mushroom,
sheep's salami and artichokes.
A tray (€15) will feed a hungry
group of four. Join the crowd
on the pavement, or mosey
down a few metres and let your
children burn off the calories in
the neighbouring playground.

IXTHYS

Pallasstr. 21 ⓤ Nollendorfplatz
☎ 030/81 47 47 69. Mon–Sat noon–10pm.
MAP OPPOSITE, POCKET MAP D8

A tiny café run by two Korean
widows (who've festooned the
walls with Biblical slogans)this
places is all about great
home-style cooking. Guests
squeeze in to enjoy the
home-made noodles with
vegetables (€5) or seafood
(€7.50) and the fiery, sizzling
bibimbap (€7.50).

KADEWE

RENGER-PATZSCH

Wartburgstr. 54 ⓤ Eisenacher Str.
☎ 030/784 2059, ⓦ www.renger-patzsch.com.
Daily 6pm–1am. MAP P.136, POCKET MAP D9

An interior of dark wood and white tablecloths forms the backdrop to an expertly prepared selection of German dishes. In spring, look for the dandelion salad with lardons (€8); in winter, the braised ox cheeks with bacon-wrapped plums, turnips and mashed potatoes (€18). The perfect place for a celebration.

TAVERNA OUSIES

Grunewaldstr. 16 ⓤ Eisenacher Str.
☎ 030/216 79 57, ⓦ www.taverna-ousies.de.
Daily from 5pm. MAP P.136, POCKET MAP D9

This kitschy, raucous Greek taverna is a perennial favourite. There are no real duds, so go wild with the meze menu (€4–7) and be entertained by the jolly staff. Reservations essential at weekends.

Cheap eats

EBBES

Crellestr. 2 ⓢ Julius-Leber-Brücke ☎ 030/70 09 48 13. Mon–Fri 10am–7.30pm, Sat 9am–4pm. MAP P.136, POCKET MAP D9

This quirky Swabian deli is crowded with rings of venison salami and trays of fresh *spätzle* (pasta). Owner Wolfgang Steppes finds his suppliers on trips to southern Germany. Buy a picnic and wander north to Kleistpark, or grab a stool outside and try one of the daily specials, including *Maultaschen* (ravioli) in broth (€2.50).

INKA EIS

Belziger Str. 44 ⓤ Eisenacher Str. ☎ 030/78 09 70 50. Daily 11am–8pm. Closed Jan & Feb. MAP P.136, POCKET MAP D9

A little taste of Latin America in a quiet corner of Schöneberg,

Inka Eis serves scrumptious scoops of tamarind ice cream, Peruvian grilled chicken (€5) and empanadas (€3.50).

WITTY'S

Wittenbergplatz 5 ⓤ Wittenbergplatz
☎ 030/211 94 96. Mon–Sat 11am–8pm, Sun noon–7pm. MAP P.136, POCKET MAP C7

One of the city's first and finest organic sausage stands, *Witty's* has customers lined up along the square for their *Currywurst* (€3.30) and crispy fries. Eat up here, then cross the street to buy an exquisite chocolate or two from KaDeWe.

Cafés and bars

CAFÉ EINSTEIN

Kurfürstenstr. 58 ⓤ Nollendorfplatz ☎ 030/261 50 96. Daily 8am–1am. MAP P.136, POCKET MAP D7

The staff can be brusque and a latte costs double what it does elsewhere, but there's no denying the parquet floors and leather banquettes have their charm. The cakes (€3.90) are a good bet. On sunny days make a beeline for the spacious garden and sip bellinis while the shadows lengthen.

FELSENKELLER

Akazienstr. 2 ⓢ Julius-Leber-Brücke
☎ 030/781 34 47. Mon–Fri 4pm–1am, Sat noon–2am. MAP P.136, POCKET MAP D9

The perfect destination when you're nostalgic for old Berlin. Founded in 1923, this bar is famous for its eight beers on tap (€2.70); they're drawn the old-fashioned way, so be prepared to wait. There's hearty, simple food, such as lentil soup and swede stew (€5). No music, but plenty of atmosphere.

GREEN DOOR

Winterfeldtstr. 50 ⓤ Nollendorfplatz
☎ 030/215 25 15. Sun–Thurs 6pm–3am, Fri & Sat 6pm–4am. MAP P.136, POCKET MAP D8

GREEN DOOR

This gay-friendly café will take you straight back to the 1950s. There's Hawaiian-style toast on the menu and Bing Crosby on the speakers. The Bakelite radios and kidney-shaped tables aren't just for decoration – most of the items are for sale.

WINTERFELDT SCHOKOLADEN

Goltzstr. 23 ⓤ Nollendorfplatz ☎ 030/23 62 32 56. Mon–Fri 9am–8pm, Sat & Sun 9am–6pm. MAP P.136, POCKET MAP D8

Once an apothecary's, this café-chocolate shop serves a lovely selection of pastries to cure all your ills. Scones with clotted cream and jam and warm chocolate fondant cake (both €3) are popular.

Ring the bell and enter one of Berlin's best-loved cocktail bars. The expert but unpretentious staff will recommend the perfect drink. An older crowd fills the cosy room. Happy hour till 9pm (cocktails €7).

KNEIPE LEUCHTTURM

Crellestr. 41 ⓤ Kleistpark ☎ 030/781 85 19. May–Sept daily 4pm–late; Oct–April Mon–Fri & Sun 6pm–late, Sat 8pm–late. MAP P.136, POCKET MAP D9

If you think beer just isn't the same without a cigarette, head for the "Lighthouse", with its unpretentious, welcoming atmosphere favoured by former hippies and locals. The wines can be middling so go for one of the beers on tap.

MAMSELL

Goltzstr. 48 ⓤ Eisenacher Str. ☎ 030/92 12 29 00. Mon–Fri 10am–7pm, Sat 10am–5pm, Sun 2–6pm. MAP P.136, POCKET MAP D8

Those with a penchant for pink will be delighted by this sweet café/shop. The addictive real hot chocolate is served with a dusting of freshly grated ginger (€3.40).

SORGENFREI

Goltzstr. 18 ⓤ Nollendorfplatz ☎ 030/30 10 40 71. Tues–Fri noon–7pm, Sat 10am–6pm, Sun 1–6pm. MAP P.136, POCKET MAP D8

Clubs and venues

HAVANNA

Hauptstr. 30 Ⓢ Julius-Leber-Brücke ☎ 030/784 85 65, ⓦ www.havanna-berlin.de. Wed from 9pm, Fri & Sat from 10pm. MAP P.136, POCKET MAP D9

With four floors and seven bars, this magnet for Latin American music fans draws a diverse clientele. Serious salsa and tango fans will find like-minded devotees to shake it on the dance floor.

HEILE WELT

Motzstr. 5, ⓤ Nollendorfplatz ☎ 030/21 91 75 07. Daily from 6pm. MAP P.136, POCKET MAP D7

A much-beloved destination for gay men and the women who love them. Music runs the gamut from soul and dance to house and home-brewed "Schlager". During the week, enjoy one of the friendly bar staff's famously strong cocktails and settle into a comfortable sofa. The action picks up at the weekend, when it gets too crowded for some, and just right for others.

Day-trips from Berlin

There's so much to do in Berlin that it's easy to forget there's a world outside the city. Berlin's surroundings are surprisingly sparse and beautiful – a bucolic swathe of lakes, forests and small villages. Amidst the vast landscape lie some of the city's highlights, many of them less than an hour from the centre. Easily accessible by public transport, areas such as Dahlem, Potsdam and Wannsee make for enjoyable and edifying visits (as well as memorials to the darker side of the city's past). The most popular day-trip is Potsdam, which includes Schloss Sanssouci and Babelsberg film studios as well as a town centre distinct from anything in Berlin. The Wannsee area offers lakeside beaches as well as historical villas and the magical Pfaueninsel, while Dahlem has botanical gardens and some excellent ethnological museums. History buffs will find journeys to Sachsenhausen concentration camp, Villa Wannsee and Hohenschönhausen Stasi prison both chilling and instructive.

SACHSENHAUSEN

Strasse der Nationen 22, Oranienburg Ⓢ Oranienburg (end of S1 line, then follow signs for Gedenkstätte Sachsenhausen) ☏ 033/01 20 02 00, Ⓦ www.stiftung-bg.de. Daily: March 15–Oct 14 8.30am–6pm; Oct 15–March 14 8.30am–4.30pm. Museums, archive and library closed Mon, but the open-air exhibition, "Station Z" memorial and visitor information centre remain open. Free. Guided tours available for groups (€15–€25) in a range of different languages.

Located in Oranienburg, 35km north of the city, Sachsen-hausen ranks among Berlin's most emotionally wrenching wartime memorials – which is saying a lot for a city like this. Established in 1936, it was first used as a prison for political opponents. It became a training ground for SS officers, and from 1938 to 1945 the central administration for all concentration camps was located here. After the war started, tens of thousands of prisoners were brought here. In 1943 a small gas chamber was added. By 1944 some 200,000 people had passed through the prison, with tens of thousands dying of starvation, disease, mistreatment and systematic extermination. In April 1945 more than 33,000 prisoners were sent on the notorious

SACHSENHAUSEN

death marches, during which more than a thousand died – those who collapsed en route were routinely shot. When the camp was liberated by Russian soldiers on April 22, 1945 only three thousand prisoners remained, many of whom who died in the days afterwards. The camp became a Soviet-run prison and in 1948 it was renamed "Special Camp No. 1". Sixty thousand people were interned here over five years, including six thousand German officers transferred from Western Allied camps. By the time the camp closed in the spring of 1950, 12,000 had died of malnutrition and disease. In 1956, the GDR turned the site into a memorial, removing many of the original buildings and constructing an obelisk, statue and meeting area. Today the memorial is a place of commemoration as well as a museum that includes a wealth of information on the camp, artwork by inmates, models, pictures and more. Following the discovery in 1990 of mass graves from the Soviet period a separate museum was opened about the Soviet-era history.

POTSDAM

S7 S-Bahn line (just under 1hr; ticket for zones A,B and C); or regional trains (RE1) to Potsdam and Bablesberg. You can cover most of Potsdam by foot but a Potsdam Card (€9.50), available from the tourist centre at the train station, gives free public transport and discounts on most main attractions.

Located 24km southwest of Berlin, Potsdam makes for an easy and pleasant day-trip, with plenty to see and do, from the wonderful Schloss Sanssouci and its gardens (see p.142) to the Babelsberg film studios. There are two quaint historic quarters in the city itself that are worth seeking out. The

DETAIL ON THE CHINESE TEAHOUSE, SANSSOUCI

DAY-TRIPS FROM BERLIN

Russian Colony Alexandrowka (Alexandrowka 2; ☎0331/817 02 03, 🌐www .alexandrowka.de; check website for opening hours; €3.50), created in 1826–27 on the request of Friedrich Wilhelm III in memory of his friend Czar Alexander I, is an artist's village of twelve picturesque wooden houses and a small Russian Orthodox chapel (1829) on Kapellenberg hill to the north. Check out the Russian tearoom in the warden's house. The **Holländisches Viertel**, or Dutch quarter (🌐www.hollaendisches -viertel.net), consists of around 150 three-storey redbrick houses, and was built between 1734 and 1742 for Dutch craftsmen invited to Potsdam by Friedrich Wilhelm I. The houses are built in the classic Dutch style with shuttered windows and slanted roofs. Jan Bouman, head of construction, has his own museum at Mittelstr. 8 (☎0331/28 03 773; Mon–Fri 10am–6pm, Sat & Sun 11am–6pm; €2) and another museum about the area is at Benkertstr. 3 (☎0331/289 68 03; daily 10am–6pm; €3).

SCHLOSS SANSSOUCI AND PARK

Park Sanssouci ◉ Potsdam. Around 5km from Potsdam train station; bus #695 goes from the train station, with stops at Schloss Sanssouci, the Orangerie and Neues Palais (among others). ☏ 0331/969 41 90, ⓦ www .spsg.de. Palace Tues–Sun: April–Oct 9am–5pm; Nov–March 9am–4pm, timed guided tours only, Park daily 9am–dusk. Admission to palace €12 (€8 in winter); other attractions individually priced, or €19 day ticket for all buildings. Park: free.

The highlight of any trip to Potsdam, Schloss Sanssouci was built for Frederick the Great by the magnificently titled Georg Wenzeslaus von Knobelsdorff between 1745 and 1747. It was his summer residence – the place he came for some peace and quiet and to be with his beloved dogs (*San Souci* means "without worries" in French); the parkland, buildings and palaces dotted around it were added to by later Prussian kings. Having survived unscathed from the War, the palace is considered one of the most significant examples of Rococo architecture – much of the original artworks were moved to Rheinsberg during the War or were transferred as booty to the Soviet Union, though

Frederick's library and 36 oil paintings were returned and can be viewed today alongside furnishings and decorations from the original rooms. The adjacent **picture gallery** exhibits works by Rubens, van Dyck, Caravaggio and other renowned artists, and the historic windmill – built in the Dutch style and rebuilt in 1993 – is worth a visit, as is the **Chinese Teahouse** and the **New Palace** (Neues Palais; Mon & Wed–Sun 10am–5/6pm; €6), a larger Baroque-style palace intended to display Frederick's power to the world. Best of all is the surrounding park, an inspiring display of terraced vineyards, flamboyant flower beds, hedges and abundant fruit trees. Note that the palaces are highly popular in summer and tours inside the main palace are limited, so arrive early or book ahead.

BABELSBERG FILMPARK

August-Bebel-Str. 26–53 (entrance Grossbeerenstr.) ◉ Babelsburg, then bus #601, #619, #690 to Filmpark or RE1 to Medienstadt ☏ 0331/ 721 27 50, ⓦ www.filmpark.de. April 15–Oct 31 daily 10am–6pm €21.

Some of Germany's most famous films were created at

SCHLOSS SANSSOUCI

Babelsberg, including masterpieces such as *Metropolis* (1927) and *The Blue Angel* (1930), starring Marlene Dietrich – in its heyday the studios were Europe's version of Hollywood. Today it feels more like a slightly tacky theme park than anything else, as you roam sets from old films, witness stuntmen in action and marvel at the special effects. It's especially good (if not better) for kids, who will enjoy the Jungle Playground and the Animal Farm.

DAHLEM MUSEUMS

🚇 Dahlemdorf 📞 030/830 1438, 🌐 www.smb .museum.com. Tues–Fri 10am–6pm, Sat & Sun 11am–6pm, €6 (free Thurs 2–6pm).

The district of Berlin-Dahlem, located in the south of the city, is a green and pleasant place. It offers a collection of museums that comprise one of Germany's best ethno-cultural collections, as well as a splendid botanical gardens (see p.144).

The main **Ethnological Museum** (Ethnologisches Museum) holds around a million items, including artworks from Africa, exhibits from North-American Indians, full-scale wooden huts and boats from the South Pacific, a large collection of ceramic and stone sculptures from the Mayas, Aztecs and Incas and an intriguing assemblage of pre-Columbian relics, including gold objects and antiquities from Peru. There's also a great **Department of Music** where you can hear folk music recordings from around the globe.

The Museum for Asian Art includes both the Far Eastern collection and the Museum of Indian Art. It is devoted to one thousand years of Asian culture, and features lots of porcelain and lacquer from Korea, China and Japan, green jade, a seventeenth-century imperial throne from China and Japanese woodblock prints – all plundered during a massive "shopping expedition" the Germans undertook in Asia. Outside the main complex (a 5min walk away), the **Museum of European Cultures** (Museum Europäischer Kulturen) is devoted to the German people themselves – not the aristocrats but the middle class and the peasant stock who built the country. The exhibits go back four centuries, tracing how artisans and homemakers lived and worked. Household items are displayed along with primitive industrial equipment such as a utensil for turning flax into linen. Furnishings, clothing, pottery and even items used in religious observances are shown, along with some fun and whimsical exhibits, including depictions of pop culture from the 1950s to 1980s.

DOMÄNE DAHLEM

Königin-Luise-Str. 49 📞 030/666 30 00, 🌐 www.domaene-dahlem.de. Mon & Wed–Sun 10am–6pm, €2.

Just over the road from the museums is a working farm and handicraft centre known as Domäne Dahlem. Intended to showcase something of Germany's pre-industrial era, the complex includes an old estate house, a collection of agricultural instruments and demonstrations of artisan trades such as wood carving, ceramics and wool spinning. The best time to come is at the weekend when more of the machines and workshops are on display and there's a small organic market.

DAHLEM BOTANIC GARDENS

Königin-Luise-Str. 6–8 ⚇/Ⓢ Rathaus Steglitz, and 15min walk or bus #X83 to Königin-Luise-Str./Botanischer Garten. ☎ 030/838 50 100, Ⓦ www.bgbm.org. Daily: museum 10am–6pm; garden Jan, Nov & Dec 9am–4pm; Feb 9am–5pm; March & Oct 9am–6pm; April & Aug 9am–8pm; May, June & July 9am–9pm; Sept 9am–7pm. Gardens €5; museum €2.

Founded as an extension to the kitchen garden of the Berlin palace by the Elector of Prussia, by 1815 the royal herbarium had developed hugely thanks to extensive botanical research by C.L. Willdenow. The collection was moved to Dahlem in 1907 and today hosts 22,000 species of plants over 43 hectares, making it one of the largest and most diverse botanical gardens in the world. The sixteen greenhouses (Gewächshäuser) feature an array of specialist areas such as a garden of aquatic and marsh plants, an aroma and touch garden and medicinal plants. The attached museum features sections of preserved fossils and plant-formations on artificially constructed landscapes.

PFAUENINSEL

Ⓢ Wannsee, then bus #208 to the passenger ferry (€2). Museum: April–Oct Tues–Sun 10am–5pm. €3.

Formerly known as *Kanninchenwerder* ("Rabbit Island"), Peacock Island features a castle built by Prussian king Frederick William II in 1793 for him and his mistress Wilhelmine Enke. His successor Frederick William III turned the island into a model farm and from 1821 had the park redesigned by Peter Joseph Lenné and Karl Friedrich Schinkel, who planned several buildings (one of which now houses a small museum). The king also laid out a menagerie modelled on the Ménagerie du Jardin des Plantes in Paris, in which exotic animals and birds including peacocks were housed. In addition to several free-ranging peacocks, other native and exotic birds can be found in captivity, complemented by a rich variety of flora. The entire island is designated as a nature reserve.

HOUSE OF THE WANNSEE CONFERENCE

Ⓢ Wannsee, then bus #114 (direction "Krankenhaus Heckeshorn") to Haus der Wannsee-Konferenz ☎ 030/80 50 010, Ⓦ www.ghwk.de. Daily 10am–6pm. Free (guided tour €2)

It's hard to imagine that this handsome villa at Wannsee lake has an iniquitous history, but it was here that the "Final Solution of the Jewish Question" was discussed – and decided – by fifteen high-ranking Nazi officials, who agreed to exterminate the entire Jewish population of Europe. Since 1992 it has served as a memorial and documentation centre, with a permanent exhibit that draws on detailed historical research to profile the conference and the process of deporting Jews to the ghettoes and camps.

STRANDBAD WANNSEE

A library on the second floor (named after Joseph Wulf, an Auschwitz survivor and campaigner for this memorial) holds thousands of books on Nazism, anti-Semitism, the Holocaust, as well as Nazi-era documents such as children's books promoting Nazism. However, the most spine-tingling experience is simply standing in the room where the plans were made for the murder of millions.

STRANDBAD WANNSEE

Wannseebadeweg 25 ⑤ Wannsee/Nikolaisee Ⓦ www.strandbadwannsee.de. Daily May–Sept 7am–8pm, €4.

Strandbad Wannsee's impressive 1275-metre long (and 80-metre wide) sweep of sandy beach has long been a venerable summer destination for Berliners. Officially the largest lido in Europe, it's located on the eastern side of the Wannsee, just a twenty-minute train ride from the city centre. Its current "look" was formulated by architects Martin Wagner and Richard Ermisch. Today the "Mother of all Lidos" attracts up to 230,000 visitors per year and has been designated a cultural heritage site. Between 2004 and 2007, it underwent a €12.5 million refurbishment for its centenary celebrations.

MAX LIEBERMANN VILLA

Colomierstr. 3 ⑤ Wannsee then either bus #114 toward Heckeshorn to Liebermann-Villa (5min) or 20min walk ☏ 030/805 85 900, Ⓦ www.liebermann-villa.de. Mon & Wed–Sun: April–Sept 10am–6pm, Thurs till 8pm; Oct–March Mon & Wed–Sun 11am–5pm. €6.

German Impressionist Max Liebermann's "castle by the sea", built in 1909, and particularly its expansive, 7000-square-metre garden, was the subject of more than two hundred of his paintings. An exhibition documents Liebermann's life here, with prints and photographs. On the upper floor are around forty paintings, pastels and prints that revolve around his Wannsee works – pictures of the flower terrace, perennial garden, birch grove and the lawn leading down to the lake – plus portraits of family and personalities. The garden has been reconstructed today as it was originally planned by Liebermann, and brims with rare and diverse species.

GEDENKSTÄTTE BERLIN-HOHENSCHÖNHAUSEN

Genslerstr. 66 ⑤ Freienwalder Str. (then 10min walk) or #M6 from Hackescher Markt Genslerstr. (then 10min walk) ☏ 030/98 60 82 30, Ⓦ www.stiftung-hsh.de. Daily 9am–4pm, English tours 2.30pm €5.

With its intact buildings, equipment and furniture, the Stasi prison at Hohenschönhausen provides a particularly authentic – and grisly – portrait of public persecution during GDR times. The Stasi used it to detain and physically and psychologically torture dissenters. The prison, which remained largely a secret until the Wall fell in 1989, was turned into a memorial in 1994, and since 2000 has been an independent foundation that researches the history of the prison and produces exhibitions, events and publications. The only way to see the memorial is via a guided tour, available in German, English, and other languages; tours with former inmates are also available, though mostly in German. The tour includes a survey of the older and newer prison blocks and detailed descriptions of daily life in the prison.

Accommodation

Berlin's accommodation options run the gamut from cheap and cheerful hostels to corporate hotels, super-deluxe five stars and intimate boutique and "art" hotels. Prices quoted usually include taxes and service charges, though breakfast and parking are sometimes extra – it's worth double-checking when booking. While there are many rooms in the city, there are also a lot of visitors; booking ahead in the warmer, more popular months is recommended, especially during large events such as the film festival (see p.161).

Spandauer Vorstadt

CIRCUS HOSTEL > Weinbergsweg 1a ⓤ Rosenthaler Platz ☎ 030/20 00 39 39, ⓦ circus-berlin.de. MAP P.32–33, POCKET MAP D11. One of the most popular hostels in the city, *Circus* offers pleasant, clean dorms, private rooms – even penthouse apartments – and a convivial, upbeat vibe right on buzzing Rosenthaler Platz. Bicycles for rent and free walking tours too. Buffet breakfast €2.50–€5. **Dorms from €19, doubles from €56.**

CIRCUS HOTEL > Rosenthalerstr. 1 ⓤ Rosenthaler Platz ☎ 030/20 00 39 39, ⓦ circus-berlin.de. MAP P.32–33, POCKET MAP E10. The sister establishment of the Circus hostel (located just over the road) is a more upmarket and more eco-friendly place. Sixty rooms include junior suites and apartments, decorated in striking colours with wooden floors and antique furniture. Restaurant *Fabisch* serves organic and locally sourced German cuisine. Buffet breakfast €4–€8. **Doubles from €70.**

HEART OF GOLD > Johannisstr. 11 ⓢ Oranienburger Str. ☎ 030/29 00 33 00, ⓦ heartofgold-hostel.de. MAP P.32–33, POCKET MAP C12. Good-value and friendly hostel near one of the busiest strips in Mitte. Dorms and rooms are basic but clean, and staff go the extra mile to make staying here fun. Expect lots of space-themed decorative touches. Buffet breakfast €3.50. **Dorms from €10, rooms from €40.**

KASTANIENHOF > Kastanienallee 65 ⓤ Senefelderplatz ☎ 030/44 30 50, ⓦ kastanienhof.biz. MAP P.32–33, POCKET MAP H2. This slightly old-fashioned hotel has 35 rooms in an elegant house, with decorative touches that nod to Berlin's fascinating history, including photos, illustrations and maps. Great location for Prenzlauer Berg and Mitte. Breakfast not included. **Doubles from €87.**

SOHO HOUSE > Torstr. 1 ⓤ Rosa-Luxemburg-Platz ☎ 030/40 50 440, ⓦ www.sohohouseberlin .com. MAP P.32–33, POCKET MAP F11.

Apartment rentals

Private apartments are a popular, and often good-value choice for many travellers to Berlin, and a plethora of options exist all over the city. The best apartments offer value for money, are well-located and usually stylish or interestingly decorated. ⓦ www.be-my-guest.com, ⓦ www.all-berlin-apartments.com and ⓦ www.brilliant-apartments.de all have a good spread of apartments and regular special deals.

Private members' club in a restored Bauhaus building with forty rooms that range from tiny to extra large. Decor is quirky and fun, and hints at the faded glamour of the late 1920s. There's also a lovely spa, gym, rooftop pool, restaurant, bars, screening room and private dining area. Cheap offers, from €100, possible. **Doubles from €210.**

WEINMEISTER > Weinmeisterstr. 2 Ⓤ Weinmeisterstr. ☎ 030/75 56 670, Ⓦ the-weinmeister.com. MAP P.32–33, POCKET MAP E11. This new hotel features 88 spacious rooms with large beds, a stylish design ethic – Apple TVs in the rooms and iPads for rent – plus a decent restaurant-bar serving German cuisine and a sixth floor beauty spa. Breakfast from €5. **Doubles from €90.**

Unter den Linden

ADLON KEMPINSKI > Unter den Linden 77 Ⓤ/Ⓢ Brandenburger Tor ☎ 030/226 10, Ⓦ hotel-adlon.de. MAP P.54–55, POCKET MAP B14. Probably the most famous hotel in the city, and definitely one of the most luxurious, the *Hotel Adlon Kempisnki* matches a wealth of history (previous guests include Emperor Wilhelm II, Albert Einstein and Michael Jackson, who famously dangled a baby from one of the hotel balconies) with serious five-star swagger and an enviable location overlooking the Brandenburg Gate on the Unter den Linden. Breakfast €39. **Doubles from €220.**

ARCOTEL JOHN F > Werderscher Markt 11 Ⓤ Hausvogteiplatz ☎ 030/40 50 460, Ⓦ arcotelhotels.com. MAP P.54–55, POCKET MAP D14. Close to Gendarmenmarkt, this 190-roomed hotel is a slightly cheaper option than the neighbouring big guns but has all the facilities you'll need – gym, sauna, meeting rooms, restaurant, bar. Breakfast not included. **Doubles from €90.**

ARTE LUISE KUNSTHOTEL > Luisenstr. 19 Ⓤ/Ⓢ Friedrichstr. ☎ 030/28 44 80, Ⓦ luise-berlin.com. MAP P.54–55, POCKET MAP B12. Walking

distance to the Reichstag and Unter den Linden, this art hotel has fifty charmingly appointed and highly individual rooms, Dutch sculptures in the large lobby and an in-house restaurant serving German-Mediterranean cuisine. Breakfast €11. **Doubles from €99.**

HOTEL DE ROME > Behrenstr. 37 Ⓤ Französische Str. ☎ 030/46 06 090, Ⓦ roccofortecollection.com. MAP P.54–55, POCKET MAP C14. Occupying a nineteenth-century former Dresdner Bank building, this high-class hotel mixes history with a swanky interior, luxurious rooms, an expansive spa and a fantastic restaurant (*Parioli*) and cocktail bar. Breakfast €30. **Doubles from €180.**

WESTIN GRAND > Friedrichstr. 158–164 Ⓤ Französische Str. ☎ 030/20 270, Ⓦ westingrandberlin.com. MAP P.54–55, POCKET MAP C13. Built during the GDR, this large hotel, well positioned on Friedrichstrasse and close to the Brandenburg Gate, has been refurbished to feature a refined Belle Époque interior and beautifully appointed rooms and suites. Breakfast not included. **Doubles from €120.**

Alexanderplatz

ART'OTEL > Wallstr. 70–73 Ⓤ Märkisches Museum ☎ 030/24 06 20, Ⓦ www.parkplaza.com. MAP P.65, POCKET MAP F14. With its impressive range of paintings by Georg Baselitz (and others), this art hotel has reasonable rates, good in-house food and drink options and friendly staff. Breakfast not included **Doubles from €105.**

CITYSTAY HOSTEL > Rosenstr. 16 Ⓢ Hackescher Markt ☎ 030/23 62 40 31, Ⓦ citystay.de. MAP P.65, POCKET MAP E12. Close to Hackescher Markt, the *Citystay* is a big, loft-style space in a nineteenth-century building with dorms and private rooms. No leisure facilities but the restaurant (summer only) serves tasty *Flammkuchen* and there's a nice courtyard (until 10pm). Breakfast buffet (partly organic) is €4.80. **Dorms from €12 (bedding an extra €2.50), doubles from €50.**

LUX 11 > Rosa-Luxemburg-Str. 11 Ⓤ Weinmeisterstr. ☎ 030/93 62 800, Ⓦ lux-eleven.com. MAP P.65, POCKET MAP F12. This designer apartment-hotel oozes style and has big, comfy rooms (with kitchenettes and spacious, open bathrooms), a decent restaurant–bar (*Luchs*) and – in case you need a haircut – an Aveda salon. Breakfast buffet €16. Doubles from €120.

PARK INN > Alexanderplatz 7 Ⓤ/Ⓢ Alexanderplatz ☎ 030/23 89 43 05, Ⓦ parkinn-berlin.de. MAP P.65, POCKET MAP F12. This towering 37-floor GDR-era building looks better on the inside than the out. Unexciting but comfortable rooms feature cosy beds, marble bathrooms and, past the twentieth floor, panoramic views across Berlin. Gym, sauna and top-floor casino too. Breakfast not included. Doubles from €84.

Potsdamer Platz and Tiergarten

HOTEL ALTBERLIN AT POTSDAMER PLATZ > Potsdamer Str. 67 Ⓤ/Ⓢ Potsdamer Platz ☎ 030/26 06 70, Ⓦ www.altberlin.de. MAP P.74–75, POCKET MAP E7. A turn-of-the-twentieth-century, Wilhelminian-era hotel with "grandma" style rooms, old-world decor and long-forgotten Berlin specialities served at its restaurant, *Rike's*. Breakfast included. Rooms from €110.

GRAND HOTEL ESPLANADE > Lützowufer 15 Ⓤ Nollendorfplatz ☎ 030/ 25 47 80, Ⓦ www .esplanadeberlin.com. MAP P.74–75, POCKET MAP D6. Smack between Ku'damm and Unter den Linden, this large, fancy hotel has three restaurants, a New York-style cocktail bar and spa – you can even rent a private yacht, *the MS Esplanade*. Breakfast €19. Doubles from €89.

HOTEL HANSABLICK > Flotowstr. 6 Ⓤ Tiergarten ☎ 030/39 04 800, Ⓦ hansablick.de. MAP P.74–75, POCKET MAP B5. The *Hansablick*, located right on the water, has rooms with balconies and/ or river views and a traditional interior that features artworks by the likes of Otmar Alt and Heinrich Zille. Rates include breakfast, wi-fi and parking. Doubles from €95.

MANDALA > Potsdamer Str. 3 Ⓤ/Ⓢ Potsdamer Platz ☎ 030/590 05 00 00, Ⓦ themandala.de. MAP P.74–75, POCKET MAP A15. The *Mandala* is a haven of hipness in commercial Potsdamer Platz. The apartment-style rooms are sleek and well thought out and there's a seductive lounge (the *Qiu*), great spa (ONO) and one of Berlin's best restaurants (*Facil*). Doubles from €130.

RITZ CARLTON > Potsdamer Platz 3 Ⓢ/Ⓤ Potsdamer Platz ☎ 030/33 77 77, Ⓦ ritzcarlton.com. MAP P.74–75, POCKET MAP A15. This distinctive skyscraper hotel has 303 rooms with expensive cherry wood closets and watercolour paintings, a glamorous spa (*La Prairie*), a great brasserie, lounges and fantastic five-star service. Breakfast included. Doubles from €325.

Prenzlauer Berg

HOTEL TRANSIT LOFT > Immanuelkirchstr. 14 Ⓤ Senefelderplatz ☎ 030/48 49 37 73, Ⓦ transit-loft.de. MAP P.86–87, POCKET MAP K3. A modern hotel set in a nineteenth-century, yellow-brick factory and well located for Kollwitzplatz (see p.88). The 47 rooms (dorms included) are airy and well lit with basic furnishings and en-suite showers. The same owners run *Hotel Transit* in Kreuzberg (see p.152). Breakfast included. Dorms from €21, doubles from €69.

LETTE'M SLEEP > Lettestr. 7 Ⓢ Prenzlauer Allee ☎ 030/44 73 36 23, Ⓦ backpackers.de. MAP P.86–87, POCKET MAP J3. Located directly on Helmholtzplatz, this vaguely hip backpacker hostel has basic but clean dorms (four-to-seven bed) as well as twins and private apartments. There's a common room with DVD evenings, kitchen, free wi-fi and a beer garden in summer. Dorms from €11, doubles from €45.

PRECISE MYER'S HOTEL > Metzer Str. 26 Ⓢ Senefelderplatz ☎ 030/44 01 40, Ⓦ grandcityhotels.de. MAP P.86–87, POCKET MAP J3. Set in a nineteenth-century Neoclassical building, this tasteful "boutique" hotel has 51 rooms in a range of shapes and sizes, a glass-roofed courtyard with lounge and gallery with changing exhibitions. There's also a garden with terrace. Breakfast not included. **Doubles from €67.**

Friedrichshain

A&O HOSTEL FRIEDRICHSHAIN > Boxhagener Str. 73 Ⓢ Ostkreuz ☎ 030/809 47 54 00, Ⓦ aohostels .com. MAP P.102–103, POCKET MAP B17. *A&O* is especially good for families, since, alongside dorms, singles and doubles it has family rooms plus a children's game room and large garden – there's even childcare available at weekends. Breakfast €4. **Dorms from €12, doubles from €49.**

ANDEL'S HOTEL BERLIN > Landsberger Allee 106 Ⓢ Landsberger Allee ☎ 030/453 05 30, Ⓦ andelsberlin.com. MAP P.102–103, POCKET MAP M3. This sprawling design hotel has 557 small and retro-ish rooms with full amenities and spacious bathrooms. The top-floor *Sky* café/bar has great city views and there's a 550-square metre spa. Breakfast included. **Doubles from €99.**

JUNCKER'S HOTEL GARNI > Grünberger Str. 21 Ⓤ Frankfurter Tor ☎ 030/29 33 550, Ⓦ junckers-hotel .de. MAP P.102–103, POCKET MAP A16. A small, family-run hotel with medium sized but good-quality rooms, friendly staff and a quiet atmosphere only occasionally interrupted by the hostel next door. Breakfast €8. **Doubles from €48.**

MICHELBERGER > Warschauer Str. 39 Ⓤ Warschauer Str. ☎ 030/29 77 85 90, Ⓦ michelbergerhotel.com. MAP P.102–103, POCKET MAP M7. This is the hotel Friedrichshain has needed for some time – creative, welcoming and trendy. The 119 rooms are imaginatively and individually designed, the stylish lounge area has regular gigs and the drinks and food are good. **Doubles from €59.**

NHOW > Stralauer Allee 3 Ⓢ Warschauer Str. ☎ 030/29 02 990, Ⓦ nhow-hotels.com. MAP P.102–103, POCKET MAP M7. This four-star concept hotel merges a music theme with designer hotel rooms. Recreational amenities include a health club, sauna and fitness facility and some rooms have great views over the river. **Doubles from €120.**

NU HOTEL BERLIN > Gubener Str. 46 Ⓤ Frankfurter Tor ☎ 030/68 81 12 20, Ⓦ nu-hotel.de. MAP P.102–103, POCKET MAP M6. Close to the East Side gallery and O2 World, this 28-room, three-star hotel has rooms that are functional but feature lots of natural light and decent amenities. **Doubles from €79 (breakfast included).**

OSTEL > Wriezener Karree 5 Ⓤ Ostbahnhof ☎ 030/25 76 86 60, Ⓦ www.ostel.eu. MAP P.102–103, POCKET MAP L6. This shrine to "Ostalgie" – nostalgia for the old Communist GDR – is kitted out with a wealth of GDR memorabilia like brown floral wallpaper, 1970s radio clocks and photographs of GDR leaders. Prices will satisfy contemporary communists too. Breakfast from €7.50. **Dorms from €15, doubles from €54.**

West Kreuzberg

ANGLETERRE HOTEL > Friedrichstr. 31 Ⓤ Kochstr. ☎ 030/20 21 37 00, Ⓦ hotel-angleterre.de. MAP P.109, POCKET MAP G7. Close to Checkpoint Charlie and the Jewish Museum, the "English Hotel" has a restaurant and bar/lounge, 24-hour room service and lots of charming old detailing, including restored murals, stuccoed ceilings, wood finishes and wall mirrors. Breakfast not included. **Doubles from €88.**

HOTEL TRANSIT > Hagelberger Str. 53 ⓘ Mehringdamm ☎ 030/78 90 470, Ⓦ hotel-transit.de. MAP P.109, POCKET MAP F8. This bright, breezy hostel occupies a former factory building and has basic but decently sized rooms and an upbeat atmosphere. Breakfast included. Dorms from €21, doubles from €59.

JOHANN HOTEL > Johanniterstr. 8 ⓘ Prinzenstr. ☎ 030/22 50 740, Ⓦ hotel-johann-berlin.de. MAP P.109, POCKET MAP H8. Close to Bergmannstr. and the Jewish Museum, the *Johann* is a fairly nondescript but friendly hotel, with spacious rooms and a peaceful garden. Breakfast included. Doubles from €95.

MÖVENPICK HOTEL > Schöneberger Str. 3 Ⓢ Anhalter Bahnhof ☎ 030/23 00 60, Ⓦ moevenpick-berlin.com. MAP P.109, POCKET MAP F7. This former Siemens office has a unique mix of contemporary and industrial decor: Philippe Starck pieces in the rooms, wood and glass in abundance and a pleasant courtyard restaurant (*Hof zwei*) and bar. Breakfast €8. Doubles from €66.

RHIEMERS HOFGARTEN > Yorckstr. 83 ⓘ Mehringdamm ☎ 030/78 09 88 00, Ⓦ riemmershofgarten.com. MAP P.109, POCKET MAP F8. There's a low-key, residential atmosphere at this hotel in a historically protected building. The 23 rooms and apartments have a correspondingly nineteenth-century feel and there's a delightful living room for relaxation. Doubles from €123.

East Kreuzberg

BAXPAX KREUZBERG HOSTEL > Skalitzer Str. 104 ⓘ Görlitzer Bahnhof ☎ 030/ 69 51 83 22, Ⓦ baxpax.de. MAP P.116–117, POCKET MAP K7. This artsy, laid-back hostel offers themed rooms (check the bed inside a VW Beetle in the Berlin room), a casual vibe and dorm and private rooms. Dorms from €10, doubles from €40.

MOTEL ONE BERLIN-MITTE > Prinzenstr. 40 ⓘ Moritzplatz ☎ 030/70 07 98 00, Ⓦ motel-one .com. MAP P.116–117, POCKET MAP J7.

Well located for Alexanderplatz and the Oranienstrasse scene, this functional hotel has comfortable enough rooms with all necessary conveniences, a bar for snacks and drinks and free wi-fi in the lounge. Doubles from €64.

ROCK'N'ROLL HERBERGE > Muskauer Str. 11 ⓘ Görlitzer Bahnhof, ☎ 030/61 62 36 00, Ⓦ www .rnrherberge.de. MAP P.116–117, POCKET MAP K7. With seven rooms designed by a local artists, billiards and table football and vegan and non vegan snacks, this budget hangout is especially set up for musicians and music lovers – as the photos of Falco and Joe Strummer testify to. Rooms for up to five people (not dorms) are available. Doubles from €49.

Charlottenburg

AM SAVIGNYPLATZ HOTEL > Kantstr. 22 Ⓢ Savignyplatz ☎ 030/50 18 17 36, Ⓦ www.am-savignyplatz-hotel.de. MAP P.126–127, POCKET MAP A6. A beautiful old building that has been thoroughly modernized, the *Am Savignyplatz* is surprisingly stylish – its eleven rooms are spacious and modern, and one of them even has a small garden. Doubles from €52.

ASKANISCHER HOF HOTEL GARNI > Kurfürstendamm 53 Ⓢ Savignyplatz ☎ 030/881 80 33, Ⓦ askanischer-hof .de. MAP P.126–127, POCKET MAP A7. *Askanischer Hof* exudes an authentically vintage atmosphere with period rooms (sixteen in total), eccentric decor – gramophones, Prussian-era furnishings – and drawings and photos on the walls. Breakfast included. Doubles from €140.

BLEIBTREU > Bleibtreustr. 31 ⓘ Uhlandstr. ☎ 030/88 47 40, Ⓦ www .bleibtreu.com. MAP P.126–127, POCKET MAP A7. With an interior designed by Herbert Jacob Weinand and eco-minded furnishings handcrafted in Germany and Italy, this unique and discreet hotel has decent rooms, café, florist and a different scent on every floor. Breakfast buffet €19. Doubles from €118.

BRANDENBURGER HOF > Eislebener Str. 14 ⑪ Augsburger Str. ☎ 030/21 40 50, ⓦ www.brandenburger-hof .com MAP P.126–127, POCKET MAP B7. A mixture of modern Bauhaus and romantic intimacy, this beautiful hotel offers impeccable service, amazing (if expensive) Scandinavian dining in the Michelin-starred *Quadriga* restaurant and a Japanese-inspired Winter Garden Lounge. Breakfast €9–32. **Doubles from €265.**

HOTEL OTTO > Knesebeckstr. 10 ⑪ Ernst-Reuter-Platz ☎ 030/54 71 00 80, ⓦ www.hotelotto.com. MAP P.126–127, POCKET MAP A6. *Otto* eschews the traditional for a cheery, modern experience that's all blues, magentas and greens. The 46 rooms are chic and individually designed and the organic food at the restaurant is good too. Breakfast €13. **Doubles from €100.**

HOTEL Q > Knesebeckstr. 67 ⑪ Uhlandstr. ☎ 030/810 06 60, ⓦ www.loock-hotels.com. MAP P.126–127, POCKET MAP A6. One of west Berlin's swankiest hotels, the *Q* has bathtubs built into bed frames, elegantly minimal rooms, chocolate massages and member-only parties. **Doubles from €120.**

PENSION DITTBERNER > Wielandstr. 26, ⑪ Adenauerplatz ☎ 030/884 69 50, ⓦ hotel-dittberner.de. MAP P.126–127, POCKET MAP A7. This tastefully designed pension, made up of two connected apartments, has been run by Frau Lange since 1958. It's friendly and intimate with an antique charm and some very large and grand rooms. **Doubles from €115.**

PENSION FUNK > Fasanenstr. 69 ⑪ Uhlandstr. ☎ 030/882 71 93, ⓦ hotel-pensionfunk.de. MAP P.126–127, POCKET MAP B7. Located on a quiet, upmarket street opposite the well-known *Literaturhaus* (see p.134), this hotel was once the home of silent movie star Asta Nielsen. The house dates back to 1895 and maintains an air of domestic intimacy with fourteen large, comfortable rooms and elegant decor from the 1920s and 1930s. Breakfast and wi-fi included. **Doubles from €67.**

SWISSOTEL > Augsburger Str. 44 ⑪ Kurfürstendamm ☎ 030/22 01 00, ⓦ swissotel.com. MAP P.126–127, POCKET MAP B7. A short stroll from the Kaiser-Wilhelm-Gedächtnis-Kirche (see p.128) and Berlin Zoo (see p.124), this eco-friendly corporate hotel has 316 rooms, restaurant and a bar/lounge, sauna and fitness facilities. **Doubles from €120.**

Schöneberg

ALETTO JUGENDHOTEL > Grunewaldstr. 33 ⑪ Eisenacher Str. ☎ 030/21 00 36 80, ⓦ aletto.de. MAP P.136, POCKET MAP E9. Singles, doubles and dorms for up to eight people at this colourful and lively hostel – table football, video games and a large DVD library keeps customers entertained. Breakfast included. **Dorms from €19, doubles from €35.**

HOTEL DE ELA > Landshuter Str. 1 ⑪ Viktoria-Luise-Platz ☎ 030/23 63 39 60, ⓦ hotel-de-ela.de. MAP P.136, POCKET MAP C8. A mix of twenty-first-century design in a nineteenth-century Victorian building, *De Ela* has large, comfortable rooms with a classic feel for decent prices. Family friendly too. Breakfast and wi-fi included. **Doubles from €52.**

JUGENDHOTEL BERLINCITY > Crellstr. 22 ⑪ Kleistpark ☎ 030/78 70 21 30, ⓦ jugendhotel-berlin.de. MAP P.136, POCKET MAP E9. With 170 plain but comfy beds in a renovated factory building, this is a good option for budget-conscious travellers. Pool tables, decent rooms and a convivial bar. Breakfast included. **Dorms from €24 Doubles from €65.**

TOM'S HOTEL > Motzstr. 19 ⑪ Nollendorfplatz ☎ 030/21 96 66 04, ⓦ toms-hotel.de. MAP P.136, POCKET MAP C7. This friendly gay hangout has a great bar (*Tom's*), a vibrant café and is close to the gay scene of Nollendorfplatz. Rooms are comfortable and artistically decorated and apartments feature a flat-screen TV and free wi-fi. Breakfast not included. **Doubles from €99.**

Arrival

By air

Flying is, predictably, the cheapest and most convenient way to get to Germany from overseas, as well as from many other European countries thanks to the proliferation of discount airlines.

Both Berlin's airports (ⓦwww .berlin-airport.de) are within Berlin public transport's zone AB, so normal single (€2.30) or day tickets apply. From Berlin's **Schönefeld airport** (SXF) S-Bahn line S9 runs to Alexanderplatz, the Hauptbahnhof and Bahnhof Zoo (every 30min; 30min); bus #X7 runs to nearby U-Bahn Rudow. From **Tegel airport** (TXL) the frequent #TXL express bus runs to the Hauptbahnhof and Alexanderplatz, while #X9 express or local #109 buses run to Bahnhof Zoo. **Taxis** from Tegel tend to cost €20–24, depending on which part of the city you want to get to; from Schönefeld expect to pay more like €30–40.

In 2012 Tegel is due to close and Schönefeld extended into **Berlin Brandenburg International** airport.

By train

Germany is well connected by train with destinations throughout continental Europe. Check Deutsche Bahn's excellent website (ⓦwww .bahn.de) for international routes. From the UK, a slow but comfortable option is via Paris, with the overnight sleeper departing a couple of times a week from Paris Est (total travel time from London around 16hr); a quicker daytime route is via Brussels and Cologne (from 10hr 30min).

The huge **Hauptbahnhof** northeast of the Brandenburg Gate is well connected to the rest of the city by

S- and U-Bahn. Many long-distance routes also stop at Ostbahnhof, convenient for Friedrichshain, or Bahnhof Zoo, for Charlottenburg. All are well connected by S-Bahn.

By bus

Several private bus companies, such as BerlinLinienBus (ⓦwww .berlinlinienbus.de), Gulliver's (ⓦwww.gulliver.de), Eurolines (ⓦwww.eurolines.com) and Touring (ⓦwww.touring.de) run routes from as far afield as Barcelona and Bucharest.

Most international buses stop at the bus station (ZOB), linked to the centre by express buses #X34 and #X49, as well as regular buses #104, #139, #218, #349 and #M49; U-Bahn #2, from Kaiserdamm station; S-Bahn from Messe-Nord/ICC.

Getting around

U- and S-Bahn

BVG (ⓦwww.bvg.de) operate an efficient, integrated system of U- and S-Bahn train lines, buses and trams. U- and S-Bahn trains run daily 4.30am–12.30am (Fri & Sat all night).

Buses and trams

The city bus network – and the tram system mainly in eastern Berlin – covers most of the gaps left by the U-Bahn; several useful **tram** routes centre on Hackescher Markt, including the M1 to Prenzlauer Berg.

A night-time network of buses and trams operates, with buses (around every 30min) often following U-Bahn line routes; free maps are available at most stations.

Buses #100 and **#200** drive past many famous Berlin sights en route from Zoologischer Garten to

City tours

Original Berlin Walks ☎ 030/301 91 94, ⓦwww.berlinwalks.com. Offers a range of walking tours of between three and six hours, many of which cover the main sights and beyond. Prices vary according to tour.

Trabi Safaris ☎ 030/275 922 73, ⓦtrabi-safari.de. Drive around the city (slowly) in a Trabant, the car of choice for the GDR (with guides and without) with live information delivered to you via radio. Day and night "safaris" available. €79–89 depending on number of people (maximum four in a car).

Zille bus tour ⓦwww.bvg.de. To experience Berlin in nostalgic fashion take a Zille bus: decorated in the style of the "Golden Twenties" in tribute to the originals that operated in the city between 1916 to 1928, they even come with a driver in period uniform. Fifty minutes costs €8 for an adult, free for children up to 10. Tickets can be bought on the bus and at ticket machines on the underground. April–Oct, departs from Brandenburg Gate.

Alexanderplatz, providing a cheap alternative to a sightseeing tour.

Tickets and passes

Tickets are available from machines at U-Bahn stations, on trams (machines on trams only take coins) or from bus drivers. Zone AB **single tickets** cost €2.30; zone ABC single are €3; **short-trip tickets** (*Kurzstreckentarif*) are available for three train or six bus/tram stops for €1.30; zone AB **day tickets** cost €6.30. Validate single tickets in the yellow machines on platforms before travelling.

For two, three or five days the **WelcomeCard** (see p.158) is good value.

Bike rental and tours

Cycling in Berlin is very easy, safe and very popular. Not only is the city (mostly) as flat as a pancake, there are dedicated cycle lanes throughout.

There are also numerous rental places, including: Fat Tire (daily: March–Nov 9.30am–6pm; mid-April to Sept till 8pm; call or email out of season ☎030/24 04 79 91, ⓦfattirebiketours.com/berlin), beneath the TV tower at Alexanderplatz. They also offer half-day **bike tours** (4hr 30min; €20/students €18). Nearly all hostels rent bikes for around €12/day.

Taxis

Taxi fares are €3 flag fall then €1.20–1.55/km; if you hail a taxi on the street – rather than at a stand or by phone – you can ask for a short-trip price (Kurzstreckentarif) before the trip starts and pay €4 for a 2km ride. Taxi firms include: Taxi Funk ☎030/44 33 22 and Funk Taxi ☎030/26 10 26.

Directory A–Z

Addresses

If you are looking for an address in the former East, bear in mind house numbers run in different directions on each side of the street, as opposed to the usual odd/even system.

Children

Berlin is a surprisingly child-friendly city. There are public playgrounds all over the city (many created from transforming bombed out areas), plenty of green areas to play in such as Tiergarten, Volkspark Friedrichshain and Viktoriapark, and, in the colder months, kindercafés (see *Onkel Albert*, p.42) where parents can enjoy a frothy coffee while their kids enjoy the toys.

Cinema

Movies in English play everyday at Babylon Kreuzberg (ⓦwww.yorck.de), Cinemaxx Colloseum (ⓦwww.cinemaxx.de), Cinestar Originals (ⓦwww.cinestar.de) in the Sony Center and at Hackesche Höfe (ⓦwww.hoefekino.de).

Crime and emergencies

Serious crime is relatively low in Berlin, though petty crime such as bike theft can be rife. You can get help at any police station where English is usually spoken. Reporting thefts at local police stations is straightforward, but inevitably there'll be a great deal of bureaucracy to wade through **Emergency numbers** are: Police ☎110; fire and ambulance ☎112.

Discount passes

The **WelcomeCard** (Berlin AB: 48hr €16.90; 72hr €22.90; 5-day €29.90; Berlin and Potsdam ABC: 48hr €18.90; 72hr €24.90; 5-day €34.90; ⓦwww.berlin-welcomecard.de) includes public transport and up to fifty percent off at many of the major tourist sights. Though the standard card doesn't cover the Museum Island, a version that does include these museums is available (see p.48). Many of the discounts are the same as student prices.

Electricity

230 V, 50 Hz. The Continental two-round-pin plug is standard.

Embassies and consulates

Australia, Wallstr. 76–79 ☎030/880 08 80; Canada, Leipziger Platz 17 ☎030/20 31 20; Ireland, Friedrichstr. 200 ☎030/22 07 20; New Zealand, Friedrichstr. 60 ☎030/20 62 10; South Africa, Tiergartenstr.18 ☎030/22 07 30; UK, Wilhelmstr. 70–71 ☎030/20 45 70; US, Pariser Platz 2 (postal address Clayallee 170) ☎030/830 50.

Gay and lesbian Berlin

Berlin's diverse gay scene is spread across the city, but with a focus of sorts in Schöneberg, especially around Nollendorfplatz. The magazine *Siegessäule* (ⓦwww.siegessaeule.de) has listings and can be picked up in many cafés and shops. Club nights by GMF (ⓦwww.gmf-berlin.de) at various venues, including Sundays at *Weekend* (see p.71), are always worth checking out. The Christopher Street Day Gay Pride festival takes place every year in June (see p.161; ⓦwww.csd-berlin.de).

Health

There's an emergency room at Campus Charité Mitte (entrance Luisenstr. 65/66), ☎030/450 50. Doctors generally speak English. Pharmacies (Apotheken) can deal with many minor complaints; all display a rota of local pharmacies open 24hr, including Apotheke Haupt-bahnhof, at the Hauptbahnhof.

Internet

Free wi-fi at the Sony Center, and in many hotels; internet access in all hostels (around €1.50/30min), also NetLounge, Auguststr. 89.

Listings and websites

ExBerliner is a monthly English-language magazine focusing on arts and music listings in Berlin (ⓦ www .exberliner.com). The two main listings magazines in German are *Tip* (ⓦ www.tip-berlin.de) and *Zitty* (ⓦ www.zitty.de); all are widely available in cafés and bars. For adverts and classifications also check Craig's List Berlin (ⓦ berlin.de.craigslist.de). Useful English-language websites include ⓦ berlin.unlike.net and ⓦ www.slowtravelberlin.com.

Lost property

Allegedly only 25 percent of lost items in Berlin turn up again, but it's worth contacting Zentrales Fundbüro, Platz der Luftbrücke 6 (ⓣ 030/75 60 31 01), who will help you with the search (there are six such offices around the city). Left or lost luggage can also be reclaimed at both airports and at the Lost & Found section at the Deutsche Bahn. Look for the "Fundbüro" at Hauptbahnhof if you lost something in the subway or tram, or contact BVG-Fundbüro Potsdamer Str. 180/182 (BVG-Callcenter ⓣ 030/19 449).

Money and banks

The German currency is the euro (€). Exchange facilities are available in most banks, post offices and commercial exchange shops called **Wechselstuben**. The Reisebank has branches in most main train stations (generally open daily, often till 10/11pm) and ATMs are widespread.

Basic **banking hours** are Monday to Friday 9am to noon and 1.30 to 3.30pm, Thursday till 6pm. **Credit cards** are fairly widely accepted – but certainly not universally – with restaurants and cafés sometimes not taking them. There can be a surcharge in hostels and smaller hotels.

ATMs and exchange are at the airports, and major stations including: Reisebank, at the Hauptbahnhof (daily 8am–10pm), Zoo station (daily 8am–9pm), Friedrichstr. station (Mon–Fri 7.30am–8pm, Sat & Sun 8am–8pm) and Ostbahnhof (Mon–Fri 7am–9pm, Sat & Sun 8am–8pm).

Opening hours

Shops open at 8am and close around 6 to 8pm weekdays and 2 to 4pm Saturday, and often close all day Sunday. Exceptions are pharmacies, petrol stations and shops in and around train stations, which stay open late and at weekends. Museums and historic monuments are, with few exceptions, closed on Monday.

Phones

Call shops are the cheapest way to phone abroad, though you can also phone abroad from all payphones except those marked "National"; phonecards are widely available. The operator is on ⓣ 03.

Post office

Post offices are open Monday to Friday 8am to 6pm and Saturday 8am to 1pm. There's a convenient branch at Dircksenstr. 2, Mitte.

Smoking

After a wave of restrictions on smoking in all bars was introduced, a lawsuit from a small bar owner resulted in the law being loosened, and Berlin bars are pretty much almost all back to being smoky or having smoking areas. Expect to get smoke in your eyes in almost all bars that don't serve food. All restaurants are smoke free but many offer a smokers' lounge somewhere.

Time

Berlin is on Central European Time (CET), one hour ahead of Britain and six hours ahead of EST, with the clocks going forward in spring and back again some time in autumn – the exact date changes from year to year. Generally speaking, Berliners, like the rest of Germany, use the 24-hour clock.

Toilets

There are a few public toilets (*Öffentliche Toilette*, WC) some of which you'll find in the almost romantic-looking toilet huts in parks and close to the subway. In some, you have to put a €0.50 coin in the slot to open the door. There are mostly free toilets at petrol stations, where you have to ask the clerk for the key. Also big shopping centres have public toilets normally with a maintenance woman, who you should tip around €0.30–50. Gentlemen should head for *Herren*; ladies should head for *Damen*.

Tipping

If you're in a group, you'll be asked if you want to pay individually (*getrennt*) or all together (*zusammen*). In general, round your bill up to the next €0.50 or €1 and give the total directly to the waiter when you pay (rather than leaving it on the table afterwards).

Sports and outdoor activities

Bundesliga football (ⓦ www .bundesliga.de) is the major spectator sport in Germany, with world-class clubs playing in top-notch stadiums, many revamped for the 2006 World Cup such as the Olympic stadium (see p.129). Important matches sell out well in advance; tickets can be purchased from the clubs' websites.

Tourist offices

The main contact details are: ☏ 030/25 00 25, ⓦ www.visitberlin .de. Tourist offices at: Hauptbahnhof (daily 8am–10pm). Also at Brandenburg Gate (daily 10am–7pm); Kurfürstendamm 21 (Mon–Sat 10am–8pm, Sun 10am–6pm); and in the ALEXA shopping centre, Alexanderplatz (Mon–Sat 10am–8pm).

Travellers with disabilities

Buses and trams marked with a wheelchair symbol are equipped for disabled passengers, and a footnote on the printed schedule provided at every stop indicates which trams and buses are so equipped. Look for the words *behindert* (disabled) and *ausgestattet* (outfitted). Both buses and trams also have seat-belt-like straps to prevent a wheelchair from rolling during transit.

Festivals and events

BREAD & BUTTER

January, Tempelhof
Ⓦ www.breadandbutter.com
The city's most prestigious fashion event features a dizzying range of brands, labels and designers – and plenty of parties in the evening.

LONG NIGHT OF THE MUSEUMS (LANGE NACHT DER MUSEEN)

January Ⓦ www.lange-nacht-der-museen.de
There are two Long Nights of the Museums – one in January and one in August, when many of Berlin's museums stay open late into the night – usually until midnight or later – with special programmes and events.

BERLINALE

February Ⓦ www.berlinale.de
For two weeks each year, Berlin turns into Hollywood as the Berlinale international film festival takes over the town. Around 400 films are shown every year as part of the Berlinale's public programme, the vast majority of which are world or European premieres.

IMPRO

Ten days in March Ⓦ www.improfestival.de
Running since 2001, this event is the biggest improvisation theatre festival in Europe. Its goal is to show international developments and take part in an intercultural exchange with different ensembles.

GALLERY WEEKEND

End April/early May Ⓦ www .gallery-weekend-berlin.de
Forty galleries and small venues dedicated to design and art open for one weekend to present exclusive exhibitions and contemporary international art.

MY FEST

May 1, Kreuzberg Ⓦ www.myfest36.de
Open-air festival that's held around Kreuzberg during the day on May 1, with music and cultural events and a lot of food stalls (especially around Kottbusser Tor). Note that May Day demonstrations in the evening in the same area have a tendency to turn ugly, though the daytime is usually very safe and fun.

CHRISTOPHER STREET DAY (CSD)

June Ⓦ www.csd-berlin.de
Held in memory of the first big gay uprising against police assaults in Greenwich Village (the Stonewall riots), Berlin's biggest celebration of gay pride has been running 33 years and draws around half a million people.

CARNIVAL OF CULTURES

Mid-June Ⓦ www.karneval-berlin.de
This colourful weekend street festival has been running since 1996, with four music stages featuring acts from around the world, plus culinary delights and handmade arts and craft stands. The peak of the festivity is a street parade with around 4700 participants from eighty nations on Whitsunday.

FÊTE DE LA MUSIQUE

June Ⓦ www.fetedelamusique.de
Over ninety concerts are put on all over town to celebrate the Fête de la Musique, a hugely ambitious event that happens across 340 cities.

CLASSIC OPEN AIR

July Ⓦ www.classicopenair.de
Five days of classical music at the beautiful Gendarmenmarkt. Previous events have included the Royal Philharmonic Orchestra London

performing the complete James Bond title themes and The Scorpions performing with the German Film Orchestra Potsdam.

LONG NIGHT OF THE MUSEUMS

August Ⓦ www.lange-nacht-der-museen.de

The second instalment of the Long Night of the Museums (see p.161)

INTERNATIONAL LITERATURE FESTIVAL

September Ⓦ www.literaturfestival.com

Berlin's biggest literary event celebrates "diversity in the age of globalization" and features an eclectic and international selection of poets, short story writers and novelists over twelve days.

BERLIN FESTIVAL / BERLIN MUSIC WEEK

Mid-September Ⓦ www.berlinfestival.de

Acclaimed three-day dance and pop festival held at Tempelhof. The guests tend to be world renowned – Moby, Peaches, Robyn – and the event coincides with other music events such as Popkomm and Music Week, which feature additional showcases and shows in clubs all over town.

BERLIN MARATHON

Late September Ⓦ www.berlin-marathon.com

First held in 1974, Berlin's marathon traditionally takes place on the last weekend in September. With around 40,000 participants from around 107 countries and the most marathon world records (for men and women) set here, it's one of the largest and most popular road races in the world.

FESTIVAL OF LIGHTS

Mid-October Ⓦ www.festival-of-lights.de

Every autumn, Berlin's famous sights are transformed into a sea of colour and light, including the Brandenburg Gate, the Berlin TV Tower, Berliner Dom and more. The nightly light show comes with art and cultural events around the topic of light.

BERLIN JAZZ FESTIVAL

Early November

Ⓦ www.berlinerfestspiele.de

Running for over forty years, the Berlin Jazz Festival is a world-renowned event that presents all the diverse styles of jazz. The full and varied programme is traditional and progressive in equal parts, and has tended to focus in particular on big bands and large ensembles.

INTERNATIONAL SHORT FILM FESTIVAL

Mid-November Ⓦ www.interfilm.de

The five-day International Short Film Festival Berlin was founded in 1982 and today is Berlin's second largest international film festival. The event showcases numerous competitions across all genres, as well as workshops, discussions and parties.

Public holidays

January 1, January 6 (regional), Good Friday, Easter Monday, May 1, Ascension Day, Whit Monday, Corpus Christi (regional), August 15 (regional), October 3, November 1 (regional) and December 25 and 26.

CHRISTMAS MARKETS

December

Many public locations in Berlin, such as Gendarmenmarkt, Alexanderplatz and the Schloss Charlottenburg, are taken over by Christmas markets selling arts, crafts, Glühwein, Wurst, pancakes and more.

Chronology

720 > The region known today as Berlin is settled by Slavic and Germanic tribes.

948 > Germans take control over the area of present-day Berlin.

983 > The Slavs rebel (successfully) against German rule.

Twelfth century > Germans take over the land again.

1244 > Berlin is first mentioned in written records.

1247 > The city of Cölln is founded right next to Berlin.

1307 > Cölln and Berlin become known simply as "Berlin", the larger of the two cities.

1451 > Berlin becomes the royal residence of the Brandenburg electors and has to give up its status of a free Hanseatic city.

1539 > The city becomes officially Lutheran.

1576 > Nearly five thousand inhabitants of Berlin are wiped out by the bubonic plague.

1618 > The Thirty Years' War begins. It has a devastating impact on Berlin with a third of houses damaged and half of the population left dead.

1685 > Friedrich Wilhelm offers asylum to the Huguenots. More than 15,000 come to Brandenburg and six thousand settle in Berlin.

1699 > Inauguration of Schloss Charlottenburg, commissioned by Sophie Charlotte, wife of Friedrich I.

1701 > Berlin becomes the capital of Prussia.

1740 > Friedrich II – known as Frederick the Great – comes to power and rules until 1786. He turns Berlin into a centre of Enlightenment.

1745–47 > Sanssouci Palace is built as the summer palace of Frederick the Great.

1788–91 > The Brandenburg Gate is built by Carl Gotthard Langhans.

1806 > Napoleon conquers Berlin but grants self-government to the city.

1810 > Humboldt University is founded by Prussian educational reformer and linguist Wilhelm von Humboldt.

1841 > The Museum Island is dedicated to "art and science" by Friedrich Wilhelm IV of Prussia.

1861 > Wedding, Moabit and several other suburbs are incorporated into Berlin.

1871 > Berlin becomes the capital of a unified German Empire, under Otto von Bismarck's chancellorship.

1894 > The Reichstag opens.

1918 > Berlin witnesses the end of World War I and the proclamation of the Weimar Republic.

1920 > Berlin is established as a separate administrative zone with the Greater Berlin Act. A dozen villages and estates are incorporated into the city to expand it.

1923 > Tempelhof is officially designated an airport.

1933 > Adolf Hitler comes to power shortly after the Reichstag building fire.

1939 > The beginning of World War II.

1938–45 > Thousands of Jews (and other minorities) living in Berlin are sent to death camps.

1943–45 > Seventy percent of Berlin is destroyed in air raids.

1945 > The Allies take Berlin, and divide it into four zones.

June 1948 > The Berlin airlift begins, with Allied planes delivering essential supplies to an isolated West Berlin.

1949 > The Federal Republic of Germany is founded in West Berlin and German Democratic Republic in East Berlin.

June 1953 > An uprising of industrial workers against the Communist regime is brutally put down.

August 1961 > The tension between East and West culminates in the building of the Berlin Wall.

June 1963 > US President John F. Kennedy visits West Berlin, delivering his famous speech, "*Ich bin ein Berliner*".

1971 > Access is guaranteed across East Germany to West Berlin with the Four Powers agreement.

1982 > US President Ronald Reagan visits Berlin for the first time.

1987 > During his second Berlin visit, Reagan makes a speech in front of the Brandenburg Gate, demanding Mr Gorbachev "tear down this Wall!".

1989 > Following mass demonstrations across East Berlin, the border crossings are finally opened on November 9.

October 3, 1990 > The two parts of Berlin are unified as part of the Federal Republic of Germany.

1999 > Berlin becomes capital of reunified Germany and the German government and parliament begin their work in Berlin.

1997 > Peter Eisenman's controversial design for a Memorial to the Murdered Jews of Europe (see p.58) is chosen.

2005 > Openly gay mayor Klaus Wowereit dubs Berlin "poor but sexy", which becomes a slogan for the city.

2006 > Demolition begins on the former East German parliament, the Palast der Republik (see p.50).

2006 > The new Hauptbahnhof is opened.

2008 > Tempelhof airport is officially closed; the surrounding area is later turned into a public park (see p.112).

2009 > Twenty years since the fall of the Wall is celebrated. In preparation, work begins on a major restoration of the original 106 paintings at the East Side Gallery (see p.100). Ninety-nine are fully restored, mostly by the original artists.

German

Being the cosmopolitan city it is, it's fairly easy to get around Berlin using English. That said, it's worth learning some basics in case you find yourself needing to communicate in the native language. Needless to say, any attempt at speaking German often goes a long way.

Alphabet

Umlaut: ä, ö, ü are the letters that have the mysterious Umlaut in the German language, which can also be spelled as ae, oe or ue. The ä is pronounced like the English a, the others are comparable to speaking the German o or u with a ping-pong ball in the mouth.

The "Sharp S": Whenever the s is supposed to be emphasized in German, the "sharp s", **ß**, is used, which is pronounced like the English double s. Since the spelling reform in 1996 there have been some discussions about whether to retain ß or use ss, but for now both variations are accepted.

Pronunciation

Consonants: "w" is pronounced like the English "v"; "sch" is pronounced "sh"; "z" is "ts". The German letter "ß" is basically a double "s".
Vowels: "ei" is "eye"; "ie" is "ee"; "eu" is "oy".

Basic words and phrases

Yes	Ja
No	Nein
Please	Bitte
Thank you	Danke
Good morning	Guten Morgen
Good evening	Guten Abend
Hello/Good day	Güten Tag
Goodbye	Tschüss, ciao, or auf Wiedersehen
Excuse me	Entschuldigen Sie, bitte

Today	Heute
Yesterday	Gestern
Tomorrow	Morgen
Day	Tag
Week	Woche
Month	Monat
Year	Jahr
Weekend	Wochenende
Monday	Montag
Tuesday	Dienstag
Wednesday	Mittwoch
Thursday	Donnerstag
Friday	Freitag
Saturday	Samstag/ Sonnabend
Sunday	Sonntag
I don't understand	Ich verstehe nicht
How much is...?	Wieviel kostet...?
Do you speak English?	Sprechen Sie Englisch?
I don't speak German	Ich spreche kein Deutsch
I'd like a beer	Ich hätte gern ein Bier
Where is?	Wo ist?
entrance/exit	der Eingang/der Ausgang
Toilet	das WC/die Toilette
Women	Damen
Men	Herren
Hotel	das Hotel
HI hostel	die Jugendherberge
Main train station	der Hauptbahnhof
Bus	der Bus
Plane	das Flugzeug
Train	der Zug
Cheap	billig
Expensive	teuer
Open	offen/auf
Closed	geschlossen/zu
Entrance	Eingang
Exit	Ausgang
Smoking/no smoking	rauchen/nicht rauchen

1	Eins
2	Zwei
3	Drei
4	Vier
5	Fünf
6	Sechs
7	Sieben
8	Acht
9	Neun
10	Zehn
11	Elf
12	Zwölf
13	Dreizehn
14	Vierzehn
15	Fünfzehn
16	Sechszehn
17	Siebzehn
18	Achtzehn
19	Neunzehn
20	Zwanzig
21	Ein-und-zwanzig
22	Zwei-und-zwanzig
30	Dreissig
40	Vierzig
50	Fünfzig
60	Sechzig
70	Siebzig
80	Achtzig
90	Neunzig
100	Hundert
1000	Tausend

Food and drink

TERMS AND PHRASES

Breakfast	Frühstück
Lunch	Mittagessen
Coffee and cakes	Kaffee und Kuchen
Dinner	Abendessen
Knife	Messer
Fork	Gabel
Spoon	Löffel
Plate	Teller
Cup	Tasse
Glass	Glas
Menu	Speisekarte
Starter	Vorspeise
Main course	Hauptgericht
Dessert	Nachspeise
The bill	Die Rechnung

Bio	organic
Vegetarian	Vegetarisch

BASICS

Brot	bread
Brötchen	bread roll
Butter	butter
Ei	egg
Essig	vinegar
Honig	honey
Joghurt	yoghurt
Käse	cheese
Kuchen	cake
Marmelade	jam
Milch	milk
Öl	oil
Pfeffer	pepper
Reis	rice
Sahne	cream
Salz	salt
Scharf	spicy
Senf	mustard
Sosse	sauce
Suppe	soup
Zucker	sugar

DRINKS

Bier	beer
Eiswürfel	ice cube
Flasche	bottle
Kaffee	coffee
Leitungswasser	tap water
Mineralwasser	mineral water
Saft	juice
Sprudelwasser	sparkling mineral water
Stroh	straw
Tee	tea
Teekanne	tea pot
Wein	wine
Weissbier/ Weizenbier	wheat beer

MEAT (FLEISCH) AND FISH (FISCH)

Currywurst	sausage served with a curry powder and tomato ketchup

Forelle	trout
Garnelen	prawns
Huhn, Hähnchen	chicken
Kabeljau	cod
Lachs	salmon
Lamm	lamb
Lammkotelett	lamb chop
Leber	liver
Leberkäse	meatloaf
Makrele	mackerel
Rindfleisch	beef
Schinken	ham
Schweinefleisch	pork
Speck	bacon
Thunfisch	tuna
Wiener Schnitzel	breadcrumb-coated cutlet, usually veal but sometimes pork
Wurst	sausage
Zander	pike perch

VEGETABLES (GEMÜSE)

Blumenkohl	cauliflower
Bohnen	beans
Bratkartoffeln	fried potatoes
Erbsen	peas
Gurke	cucumber or gherkin
Grüne Bohnen	green beans
Karotten, Möhren	carrots
Kartoffel	potatoes
Knoblauch	garlic
Lauch (or Porree)	leeks
Maiskolben	corn on the cob
Paprika	peppers
Pilze or Champignons	mushrooms
Pommes frites	chips or fries
Rosenkohl	Brussels sprouts
Rotkohl	red cabbage
Salat	salad
Salzkartoffeln	boiled potatoes
Sauerkraut	pickled cabbage
Spargel	asparagus (white asparagus is particularly popular in season)

Tomaten	tomatoes
Zwiebeln	onions

FRUIT (OBST)

Ananas	pineapple
Apfel	apple
Aprikose	apricot
Banane	banana
Birne	pear
Erdbeer	strawberry
Himbeer	raspberry
Kirsch	cherry
Melone	melon
Orange	orange
Pfirsch	peach
Pflaum	plum
Trauben	grapes
Zitrone	lemon

DESSERTS AND CAKES

Eis	ice cream
Keks	biscuits
Käsekuchen	cheese cake
Kuchen	cake
Schokolade	chocolate
Torte	cake/tart

GERMAN SPECIALITIES

Knödel/Klösse	Poached or boiled potatoes or bread dumplings
Maultaschen	stuffed noodles similar to ravioli
Quark	A type of strained fresh cheese
Sauerbraten	Pot roast, usually beef
Schweinsbraten	Pot-roasted pork
Spätzle	Egg noodles of soft texture

PUBLISHING INFORMATION

This first edition published March 2012 by **Rough Guides Ltd**

80 Strand, London WC2R 0RL

11, Community Centre, Panchsheel Park, New Delhi 110017, India

Distributed by the Penguin Group

Penguin Books Ltd, 80 Strand, London WC2R 0RL

Penguin Group (USA) 375 Hudson Street, NY 10014, USA

Penguin Group (Australia) 250 Camberwell Road, Camberwell, Victoria 3124, Australia

Penguin Group (NZ) 67 Apollo Drive, Mairangi Bay, Auckland 1310, New Zealand

Rough Guides is represented in Canada by

Tourmaline Editions Inc., 662 King Street West, Suite 304, Toronto, Ontario, M5V 1M7

Typeset in Minion and Din to an original design by Henry Iles and Dan May.

Printed and bound in China

© Rough Guides 2012

Maps © Rough Guides

176pp includes index

A catalogue record for this book is available from the British Library

ISBN 978-1-40538-535-0

The publishers and authors have done their best to ensure the accuracy and currency of all the information in **Pocket Rough Guide Berlin**, however, they can accept no responsibility for any loss, injury, or inconvenience sustained by any traveller as a result of information or advice contained in the guide.

11 12 13 14 8 7 6 5 4 3 2 1

ROUGH GUIDES CREDITS

Text editor: Alice Park

Layout: Ankur Guha

Cartography: Ed Wright

Picture editor: Nicole Newman

Photographer: Roger d'Olivere Mapp

Production: Rebecca Short

Proofreader: Serena Stephenson

Cover design: Nicole Newman, Dan May

THE AUTHOR

Paul Sullivan is an itinerant British writer and photographer who's been based in Berlin since 2008. His words and images have appeared in *The Guardian, The Independent, The Telegraph* and *The National* and he's authored several guidebooks for publishers like Time Out, HG2, Cool Camping and Wallpaper, as well as a couple of books on Icelandic and Jamaican music. He runs niche travel site www.slowtravelberlin.com and also runs photography tours in the city. This is his first Rough Guide.

ACKNOWLEDGEMENTS

Paul Sullivan would like to thank Sylee Gore and Sabrina Boller for additional research and writing.

Thanks also to Nicola Brown and Lewis Bush for their assistance on this title.

HELP US UPDATE

We've gone to a lot of effort to ensure that the first edition of the **Pocket Rough Guide Berlin** is accurate and up-to-date. However, things change – places get "discovered", opening hours are notoriously fickle, restaurants and rooms raise prices or lower standards. If you feel we've got it wrong or left something out, we'd like to know, and if you can remember the address, the price, the hours, the phone number, so much the better.

Please send your comments with the subject line "**Pocket Rough Guide Berlin Update**" to ✉ mail@roughguides.com. We'll credit all contributions and send a copy of the next edition (or any other Rough Guide if you prefer) for the very best emails.

Find more travel information, connect with fellow travellers and book your trip on Ⓦ www .roughguides.com

PHOTO CREDITS

All images © Rough Guides except the following:

Front cover Brandenburg Gate © SuperStock
Back cover People relaxing and drinking at riverside bars, River Spree © Roger d'Olivere Mapp/Rough Guides
Best of Berlin
p. 21 Clärchens Ballhaus © Paul Sullivan

p.21 White Trash Fast Food © Paul Sullivan
p.21 Club der Visionaere © travelstock44/Alamy
Places
p.55 Bebelplatz © Superstock
p.142 Sanssouci palace © James Tye/DK Images

Index

Maps are marked in **bold**.